SPECIAL F
Pastor'
Comm

MW01002395

A Pastor's Manual on Doing Church

General Editor

Mal Couch

21stCENTURYPRESS.com
Springfield, MO 65807

A Pastor's
Manual on
Doing Church

Copyright © 2002 *by Mal Couch*
Fort Worth, Texas

Published by 21st Century Press
2131 W. Republic Rd.
PMB 41
Springfield, MO 65807

Unless otherwise indicated, Scripture quotations are from the New American Standard Bible, © the Lockman Foundation 1960, 1962, 1963, 1968, 1971,1972, 1973, 1975, 1977.

For more information about 21st Century Press visit our web site: www.21stcenturypress.com

ISBN 0-9717009-4-X

Cover and Book Design: Lee Fredrickson

Contributors

Mal Couch, MA, Th.M., Th.D., Ph.D., DD, is founder and president of Tyndale Theological Seminary and Biblical Institute, Ft. Worth, TX.

Dave Kooyers is in the DCS program at Tyndale and is a pastoral and church leadership consultant to Bible churches in Northern California.

Hal Molloy, BS, is an elder/teacher at Holly Hills Bible Church, Denver, CO.

Eric Peterman is the CTS Online Editor, Dean of Administration for Tyndale, where he is in the biblical languages program. He is an author, conference speaker, and a former software designer.

Vern Peterman, BA, MBA, D.Min., is pastor/elder at Holly Hills Bible Church, Denver, CO.

Karl Poppelreiter, BS, is in the graduate program in systematic theology at Tyndale, and is a conference speaker and an author.

Charles Ray, Th.M., Th.D., Editor of the *Conservative Theological Journal*.

Foreword

For sometime now, I have felt there needed to be a quick reference Handbook, a volume of wisdom, experience, and verses of Scripture to help busy pastors think through tough problems. Though this book is certainly not exhaustive concerning all the issues pastors face, it may start the thinking process in order to find answers.

This book was put together by a handful of like-minded, conservative Bible teachers. By saying like-minded, we do not mean that there is agreement on every fine point, but that we all respect the Word of God, and desire to follow what it says. In the same manner, you the reader will not agree on all of our biblical perspectives and suggestions, but we hope and pray that you give what we write a thoughtful reading!

The pastorate is under fire today! Outside secular forces are bending and reshaping the attitudes of the average layman. The church-growth movement, the hyper-faith movement, secular psychology, and other forms of biblical departure, are all spinning their webs of destruction on many congregations. "To let the Bible speak" should be the watchword for safeguarding the integrity of local churches. The reader will see that we often reference my book *A Biblical Theology of the Church* (Kregel). This is because many of the subjects referred to in this Handbook are dealt with in that volume. Readers would benefit from having this Biblical Theology for more in-depth study.

This Handbook is divided into two parts. The first is our quick reference helps, and the second half is a critical commentary on Titus, Paul's words to this younger apostle as he set about appointing pastors and supervising their work in the ministry. While both parts are different, we pray they will work together in behalf of your needs as a leader. I have selected two verses from Titus that will help set the direction for this Handbook. May God use these words to encourage you in your ministry. The apostle Paul writes to elders that they should be:

> *Holding fast the faithful word, which is in accordance with the teaching that he may be able both to exhort in sound doctrine and to refute those who contradict (1:9).*

> *This is a trustworthy statement; and concerning these things, I want you to speak confidently, so that those who have believed God may be careful to engage in good deeds. These things are good and profitable for men (3:8).*

Mal Couch, General Editor

5

Table of Contents

Part I – Common Subjects With Which Pastors Deal

Part II – Commentary on Titus

Part III – Suggested Doctrinal Statement for Churches

Part I

Common Subjects With
Which Pastors Deal

Abortion

Though not a verse about abortion, Proverbs 24:11 is certainly applicable to the issue:

> *Deliver those who are being taken away to death, and those who are staggering to slaughter, Oh hold them back. If you say, 'See, we did not know this,' does He not consider it who weighs the hearts?*

Better yet is Psalm 139 that tells us plainly how God formed our inward parts, and weaved us in our mother's womb (v. 13). The passage continues and describes the fact that our frame (probably meaning skeleton) was made in secret (v. 15) and that all our unformed substance was written in the Lord's book (v. 16).

There is no doubt that the psalmist David is saying, we were known by the Lord while being crafted in the womb. We were not simply a piece of flesh or biological tissue that could be easily disposed of, as the abortionists argue, but we were living human beings, marvelously fashioned by the God who creates the living!

Abortion is Murder

If God is the author of life, then whoever destroys life is a murderer! This has always been the view of the nation that honored biblical ethics. It has only been in the last thirty years, since the creation of the abortion pill, that ethics have been removed from the decision to abort.

Arguments for Abortion

Rational and unbiblical arguments go something like this: (1) If abortion is not allowed, there will be the back alley coat hanger abortions all over again; (2) Abortion prevents unwanted children; (3) A child is too much of a burden on a girl who will likely be abandoned by the father.

Pro-abortionists move the target from one immoral act over to another immoral act! Two principles come to play: (1) People must be held responsible for their acts no matter how devastating the consequences; (2) There are ways, no matter how difficult to preserve a life that is brought into the world.

Though certainly not the ideal, there are thousands of godly couples waiting to adopt unwanted children! Pastors, and all counselors working with them, will be blessed by sparing a child from the surgeon's knife! From the Scriptures, our Judeo-Christian heritage considers all life sacred, since all humans are created in the image of God. Because of this, whoever takes a life, forfeits his own life (Gen. 9:6).

Counseling those considering abortion. (1) If it is an unmarried couple considering abortion, the pastor should counsel with his wife as the voice that speaks to the girl; (2) If it is a single girl considering abortion, the pastor should seek a woman, such as his wife or a godly Christian abortion counselor to deal with the girl alone.

In abortion counseling, (1) The gospel should always be made clear; (2) The fact that the life of a child is at stake, should be stressed; (3) The motherly instinct should be emphasized so that the one considering abortion understands that she is killing the life of her own child.

Appropriately, the grace of the Lord Jesus Christ should be emphasized. There can be confession of sin, and restoration. Help can be arranged for those who feel helpless and alone, because of their sin.

Many godly Christian agencies provide compassionate and professional help so that an abortion is no longer an option. Arrangements can be made for the girl to keep her baby. Godly Christian women can give comfort and guidance so that the pregnant girl can sense that, "the worst way out, is not the way out!"

Recommended Books

Jean Staker Garton, *Who Broke the Baby?* (Minneapolis, MN: Bethany House); David C. Reardon, *Aborted Women, Silent No More* (Westchester, ILL: Crossway); George Grant, *Grand Illusions* (Brentwood, TN: Wolgemuth & Hyatt).

Advertising

Introduction: The New Testament church did not have the variety and scope of media for advertising that is available to today's churches. In contrast, today we are blessed with an abundance of Bibles, and Bible study tools that can provide essential principles to guide the use of the ever-expanding capacity for advertising in the promotion of the church. A great many churches today are making more use of the spectrum of advertising capacity available to them, than to the tools available for sharpened biblical discernment, so setting forth some key principles to govern the use of advertising is in order.

What is the Goal?

Since the capacity for advertising is technology-driven, it is essential to discern which are biblical purposes for advertising and which are not. To arrive at those purposes which are biblical, we must first look at the goal toward which the church of Jesus Christ is to be focusing: We are seeking to make disciples, presenting every man mature in Christ, and teaching those who will be faithful to teach others also (Matt. 28:19,20; Col. 1:28,29; 2 Tim. 2:2). It is within the specific biblical definition of a pastor-teacher (i.e., shepherd) to equip the saints for works of service (Eph. 4:11, 12). That equipping is to make them interdependently dependent upon the Lord. In consideration of when and how the church should advertise then, it is most critical to first understand God's purpose for the church and the intended role of its shepherds.

Advertising that is consistent with the above-stated goal might be produced for a marriage class, new media resources, church assistance, opportunities for service, retreat, conference, etc. The scope of the information provided in the advertising might be outside what can be communicated in a church bulletin or general announcement to the congregation, either by capacity or by intended audience.

What is Not the Goal?

It is the purpose of the church to make disciples and not just converts and most decidedly not just seat warmers and spectators. The Scriptures say, in contrast, that the aim should be to teach faithful men who will in turn teach others [who are faithful] also (2 Tim. 2:2). In line with the modern focus on statistics, the church at large has tended to be increasingly intent on growing numbers of people and financial aspects of ministry – the "nickels and noses". Decades of maintaining this skewed focus on statistical information has tended to emphasize getting people in the door, by whatever means. Because biblical depth does not yield well to statistical measure, the true aim of ministry has been overwhelmed by popular appeal – whatever brings in the numbers. Consequently, the church at large has tended to be "a mile wide and an inch deep". Should there be evangelism in the church? Absolutely!

But the events that involve the gathering of believers should not be directed towards evangelism or getting many people in the door, but rather deepening the growth of the believers both individually and as a church body.

Advertising should never be used to bring unbelievers into a meeting that is or should be designed for the gathering and building up of believers. Unbelievers coming into such a gathering of believers is incidental, and may be productive, but should not be the focus (1 Cor. 14:23-26). If pastors truly desire to be effective in seeing people saved, they are called upon to watch their own life and doctrine closely (1 Tim. 4:16). It is God's place to add to the church (Acts 2:41, 5:14).

So what are the biblical parameters for advertising? Once having determined that advertising is to be used to forward genuine biblical goals for the church, we are in a position to examine other biblical parameters that can guide the use of advertising for the church.

Not only must the purpose of the advertising be biblical, but also the content must be biblical. The content of any advertising must reflect the same care for biblical life and doctrine as is the concern regarding biblical purpose in the advertising. In practical terms, advertising needs to be reviewed for doctrinal and practical quality of content. Scripture, as in every other area, needs to be the measure of content (I Thess. 5:21; 2 Tim. 3:16, 17). See to it that content is consistent with the biblical goal of advertising. Entertainment and amusement of the masses or the flock is no substitute for biblical instruction and biblical worship among believers.

Advertising is Intended to Inform and Persuade

Whatever advertising the church does should be designed to accomplish those goals. The information provided should of course be complete, concise and truthful. The means and direction of the persuasion is a matter of careful discernment. Is the persuasive appeal to fleshly motivations or to spiritual motivations? Is it truthful? Since some matters are not clearly biblical in a "black and white" sense, it is then appropriate to ask if the advertising content is helpful to those receiving it. In other words, is there a potential for the content of the advertisement to violate the conscience of those reading it or to create unnecessary conflict (1 Cor. 6:10, 16:23)?

Pray about it during its planning, distribution, and for those who will receive it. The advertising that will be of value will be God's good works prepared in advance that we might walk in them (Eph. 2:10). Advertising, like any other aspect of ministry, should be the subject of prayer throughout.

See **Promoting, of Church.**

Baptism, Infant

It is the high ritualistic churches that mainly advocate infant baptism: Roman Catholic, Eastern Orthodox, Lutheran, and Reformed. The first three place a degree of salvation on such a visual rite, at least temporarily, until the child has reached an age of accountability. Then, many groups have what they call *confirmation* that supposedly means the child is now a full member in the church, and that he has been kept secure until he had a chance to make an intellectual assent in accepting Christ as his Savior.

Those who promote infant baptism used the words of Jesus in passages such as Mark 10:14: "Permit the children to come to Me; do not hinder them; for the kingdom of God belongs to such as these." They fail to note that the Lord is speaking about children who are old enough to make a decision to go up to Him. He is not referring to a passive infant!

Those who hold to infant baptism also use Acts 10:44-48 and the fact that those in the household of Cornelius believed in Christ, and this must have included small infants. The text says that, "everyone who believes in Him receives forgiveness of sins" (v. 43), with the response attributed to "all those who were listening to the message" (v. 44). Again, this would not include passive, immature infants!

They also refer to the account of Paul and Silas witnessing to the jailer and his household: "Believe in the Lord Jesus, and you shall be saved, you and your household" (16:32). The story concludes with the fact that the jailer was "baptized, he and all his household" (v. 33), and that he "believed in God with his whole household" (v. 34). His household included those old enough to make a decision for Christ. The passage is not implying in any way that there were infants in the household who believed.

Some attempt to argue that infant baptism replaces the Old Testament rite of infant circumcision, where the males were circumcised on the eighth day after birth. The problem with this line of reasoning is that only the little boys are circumcised and this would leave the infant girls out of the picture. In addition, circumcision was never shown in the Old Testament as a sign of salvation, but instead as a sign of the Jewish covenant. Circumcision never saved a Jewish male!

See **Dedication, Ceremony of children; Baptism, Water.**

Baptism, Modes of

Some churches use sprinkling from a laver; others pour water from the laver over the head of the one being baptized. But from *baptizo* and *bapto* we get the concept to dip, immerse. When the priests washed at the laver, they more than likely sloshed and dipped water on their hands, and then their feet (Exod. 30:21). This cleansing pointed to their sanctification as ministers unto the Lord.

Because early churches had to meet in secret, some catacomb drawings show people simply standing ankle deep in water, with the water poured on their heads from a vessel. We know the early church also sprinkled with what was called "clinical" baptism for the sick. However even non-immersionists, such as John Calvin admit that immersion was the universal practice of the apostolic church (See Calvin Institutes IV.XV, 19).

The future washing of the Holy Spirit would inaugurate the New Covenant for Israel (Ezek. 36:24-28). Many English texts say the Lord will sprinkle clean water on the Jewish people, but the Hebrew word *za'rach* is better-translated slosh. This symbolically cleanses Israel "from all your filthiness and from all your idols" (v. 25). The Lord adds, on that day "I [will] cleanse you from all your iniquities" (v. 33).

Following menstruation, women were to be cleansed in a bath called a *mik'vah*. The *mik'vah* was about the size of a bathtub in which the women kneeled and completely immersed their whole body.

All of these actions are types or pictures of baptism, with the more compelling thought of a cleansing or washing. Because of the fact that Philip and the Ethiopian eunuch "both went down into the water, Philip as well as the eunuch," and they both "came out of the water" (8:38-39), immersion remains the greatest picture of the cleansing work of the Holy Spirit, based on the sanctifying ministry provided by Christ's death on the cross.

Paul writes about this spiritual transaction: "Having been buried with Him in baptism, in which you were raised up with Him through faith in the working of God, who raised Him from the dead ... He made you alive together with Him, having forgiven us all our transgressions" (Col. 2:12-13).

While immersion should be used for baptism, pastors need to avoid a certain legalism on the matter. A profession of faith is what saves not baptism, no matter what form is used.

Recommended Books
Charles Ryrie, Basic *Theology* (Chicago: Moody).

See **Baptism, Spiritual; Baptism, Water.**

Baptism, Spiritual

The apostle Paul says that all believers in Corinth, both the spiritual and the carnal, were baptized into the body of Christ. This is clearly something that happens at the time of salvation. At the time of the transition of the new dispensation of the church, replacing the dispensation of law, there were those, such as the apostles, who were "saved" in Old Testament terminology. They received the Holy Spirit in Acts 2, just as Jesus had predicted before His ascension (1:5). Though 2:4 only mentions the filling of the Spirit, Peter said the coming of the Spirit at Pentecost also included the baptism of the Spirit as well (11:15-16).

Spiritual baptism, not water baptism, is obviously in view also in Colossians 2:11-14. This spiritual baptism brings about a "spiritual" circumcision (v. 11). The results of this baptism also bring about a "spiritual" burial with Christ (v. 12a); this leads to a "spiritual" resurrection with Him as well (v. 12b).

Local Church Issues

Some try to claim that there is a second blessing for the believer in the baptism of the Holy Spirit. They take this view because they fail to see Acts as a transition book, in that people who were already "saved" under the dispensation of the law, needed to be placed in the body of Christ when the Holy Spirit came to launch the church age.

Some pastors believe that speaking in tongues (linguistics) is necessary to prove that one has been baptized by the Spirit. They feel a "manifestation" is required to demonstrate to the local church that the Holy Spirit is present. But this is not biblical when all the verses are studied.

Such views keep believers in Christ in constant anxiety in order to "prove" their salvation. They end up spiritually frustrated, or simply fabricating a claim that they have "experienced" the work of the Spirit of God by an imagined tongues manifestation.

> When all the pieces are assembled (Acts 1:5, 8; 2:4; 10:44-48; 11:15-18; 1 Cor. 12:13), it becomes clear that Spirit baptism occurs every time someone into the body of Christ, placed into organic union with Christ, and is actually identified with Christ in His death, burial, and resurrection (Rom. 6:1-11). Moreover, that person is identified with every other believer who is in Christ. He, or she, becomes a member of the body of Christ. (*A Bible Handbook to the Acts of the Apostles*, p. 161)

The baptism of the Spirit also included the giving of spiritual gifts, by the Holy Spirit (1 Cor. 12:12-31). Those gifts are not delayed but are imparted at the moment of belief, though they must be cultivated and exercised as the believer matures.

Recommended Books

Mal Couch, gen. ed., *A Bible Handbook to the Acts of the Apostles* (Grand Rapids: Kregel); Charles Ryrie, *The Holy Spirit* (Chicago: Moody); Thomas Edgar, *Satisfied by the Promise of the Spirit* (Grand Rapids: Kregel); Mal Couch, *The Holy Spirit* (Ft. Worth, TX: Tyndale Seminary).

Baptism, Water

While *baptizo* and *bapto* means technically to dip, immerse, the thought behind these words simply means to wash, cleanse. Washing with water was indeed a physical cleanser that became in time a symbol for spiritual purification. This picture was coupled to the dynamic spiritual work of the Holy Spirit in sanctifying the believer.

There is a long progression of teaching about water purification. To wash the feet that may get dirty is first mentioned in Genesis 18:4. The first consecration washing took place when Israel came out of Egypt. Moses told the people to wash their clothes (Exod. 19:10). Leviticus 11-17 gives the full teaching on the washings required of the priests. In the Septuagint, the Greek translation of the Old Testament, the word is often used. Naaman was told to dip himself (2 Kings 5:14). To plunge, dip, or wash, using various forms of *bapto*, are found in Exodus 12:22; Leviticus 4:6, 17; and Judges 12:7.

John baptized in the Jordan River the repentant (Mark 1:4; Luke 3:3; and elsewhere) as a sign of cleansing, but he prophesied that Jesus the Messiah would someday baptize with the Holy Spirit (Mt. 3:11). Before His ascension, Jesus reminded His disciples of this Spirit baptism coming (Acts 1:5), that indeed took place at Pentecost (2:1-4; 11:15-16).

Almost no evangelical leaders hold that water baptism is required for salvation, though some mistakenly try to use Acts 2:38 to prove that this is so. This passage is not translated well from the Greek text. By grouping the second and third persons separately in the grammar construction, the passage becomes clearer. It should read:

> *Repent all of you for the forgiveness of all of your sins; and all of you shall receive the gift of the Holy Spirit.*
>
> *Then let each of you individually be baptized in the name of Jesus Christ.*

Water Baptism and the Gospel

Two important passages tell us that water baptism is not a requirement for salvation. In Paul's great definitive passage about the gospel "by which also you are saved" (1 Cor. 15:1-5), he does not include baptism. And in his bringing the gospel to the Corinthians, as mentioned in 1:12-17, he actually separates water baptism from the gospel message. Here, the apostle writes that, though he baptized Crispus and Gaius, he was not sure whom else he baptized in Corinth; then he remembers that he baptized the household of one called Stephanas (v. 15). But he comes back and adds, "I do not know whether I baptized any other." Verse 17 is the key:

For Christ did not send me to baptize, but to preach the gospel, not in cleverness of speech, that the cross of Christ should not be made void.

If water baptism were essential for salvation in the dispensation of the church, Paul could not have written these words.

Water Baptism and the Local Church

Some churches wrongly hold to the belief that water baptism should be tied to membership in the local church, but this is proven wrong by the account of the baptism of the Ethiopian eunuch by Philip (Acts 8:36-39). There were no indications that any church membership was involved when the man believed in the Lord and then was baptized (vv 36-37).

Recommended Books

Charles Ryrie, *Basic Theology*, (Chicago: Moody).

See **Baptism, Infant; Baptism, Modes of.**

Camp, Youth

There is nothing that pulls people together like a getaway into the natural world that is the creation of God. Because of this, youth camps have been extremely successful in giving an energetic setting for teaching spiritual truth.

This writer (Mal Couch) first went to camp at the age of 12, and accepted the Lord as Savior at a weekend camp at 16. For some reason the great outdoors, and the closeness of the campers and their leaders, seem to stimulate an environment for transmitting the importance of personal salvation, and for punctuating the need for living that salvation out in life experiences.

Besides the spiritual experiences that should be central at camp, there is also the excitement of peer relationships, and the challenge of living, even if briefly, in the outdoors. Below are some advantages of camping:

- Close companionship with youth of the same age.

- Outdoor challenges.

- Focused and concentrated Bible study.

- An opportunity to learn from and look up to older camp leaders.

Below are suggestions for creating outdoor camping experiences for the church youth:

- If no formal campgrounds are available, the church can lease a camping area in a state park, and make its own camp program.

- A church may be able to lease established camping facilities and make its own program.

- In most regions of the country, there are facilities with fully planned out camping experiences to which youngsters can be sent.

There is no magic formula to "doing" camp! Planning activities and a schedule is not hard to accomplish. Dedication of "activity" and spiritual leadership is what makes a successful camping program.

- Advertising should begin early for the camping outing because many families plan ahead for their summer activities.

- Theme camps may also be successful focusing around: music, computer learning, specific sports activities, hiking, boating, etc.

The Registration sheet should have the following:

- The parents' signature

- Parents' permission to take the youngster to a hospital in case of an emergency

- The name of the medical insurance company along with the insurance account number

- Medicines listed that must be taken by the camper

- Any allergies with which the camper may have problems

- Home and work phone numbers

- Parents' permission for unusual activities, such as rock climbing, boating, etc.

- Information about the camper's ability to swim.

Finally, it would be wise to have early camp planning, along with early enlisting of camp workers.

Charismatic Issues

What is meant by the phrase "charismatic issues"? The charismatic movement has a history that goes back to the early church (e.g., I Cor. 12-14), but within the last century can be outlined in three "waves" as follows.

First Wave (about 1906)

Pentecostal movement, followed by the founding of Pentecostal denominations: Assemblies of God, Foursquare Church, etc., generally including manifestations described in the New Testament, and stipulating that the so-called gift of tongues was the evidence of having received the baptism of the Holy Spirit.

Second Wave (about 1960)

Charismatic movement, which was Pentecostalism moving into non-Pentecostal denominations and founding of new Charismatic church groups, still largely including manifestations described in the New Testament, but with less insistence that tongues specifically was an essential to spiritual growth and/or and evidence of the baptism of the Holy Spirit.

Third Wave (about 1980)

John Wimber established the Vineyard churches, with manifestations that are not described in the New Testament, flowing into other denominations and churches. This movement has tended to be very ecumenical, and the manifestations have tended to become increasingly outside of anything found among believers as described in the New Testament.

Is the Charismatic Movement or Charismatic Influence a Problem in the Church?

Charismatic elements were evident in New Testament times, when tongues and other sign gifts were in evidence, but Paul had to deal with problems of immaturity and fleshly behavior in their use in the church (I Cor. 12-14). By the latter half of the second century, the expression of charismatic utterances by Montanus and his two prophetesses was met with declarations of heresy by other church leaders. Early church records consistently and persistently indicate that no expression of the sign gifts was considered valid after the time of the apostles. Numerous manifestations expressed in the charismatic movement today have no correlation to anything described in the New Testament, and have been shown on numerous occasions to be divisive (Titus 3:10, 11).

The charismatic movement has grown substantially in recent decades, not based upon sound biblical exegesis and conviction, but rather based on the appeal to experience, emotions and special knowledge. Societal and church support for these trends can be traced to the 18th and 19th century's teachings of men such as Wesley, Schleiermacher, Kierkegaard, and others of humanistic, experiential and existential viewpoint.

The mistaken appeal of the charismatic movement that these various manifestations are biblically founded is based upon a fundamental misunderstanding of the New Testament in the following aspects.

The transition from one dispensation to another is not typical of the dispensation to follow. Noah's flood was not typical of the dispensation to follow, nor was the manner of God's giving of the Law to Moses typical of the dispensation to follow. The book of Acts, which took place over about a 30-year period, contains events that are unique to the transition it describes, and not to be applied to the centuries of the church dispensation that followed. Manifestations which pertained to the unique and time-specific role of the apostles, and the proper expression of those manifestations, ended with the apostles.

Acts describes the decades just before the execution of judgment against the Jews, chronicling the setting aside of the Jews for a time based on their prevailing and consistent rejection of the Messiah. Tongues is a sign for the Jews, especially to those who do not believe (1 Cor. 14:22). Every instance of the introduction of tongues among the early church in Acts included one or more apostles, Jews present, appeared to be singular in each population, and did not involve asking for the manifestation, practicing or coaching (Acts 2, 10, 19).

The only discussion of the gift of tongues in any of the epistles (1 Cor. 12-14) is in the context of problems, pride and immaturity (1 Cor. 3:1-3). In that same context, we are told that not all in the body of Christ are intended to have the gift of tongues (1 Cor. 12:30). All things are to be orderly in the church (1 Cor. 14:40).

The nature of God's progressive revelation from Old Testament times to the completion of the New Testament canon was such that continuing revelation, which was appropriate for the New Testament era, became eclipsed by the New Testament itself, as God's final and total revelation (1 Cor. 13:8-13; Jude 3; Rev. 22:18).

What are some of the Indicators of Charismatic Influence or Susceptibility?

Emphasis on Experience and Spiritual Events:

- *Experiencing God* and similar books

- Focus on "my experience" versus what is true

- Pursuit of excitement and/or special revelations

- Teachings and perspectives on sanctification coming out of Wesleyan, Nazarene, Holiness, or similar backgrounds that convey or promote "instant maturity"

Lack of Solid, Doctrinally-Founded Teaching:

- Believing that intensity of emotional expression is a measure of the degree of spiritual impact in the life of a believer or church body

- Shallow and/or narrow teaching

- Believers not being equipped for true ministry, but for dependence or superficiality

- Believers not able to study God's word in depth for themselves (2 Tim. 2:15)

- Lack of emphasis on discernment, reinforced by ecumenical or non-dispensational teaching (Eph. 4:11-16)

Language and practices that derive from non-Christian, perhaps even occult sources:

- Bathed in prayer, blanketed in prayer, "holy" barking, spiritual mapping, etc.

- Language that fails to recognize what God has already accomplished & blessed us with, so that believers ask for what they already have, including asking for the

Holy Spirit, whom they already have (Rom. 8:9)

Looking for Quick Results and Bending to Pressure:
- Exhausted, frustrated or discouraged pastors

- Lack of pastoral understanding and depth

- Looking for visible and impressive results

- Pragmatism instead of biblical truth

- Unwillingness to stand firm on solid doctrine for fear of negative reaction

Music Contributing to Charismatic Influence:
- Words based on Dispensation of Law and not Church Dispensation, Invitations for the Holy Spirit to come, descend, return or fall; making of human promises to God

- Repetitive words and melody lines

- Aggressive spiritual warfare in lyrics

- Appeal to feeling the Holy Spirit, subjective and human-centered lyrics

- Performance, showiness and people-pleasing given priority over worship and doctrinal depth in music

- Composition that overpowers the lyrics

Emphasis on Entertaining vs. Training:
- Believers drawn by entertainment and feeling good versus desiring of the meat of the word of God

- No expectation that involvement with the church will lead to spiritual maturity and equipping for ministry

- Musical or other performance skills given priority over spiritual maturity and understanding

- Seeking impressive and showy manifestations or other evidences

So how should pastors prevent charismatic influence and susceptibility in their church? The answer is well summarized in Paul's letter to the Ephesians (4:11-15). He says, "...pastors and teachers, for the equipping of the saints for the work of service, to the building up of the body of Christ; until we all attain to the unity of the faith, and of the knowledge of the Son of God, to a mature man, to the measure of the stature which belongs to the fullness of Christ. As a result, we are no longer to be children, tossed here and there by waves and carried about by every wind of doctrine, by the trickery of men, by craftiness in deceitful scheming; but speaking the truth in love, we are to grow up in all aspects into Him who is the head, even Christ..." This is how we should put this passage into practice as pastors in dealing with the charismatic movement:

- Teach the biblical nature of and requirements for spiritual growth (Col. 1:28,29)
- Warn believers of the tendency to follow the culture in the seeking of experiences

- Teach the whole counsel of God, including the nature of spiritual gifts (Acts 20:27)

- Teach believers how to study God's word for themselves (2 Tim. 2:15)

- Teach the character of the transition between the dispensation of Law and the dispensation of Grace as conveyed in Acts

- Warn against adopting occult practices that are sweeping through some church groups

- Urge believers to stand firm on solid doctrine (1 Tim. 6:20,21; Jude 3)

- Be discerning about music which encourages and teaches charismatic doctrines, practices, and feeling-based faith

- Seek to train rather than to entertain

Recommended Books

Thomas Baxter, *Charismatic Gift of Tongues* (Grand Rapids: Kregel); Thomas Baxter, *Gifts of the Spirit* (Grand Rapids: Kregel); Thomas R. Edgar, *Satisfied by the Promise of the Spirit* (Grand Rapids: Kregel).

Charity Issues

The church should always provide charitable help for those outside of Christ. Medical or material help has always been a part of the concern of Christians for "whoever" needs it, whether in locations overseas, or on the home front.

But as well, "charity begins at home." The New Testament has a lot to say about helping those in the body of Christ.

Through the Bible, God has placed a high priority on care for the weak and helpless. In the societal laws given for the nation of Israel, the Lord states of those who might afflict an orphan or widow, "I will surely hear his cry; and My anger will be kindled, and I will kill you with the sword; and your wives shall become widows and your children orphans" (Exod. 22:23-24). By using such words, one can see that God takes the issue of neglect, abuse, or mistreatment very seriously!

Of Himself, the Lord says, I am "a Father of the fatherless and a Judge for the widows, [because God is] in His holy habitation" (Ps. 68:5). James, in his painfully practical book, states, "This is pure religion in the sight of God and Father, to visit orphans and widows in their distress" (James 1:27). Visit here means more than simply dropping in. Throughout the New Testament, the word means "to provide for or "to care for" (Matt. 25:36, 43; Acts 7:23, 15:36).

When it comes to the care of the sick, a church with a team of concerned leaders is richly blessed. If that local church is but served by one minister, he may soon weary of calling on the many who may be ill, both in home visits and in the hospital. In order that the teaching ministry of the assembly be unhindered, it is beneficial to have those with the personal gift of relating to people and their problems carry out the main task of visitation. Though cards, letters, and phone calls may raise the spirits of those confined by infirmities, nothing can substitute for the personal touch.

Time with the sick may move slowly and drain the mental and physical resources of a single pastor. With a local congregation of any significant size, he cannot do it all. That is why Paul calls for multiple elders/pastors, and for active deacons. The two groups work together. Also, such leadership can certainly also appoint members of the congregation to help out, so that no one is neglected.

Recommended Books
Mal Couch, *A Biblical Theology of the Church* (Grand Rapids: Kregel).

Children, Training of

The spiritual training of children is mentioned early in the Bible, beginning with specific instructions given in the Torah. The commandments, statutes, and judgments were to be taught by the fathers "so that you and your son and your grandson might fear the Lord your God ... all the days of your life, and that your days be prolonged" (Deut. 6:1-2). God's laws were to be on the heart of the parent (v. 6), and were to be taught diligently when the father sat in his house, walked in the way, and when he laid down and when he arose (v. 7).

Home Defense

While the home was to be the first-line bastion for teaching spiritual truth, it was not the only one. The law was to be read to all of Israel (31:11), and taught from town to town before the men, women, children, and the stranger in their midst (v. 12). "And their children, who have not known, will hear and learn to fear the Lord your God, as long as you live on the land [of Israel]" (v. 13).

When the Jews had returned from the captivity in Babylon, Ezra set up a high podium, and then gathered a great crowd to hear the law of Moses. Men, woman, "and all who could listen with understanding [including youngsters] ... were to be attentive to the [reading of the] book of the law" (Neh. 8:2-3).

The book of Proverbs also gives guidelines to all the family members, but the first seven chapters set forth the words of a father to his son. For example, "My sons, listen to me and pay attention to the words of my mouth" (7:24). These verses are focusing on sons, so that young men may be reigned in early by their fathers in order to learn to fear God and to do what is right. If you get the son, the daughter hears also. But more importantly, you bless a future new family if that young father is trusting God!

Timothy was blessed with the home teaching and the sharing of the faith of his mother Eunice, and his grandmother Lois (2 Tim. 1:5). Because of their faithfulness, "from childhood you have known the sacred writings which are able to give you the wisdom that leads to salvation through faith which is in Christ Jesus" (3:15). In the home Paul instructs that the children are to be brought "up in the discipline and instruction of the Lord" (Eph. 6:4), and they are to "be obedient to ... parents in all things, for this is well-pleasing to the Lord" (Col. 3:20).

While the home is the most important for spiritually training children, the church plays its role also, though unfortunately, many parents leave the biblical education to the church and neglect their responsibility.

Second Line of Defense

The church teaching staff needs to make certain there is an adequate biblical diet for all ages of the children. Salvation must always be taught clearly. Sunday school curriculum must be carefully selected for doctrinal accuracy and for clarity of presenting the spiritual truths of the Scriptures.

Since many publishers of curriculum are moving to the left, this is a daunting task! However, there are certain textbooks that make good study material for the middle and older age groups (and even for adults), such as Chafer and Walvoord's *Major Bible Themes* (Zondervan), Charles Ryrie's *Basic Theology* (Moody), and Irving Jensen's two volume *Survey of the Old Testament* and *Survey of the New Testament* (Moody). Also usable for Sunday school texts: Mal Couch's *The Fundamentals for the Twenty-First Century*, and *A Bible Handbook to the Acts of the Apostles* (Kregel). Dave Noebel's *Understanding the Times* (Summit) is excellent for life-preparation for older teens about to graduate from high school, and who are going off to college. This book gives biblical answers to the philosophies and isms that are anti-biblical and that are aimed at destroying Christianity.

Children, Clubs

Youngsters are social beings that thrive on peer relationships and peer learning. Clubs such as AWANA need to be considered for training children in the church setting. The frontline of spiritual learning should be the home, but unfortunately, even among the best of Christian families, not enough is being done under the spiritual leadership of the father and the mother.

The church has become the prime base for spiritual and biblical teaching. Clubs that pull the children together around peer activities, and a reasonable amount of fun and games, really seem to service the children well.

There are other clubs besides AWANA. All clubs should be evaluated on:

- How they clearly present the gospel

- How they uphold the integrity of Scripture as the base of the Christian's authority

- How well the material applies the Bible to life issues on the various levels of the children

- How well they are holding the line against liberalism, and the hard-core Charismatic Movement.

For years, home Bible classes have been effective in teaching the Word of God and bringing youngsters to Christ. This option should still be considered for both evangelism of children and for teaching them scriptural principles. Leaders should be biblically well trained, and the material used should be scripturally solid and easy to use.

Some have warned that they see some questionable trends coming into some of the nationally well-known clubs. All churches must be the keepers at the door in watching for slippage taking place in some of these groups. Doctrinal changes can come in a most subtle way so that they are un-noticeable.

Finally, Bible-based clubs for children will not only touch the children but will also reel in their parents. If the parents who do not attend church see spiritual enthusiasm in their youngsters, they will begin coming to services and Bible studies.

Church Growth, Philosophy of

What is Church Growth?

The phrase "church growth" does not have a singular definition, but instead has come to mean several different things, including, but not limited to:

- Numerical growth of attendees in a specific congregation and location

- Numerical growth in membership in a specific congregation and location

- Numerical growth of churches originating from one congregation

- Spiritual growth of individual believers within a congregation

- Spiritual growth of interdependence between believers within a congregation

Recent trends among churches have been focused on increasing numbers of attendees and members (definitions 1 and 2), with little regard, or utter disregard, for whether those attendees are actually believers. The business model approach that targets "market segments", seeks to meet "felt needs", and endeavors to be "seeker sensitive" has been increasingly popular among "progressive" churches. Some of these churches have become the size of a municipality, and have spawned the planting of other churches in the same region and in more distant areas, fulfilling definition three above.

Church growth definitions four and five above seek to develop believers spiritually, not based upon felt needs or elements of the business model approach, but upon the biblical definition of spiritual maturity (Matt. 28:18-20; Eph. 4:11-15, Col. 1:28,29). "You therefore, beloved, knowing this beforehand, be on your guard so that you are not carried away by the error of unprincipled men and fall from your own steadfastness, but grow in the grace and knowledge of our Lord and Savior Jesus Christ. To Him be the glory, both now and to the day of eternity. Amen." (2 Peter 3:17-18).

What is the Basis of Biblical Church Growth

Biblical church growth leaves it to the Lord to add to the church, using those approaches, methods and philosophies that are consistent with the Scriptures (Acts 2:41; 5:14; 1 Cor. 3:6-9). Each member of the body of believers has his place in the building up of the body, of which but one gift is specifically given in our time for the purpose of evangelism. The pastors in particular and the church as a whole should be aiming for maturity in every believer. That growth which will be directed toward spiritual maturity will consist of:

- Knowledge and Reckoning

- Abiding and Resting

- Depending and Walking

Shepherds in each church should keep these elements in focus.

So what is wrong with the business model or seeker sensitive approach to church growth? The business model puts numerical growth in human hands instead of leaving it to God. The business model also produces programs and methods that are based on human wisdom and can easily run crosscurrent with what God has conveyed in Scripture. For data input, the business model approach gathers data on expressed needs from people who are perhaps not saved, and who may be basing their input on immaturity and fleshly character. There is nothing to gain in trying to please the flesh to grow people spiritually. Using this input to guide church strategy and direction assures that spiritual immaturity, fleshly character and unredeemed souls will steer the direction of the church. Further, the worldly trends that course their way through society will be assured of doing the same in the church. The church becomes, then, all too much like the world, instead of being in sharp contrast with it (Rom. 12:1, 2).

Seeker sensitive churches pursue bringing the un-churched into the church. Bringing unbelievers into the church is not only the norm, but also a primary focus of such efforts. There are two principle problems with this:

- Entertainment and amusement all too easily become the focus, rather than spiritual maturity.

- The church is for believers, and the presence of unbelievers is incidental, but not to be the primary intent for gathering (1 Cor. 14:23, 24).

The result of the business model and/or seeker sensitive approach is that the church all too easily becomes "a mile wide and an inch deep". The biblical goal should be to present the gospel of salvation where the unsaved who need it already are (not relying upon bringing them into the church gathering), and leave it to the Lord as to how many are added to the church (Acts 2:47). But as for church shepherds, let them focus by the Lord's enabling upon making true disciples of every one who is saved (Col. 1:28, 29). Aim for spiritual depth and doctrinal stability in every believer the Lord has given to your care.

Church, Home Groups

The New Testament Church Meeting in Homes

The New Testament church, as God formed it in Jerusalem, was centered in two places: The temple and in homes. From Acts 2 to Acts 5, the temple is mentioned almost two dozen times, then not again until Acts 21, when Paul found himself in long-term trouble over false accusations about bringing a Gentile into the temple. From Acts 2, however, we see a pattern of meeting in homes that continued throughout the New Testament era, and has continued with believers over the centuries to this day and throughout the world. There are about 30 references in the New Testament, from Acts 2 on, where believers' houses are described as an occasional or regular place of ministry, with four references to churches meeting - apparently regularly - in a house.

Two Modes of Home Church Meetings

As for regular meetings of the church in homes, there are two biblical modes of meeting in homes:

- The home meeting is the gathering of that specific local body of believers.

- The home meeting is a smaller group from a larger congregation that regularly meets elsewhere.

Each mode of meeting will be addressed separately, since each has a different form and purpose.

The "House Church"

House churches, where the meeting of believers at a home is the local meeting of that local body of believers, may be either a temporary arrangement until the church takes up more substantial facilities, or the permanent arrangement. In either case, the church should look to establishing the key elements of a biblical fellowship. Even though meeting regularly in a home, the church should seek to establish elders, consolidate its doctrine, and develop the ability to provide teaching, conduct worship and other biblically based functions within the church. There may not be a need, due to its smaller size and minimal complexity, to establish the home church as a legal entity. Indeed, the New Testament church did not even have that as an option, much less a need.

The advantage of the home is its simplicity as well as the opportunity for intimacy and regular expression of hospitality – something which many larger churches cannot offer without developing some smaller group gatherings as well. The disadvantage of the house church is its limitation by virtue of building size, configuration, parking capacity and/or zoning regulations. In some cases, there may be difficulty in identifying men who are both willing and qualified to serve as elders, though it appears the early church solved this limitation by associating with all the churches in the city, and even with other cities.

The "Home Fellowship Group"

Even larger churches will often establish home churches as means of addressing fellowship and/or other needs within the larger body of believers. These will typically serve a need that the larger congregation simply cannot offer. A larger congregation may have a network of such smaller home fellowship groups, and therefore the total church structure and provision will not be needed at each home, but there will be a need for a leader, if not a teacher at each home. Other purposes that may be designated for the gathering, such as prayer groups, young married couples, etc. will need to be accommodated by arrangements in each home or orchestrated from the larger church congregation. Even though there are elders in the larger church congregation, any smaller church gatherings in homes will need to have a shepherding function extended to the home gathering.

Church Membership

Apparently the New Testament did not have a formal church membership or inauguration into the fellowship of the congregation. By one hundred years and later, water baptism became a requirement of church fellowship, or became a kind of test, for relating with the local assembly.

In would seem biblical that those wishing to fellowship in a church would be admitted based on their profession of faith only. The apostles do not give any specific criteria for joining the group.

However, there are practical considerations, and most churches put into place some sort of check for full membership. Often it goes like this:

• The person must make a profession of faith

• He or she must agree to the written doctrinal statement.

Many churches also find it prudent to put fledgling members into a doctrinal orientation class in order to make sure they understand all of the key teachings of Scripture.

It must be admitted that these guidelines are proper, given the nature of what people need to know about doctrine, and about what they need to understand concerning their place and role in the congregation.

As far as we can tell, in the early church there was only one church for all the faithful in each city or community. Because of this, all who were interested in the gospel would come to hear the Word taught. In addition, if they accepted Christ as their Savior, they became part of the assembly. Anyone causing confusion, who was teaching false doctrine, or who was a deadbeat and living off the congregation, could be driven out of the fellowship. Those caught in immorality could be brought before the church and charged with the sin. They could also be kept from the group if there was no repentance.

The Bottom Line

The most biblical way of dealing with membership would be that the church would have no hard and fast guidelines for membership, except certainly, confession of faith. Strong elders are the "keepers" of the truth for the church, and should be able to deal with any problems that might cause conflict in the local church body.

Of course, it is understood that, if there were heresy or a violent disagreement with what the church teaches, it would be best that those people move on to other territory rather than stay and create confusion. If people with different beliefs are not comfortable, this only makes sense!

Church, The Body of Christ

While there is the local church, there is the church that is the spiritual body of Christ. This is the universal (not universalism!) church that consists of all believers worldwide who know Jesus Christ as personal Savior. Though not all such believers may speak the same earthly language, we are still brothers in Christ, united by faith around the death, burial, and resurrection of the Lord.

Christians in the local Corinthian church were walking around as fleshly, or in carnality (1 Cor. 3:2-3) and could only take milk for sustenance and not solid food (v. 2). But the apostle Paul yet says of them that they were "sanctified in Christ Jesus, saints by calling, with all who in every place call upon the name of our Lord Jesus Christ, there Lord and ours" (1:2). This great company who are scattered everywhere have been baptized by one Spirit into the body of Christ (12:12-13). However specifically, the apostle went on and described the believers in the local assembly as members "of the church of God which is at Corinth" (1:2).

Spiritual baptism has to be for all believers because it forms the basis of the actual salvation process, since every Christian has "been buried with Him in baptism, in which you were also raised up with Him through faith in the working of God, who raise Him from the dead. ... He made you alive together with Him, having forgiven us all our transgressions" (Col. 2:12-13).

Some pastors mistakenly hold to only one church, and it is formed by faith, and by the ceremony of water baptism. They even add that water baptism is the spiritual baptism of the Holy Spirit! This teaching violates the clear evidence that there is the spiritual body of Christ, and then there is the local church, the outward gathering or collection of believers in a specific city or place.

Recommended Books

Mal Couch, *A Biblical Theology of the Church* (Grand Rapids: Kregel); Charles Ryrie, *Basic Theology* (Chicago: Moody).

See **Church, The Local Assembly; Church, Government of.**

Church, The Local Assembly

All of the apostles' letters are written to local congregations. For example, Paul writes to the "saints in Christ Jesus who are in Philippi, including the overseers and deacons" (Phil. 1:1). He shows in his 1 Corinthian letter that there are saints fellowshipping in a local church, and there is the spiritual body of Christ worldwide.

> *To the church of God which is at Corinth, to those who have been sanctified in Christ Jesus, saints by calling, with all who in every place call upon the name of our lord Jesus Christ, their Lord and ours. (1 Cor. 1:2)*

In the local church there can be a mixture of believers who are walking spiritually, and those who are living fleshly (3:1-4). The problem with those who are fleshly is that they are not growing spiritually (vv. 6-8). The seven churches of Revelation 2-3 also show that people within one congregation may be walking about in spiritual integrity, or in spiritual immaturity. These churches prove as well that churches may have different problems and temptations that retard their witness. The believers in the assembly can be seduced by the culture and even be harassed by Satan.

Local assemblies may also have divisions, strife and jealously (1 Cor. 3:3), and be harboring those who teach error and heresy (Titus 1:10-14; 2 Tim. 4:14-17). Local congregations must be guided by strong elders, who watch over the spiritual growth of the flocks (Titus 1; Acts 20:17-32).

Recommended Books

Mal Couch, *A Biblical Theology of the Church* (Grand Rapids: Kregel); Charles Ryrie, *Basic Theology* (Chicago: Moody).

See **Church, The Body of Christ; Church, Government of.**

Church, Government of

The New Testament shows that the earliest churches were spiritually led by the elders, with a body of deacons who carried out very important human tasks, and who watched over the needs of charity in the congregations. Elder appointment, and elder rule—this is clearly the teaching of the New Testament. But through history, other forms of church government arose.

- While the word bishop was an alternate word to describe the church elder, in several hundred years after the apostolic church, bishops were ruling over a group of churches that had, in a sense, lost their independence.

- Federal church government and headship developed through the Roman Catholic system, with the pope controlling the bishops and cardinals, who in turn have authority over the local assemblies.

- Congregational-elder rule. Many churches have moved to this approach to church government, with varying involvement of the assembly making decisions as to how to govern the church. Elders and deacons are elected by popular vote. This may be the most popular system used with evangelical churches.

- Congregational. To the extreme, the congregation votes on almost every issue. The sheep have full control, with the shepherds only following directions.

- Elder leadership. Elders are appointed by the elder group (Titus 1:5): "For this reason [Titus] I left you in Crete, that you might set in order what remains, and appoint elders [plural] in every city as I directed you."

The congregation may have a say in the choosing of missionaries (Acts 15:19-29), and the setting forth of candidates for the office of deacon (6:1-7). However, the elders are spiritually responsible for the way they manage and take care of the church of God (1 Tim. 3:5). Despite leadership responsibilities, elders must not run over the sheep, and if they become morally stubborn, they can be brought before the assembly and rebuked, "so that the rest also may be fearful of sinning" (5:20).

In America, elder leadership is in disfavor because of the propensity toward American democracy. Most churches and even trained pastors do not even know that this is what the Scriptures teach.

Recommended Books
Mal Couch, *A Biblical Theology of the Church* (Grand Rapids: Kregel).

See Elder, **Deacon, Church.**

Church Website

The Internet – An unavoidable Fact

The Internet is an unavoidable fact with which churches, ministries and their leadership need to reckon. The "Net" is ubiquitous and interwoven into the fabric and mindset of our modern society. To put it simply, most people in North America, Europe and much of the rest of the first world *expect* to be able to read about most anything on-line and that includes Christians looking for your church and non-Christians looking for religious information. Because of the lowering price of computers, the Internet is coming into greater and greater use in less developed countries as well. The keys to the Internet are its ability to rapidly deliver information to on-line users on a vast array of subjects that they select, including your church and its beliefs, and interaction with others via e-mail and web-based libraries, discussion forums and order fulfillment systems.

For these reasons, the decision today to have a church website is roughly equivalent to a decision in the 1980's as to whether or not your church or ministry wanted to be listed in the Yellow Pages. The contrast with the Yellow Pages is that the Internet potentially extends the reach of your church worldwide. For example, *The Conservative Theological Society* website, *www.ConservativeOnline.org* has regular visits from users in Russia, Africa, Asia, South America as well as North America and has, at the time of publication, many thousands of visitors per month. Granted, many congregations are satisfied with their current level of public awareness and do not see the need for a Yellow Pages ad or an Internet presence. But for the great number of churches that want to increase their public visibility, broadcast Biblical doctrines, and enhance the services to, and interaction with their members, a website is a readily available and ideal tool.

Your Website's Purpose

By far the most important factor in the decision to have a website for your local church is to determine its *purpose*. Establishing the purpose for your website's existence will result in graduated levels of commitment on your part to develop material for it and to fund the development and maintenance of it. These commitment levels range from a one-time, one or two hour session and small setup charge for a one page, static, informational web, all the way to having a full time web developer or development team on staff. Most church websites fall somewhere between these extremes, but you need to decide why you want the website, how much you want it to do, and balance that with your financial and time resources. In general, the more a site does, and the more often it is updated, the more time and financial resources it will take.

If the decision is made to go beyond a simple one-page informational site, the name of the game is *content*, regularly updated and enhanced. Websites that attract and keep visitors are those that are regularly updated with fresh and interesting information, articles and discussion forums. The best way to grow your user base is to keep your current visitors/users coming back for more. Satisfied users will do much of the work of promoting your site.

Words to the Wise – Control the Content and the Presentation

Consider carefully too, *who* will do your website development. A static informational page or larger static informational web will require little ongoing effort, but anything beyond that will require both an ongoing input of content from you and/or your church leaders, as well as growing technical expertise, either on your part or on a staff member. Determine, before you begin, that you can sustain the push to develop the site and the expertise to grow with it. In other words, understand what you're getting into, and don't "bite off more than you can chew."

A bit of pastoral advice and Biblical warning is in order at this point: As a pastor and church leader you have responsibility for what is put on the website, just as you have responsibility for what is said from the pulpit. Don't make the mistake of relegating site content development to someone in your congregation just because they have the time and expertise and you don't. Make sure you, or another doctrinally astute leader, has direct editorial control or at least oversight. A website is like a pulpit on steroids. It is a megaphone to the world. That slip of the tongue in the pulpit, or that badly delivered sermon, or a doctrinally questionable teaching may get shrugged off by your congregation, but the same mistake on the Internet has potentially worldwide repercussions.

The Internet is a visual medium, so ensure that your web pages are attractive, the fonts easy to read, and that there are no misspellings. Good content sloppily presented reflects poorly on your church and on the Lord. A humorous word from the wise: this author has found that for some reason most programmers are poor spellers. Larger churches and ministries should have a review panel of pastors and artists and/or editors to make sure the content, grammar and presentation meet high standards. Smaller churches should have at least one person other than the web developer review the website regularly and proof all articles before they are published.

Example Website Categories

The following are some example categories of websites along with a rating for the resources required to develop and maintain them.

- Resource Rating -
1 = Simple one time fee and/or development time. Under $10/month (or free) web-hosting fee.
2 = 1-10 hours a month and up to $20/month for web-hosting and other fees.
3 = 5-10 hours a week and up to $40/month.
4 = 11-20 hours a week and >$40/month.
5 = 21-40+ hours a week and >$40/month.

Static Informational *Page*, including church name, address, phone number, meeting times, a brief statement about your church, your e-mail address and a photo or two. If you don't do the development in-house, expect to pay a one-time developer fee and perhaps a small monthly fee. Rating = 1.

Dynamic Informational *Page*, includes above, but with a regularly updated calendar of events that you supply. Rating = 2.

Semi-Static Informational *Web*, includes above, but with a web of pages that includes your statement of doctrine, various departments (youth programs, Sunday school, etc), missionaries, etc. This web could also have a page of links to other favorite and doctrinally approved websites. Rating = 2.

Dynamic Informational *Web*, includes above, but with a web of pages that are regularly updated and changed based on department activities, etc. Rating = 2-3.

Dynamic Interaction *Web*, includes above, but with a web of pages that include discussion forums, doctrinal articles, etc. The site may include the ability for users to make a donation on-line or sign up to receive sermon tapes or other light database duty. The site may also provide the ability for users to listen to sermon recordings on-line and or take classes via web interaction. Rating = 3-4.

e-Commerce *Web*, includes above, but with full ability to take orders for books, tapes and other inventoried material, including complete, high volume credit card transactions, order fulfillment, inventory control, etc. Rating = 3-5.

Of course this list contains only examples of what you might do with your web. The possibilities are limited only by your imagination and your time budget.

Web Development – What You Need

Here is a list of the tools and services for web development. You will need all or some of these:

Web development software. Up front you'll need to decide how deep technically you want to dive. Generally speaking, the more programming power, flash and flexibility you want, the deeper into programming in HTML you'll have to get. If you want to avoid learning a programming language and make your web design more accessible to other non-programmers, you can use web development programs such as Microsoft FrontPage or even MS Word.

Internet access. Of course you'll need access to the internet via a phone line or higher speed connection like DSL. A word of caution, if you develop a website using a high speed connection, make sure to test it with a phone line. A site that operates well on DSL can be so slow as to be unusable on a phone line.

Registering your Domain Name. A website is identified on the web by a unique numeric identifier, which is not very useful to your users. Domain Name Registry is a service that you pay for that registers your unique domain name (www.YourDomainName.org or .com) and associates it on the web with your unique web number. To locate one of these services, do a web search for "Domain Name Registry". Be sure to shop around for a competitive rate.

Web Hosting Service or your own Servers. Your web has to be installed on a server, either your own or on a commercially available server. Setting up your own server is beyond the scope of this article but there are certain circumstances where this may be advisable or necessary. For most webs it makes more sense to use one of the many commercial services available. These provide many valuable and even necessary services to support your website, including e-mail, handling form data, hosting CGI scripts, etc. Do some background checking on the company that is trying to sell you services. Make sure they're financially stable, have a good reputation for tech support, and make sure their up-time record is very good. You want a service with server redundancy. It is also helpful if their servers are physically located on one of the main fiber-optic lines so that they have reliability and high data bandwidth.

Website Promotion. Once your website is up and going, you'll need to promote it. If you want to reach much beyond your local church or community you'll need to consider how to get your site onto the major search engines. For help in doing this, search for "website promotion" and "search engines." These services used to be free but more and more of the major search engines are requiring an annual fee to index your website for their engines.

Those Free Web-Hosting Sites

Most churches have budget constraints, and those web hosts that offer web-hosting services for "free" may seem tempting. Some of them come at the price of your having to provide banner space for their advertisements, and some have ads that pop up when users visit your sites. Others offered by Christian organizations as a service to the church are genuinely free with no strings. However, the old adage goes, "you get what you pay for." Many of these free services offer little or no tech support, and that may be fine for a simple site, but risky for a more complex or mission critical web. Just one problem with your website and you may wish you paid the small monthly web hosting fee that comes with reliable tech support. The best hosting companies offer true 24/7 tech support and are worth the monthly fee if you have any kind of problem. Shop carefully and research thoroughly. A free site may be fine, but be sure of what you are getting into.

Constitution, Church

If a church seeks a nonprofit status with the state, or is seeking IRS tax exemption, a constitution is often required. Both the state and the IRS want to see certain guidelines of responsibility. They want to see the names and the offices of the stewards of the organization. They usually want a board with a president, vice-president, secretary, and treasurer. Often, they want stated how certain procedures will be carried out in the function of the assembly.

There is a real question if a church should so wish to "please" the state and the federal government in these matters. There is no proof of such a constitution setup in the early church. Government can be capricious. The state can turn against the church. A strong argument is made that, if the church goes the "government" way for incorporating, it is already caught in the web of state control and its spiritual mission cut or limited.

Regardless of incorporation issues, many churches "bind" themselves into heavy Wall Street business practices that hinder the work of the Holy Spirit to work through the elders in deciding spiritual matters. Many constitutions wind tightly the procedures so that church business becomes business and brings on wrangling, division, and carnal church politics!

Churches that have limited constitutional guidelines seem to simply "just get the job done" under the leadership of the elders and deacons.

Churches that are constitutionally bound are generally very democratically and congregationally operated, with copious voting and elections to committees. Again, politics may raise its ugly head, with the sheep deciding on the issues of the church, rather than the leaders who are appointed by the Holy Spirit.

Counseling, Definition of

The ministry of *counseling* today has been stolen by secular psychology and has been unduly professionalized. Some states are even going so far as to try to force all pastors to be professionally licensed or they will be unable to counsel their own church members.

There may be a place for training and helping Christians to be better prepared to counsel by the Scriptures, but there can be no cornering of the market to limit every child of God from helping a brother and sister in Christ through tough times.

The Greek verb *parakaleo* and its various other verbal and noun forms is the most common word that conveys the thought of *counseling*. The word means to call alongside someone to encourage and minister to one's needs. As the word is used in some of the contexts of the New Testament, it may also imply "to chide or correct." When used this way, it would be translated to *exhort, exhortation.*

The same word is used to describe the helping ministry of the Holy Spirit, and is often translated in different Bible versions, *Helper, Comforter, Advocate* (the *paraklatos*) (John 14:16, 26; 15:26; 16:7; see also 1 John 2:1). The word and its various forms are used approximately 135 times in the New Testament. One of the most concentrated sections using the word is 2 Corinthians 1, where it is mentioned seven times. Here Paul writes that:

- God is the Father of mercies and God of all comfort (counsel).

- God comforts us in our afflictions.

- We are comforted by Him.

- We have an abundance of comfort (counseling) to give to others through Christ.

- Our affliction helps us bring comfort to others.

- We can comfort each other.

Elsewhere Paul also writes:

- We were counseled through your comfort (2 Cor. 7:13).

- There is a gift of counseling (Rom. 12: 8).

- There is counseling from the Scriptures (15:4).

- Paul's counseling was pure and doctrinally correct (1 Thess. 2:3).

Many evangelical seminaries are teaching counseling as integrationists, mixing the Bible with secular counseling. They mix the theories of Carl Jung, Abraham Maslow, Sigmund Feud, and Carl Rogers. John MacArthur writes:

> The word psychology literally means "the study of the soul." True soul-study cannot be done by unbelievers. After all, only Christians have the resources for comprehending the nature of the human soul and understanding how it can be transformed. The secular discipline of psychology is based on godless assumptions and evolutionary foundations and is capable of dealing with people only superficially. ... Before Freud, the study of the soul was thought of as a spiritual discipline. (*Introduction to Biblical Counseling*, 8)

Because so many pastors today have been university trained, they have received large doses of secular psychological principles in psychology, biology, philosophy, and educational classes. Going on to seminary, many were bombarded again with psychology in the Christian counseling courses.

Many pastors are unaware of how anti-biblical many of the theories used in psychology such as "self-esteem," "the little child within," "self-actualization," the "hierarchy of needs" really is.

Recommended Books

John MacArthur, Introduction to Biblical Counseling (Dallas: Word); Mal Couch, A Biblical Theology of the Church (Grand Rapids: Kregel).

See Counseling, **Within the Church; Counseling, Psychological and Secular.**

Counseling, Within the Church

Counsel, within the biblical definition, will consist of admonishment, comfort, encouragement, teaching and wisdom, which should in fact be taking place between believers in the normal course of their interactions with one another (Rom. 15:14, Heb. 3:13, 1 Thess. 4:18, James 5:16, Rom. 15:1, Gal. 6:1-2, Col. 3:16). So how does a pastor counsel a person who comes to him seeking advice, guidance and resolution of some disturbing, stressful or deep emotional problem that has not found resolution within the normal course of interaction among the body of believers? There are two options; the first is to refer the client to a "Christian counselor" or psychologist, and the second option is to personally counsel the client.

Who can Counsel?

Some believe that only pastors should have the right to counsel in the church setting. Actually, "biblical" counseling has always been practiced since New Testament times. When anyone is "called alongside" for comfort, advice, and encouragement, this is biblical counseling. The so-called "professional" counselors are trying to tell the Christian public that they only have the credentials to help people with acute problems. This is of course wrong.

It is true however, that many pastors place all problems and difficulties under the broad category of sin. Their approach may be too simplistic in that they may seem to say, "Just repent of your sin and the problem will automatically go away!" While confession of sin and repentance may always be the key solution to a problem, people also need to sense patience and understanding from the one helping them. Most human problems do not go away instantly. Time is a great healer when hearts and emotions are damaged!

An ideal situation for counseling in the church setting for couples, women, and even single Christians, would be with the team of the pastor and his wife. If trust can be built with them, this would work in most churches.

See **Counseling, Definition of; Counseling, Psychological and Secular.**

Counseling, Psychological and Secular

What is the Philosophical Basis for the Approach to Counseling?

Secular psychological counseling has been developed over the last century, primarily by those who approach the development of theory with at least a non-biblical outlook, if not an anti-biblical outlook. The secular psychological approach has largely sought to explain the behavior of human beings with the following assumptions:

- Mankind originated by evolutionary processes

- Man's behavior is basically rooted in his animal ancestry

- Man is not a spiritual being, but entirely physical

- The spiritual realm, and spiritual approaches to psychology are superfluous

- God, as defined in the Scriptures, is not a necessary consideration in psychological matters

- The philosophical basis for such secular theories is therefore agnostic to atheistic

- Biblical considerations are therefore seen as irrelevant at a minimum, if not integral to mankind's psychological problems

What is the Assessment of the Problem?

At the core of the development of the approach to secular counseling theories – and there are a couple hundred theories - is the atheistic/agnostic assumption. Built into the assumptions of secular psychological theories is the concept that God is at least irrelevant to, if not a major contributing factor, to mankind's psychological problems. The assessment of the problems of mankind, corporately or individually, is exclusive of any consideration of sin, which is defined as offense against God and falling short of His holy character. Mankind's problems are to be explained entirely in the physical realm within the fields of historical anthropology, biochemistry, physiology, and psychosocial history. Spirituality becomes a vestigial relic of man's evolution or explained based on factors entirely in the physical realm. Scripture says that sin is the problem. Secular psychological theories describe man's problems entirely aside from sin.

What is the objective toward which one is counseling? Secular psychological counseling theories define the objective toward which counseling is directed in terms of human behavior and condition. Reckoning with sin or addressing any spiritual factors is excluded from the counseling process. Secular psychology focuses on what mankind can do and ignores God or deals with God as a problem. God, in the Scriptures, tells us what God has done for mankind's problem, and that the solution is to believe in who He is, what He has done, and the truths He has revealed. Secular psychology and biblical faith could hardly be more antithetical.

How should pastors address secular psychology in their counseling? Secular psychology is based upon ignoring God. Since its assumptions, assessment of mankind's problems, and proposed solutions are opposed to biblical faith, secular psychology has no place in pastoral counseling. Pastoral counseling should be founded on the assumptions, assessments, and objectives conveyed in Scripture. The apostle Paul tells us in 1 Corinthians 2:14, "But a natural man does not accept the things of the Spirit of God, for they are foolishness to him; and he cannot understand them, because they are spiritually appraised." The Greek word translated "natural" is *psuchikos*, from which our English prefix "psycho" is derived. How much more clearly can we be told that secular psychological theory is unable to address the spiritual nature or condition of mankind? Only God's word has the answers (Heb. 4:12).

Psychological counseling is corrupt for the following reasons:

- In the broad understanding, it is evolutionary, anti-God, anti-Bible, naturalistic.

- It does not propagate the ministry of the Holy Spirit.

- It does not advocate redemption, the new birth, and change that only God can bring about.

- It treats the soul from the standpoint of disease. Disease conceptions of misbehavior are bad science and are morally and intellectually deceptive.

- Sinful people are branded as sick or debilitated.

- Sanctioned by medicine, "diseased" people are permanently branded, often as incurable.

- People who think they have a disease often have more trouble "outgrowing" their problems.

Evangelical Christianity is in serious trouble. Our sin is great because we have clothed our humanism in Christian garb and claim that this is right! Psychology, with its victimization counseling methodology drawn straight from humanistic presuppositions, has become the most obvious and open expression of this accommodating worldliness.

Pastors must be extremely careful and warn their flock to avoid secular counseling at all cost!

Recommended Books

Jim Owen, *Christian Psychology's War on God's Word* (Santa Barbara, CA: EastGate Publishers); Stanton Peele, *Diseasing of America* (New York: Lexington Books); Charles J. Sykes, *A Nation of Victims* (New York: St. Martin's Press).

See **Counseling, Definition of; Counseling, Within the Church.**

Cults, Protecting the Congregation From

"The best defense is a good offense!" This little statement is packed with meaning for the church of Jesus Christ today. If people know the truth, they will be less likely to fall for error.

In his letters, the apostle Paul writes volumes about error and heresy. He writes about "those who contradict" (Titus 1:9); of those who teach a contradictory gospel (Gal. 1:8); of doctrines that are contrary "to sound teaching" (1 Tim. 1:10). Luke as well writes about those who "begin contradicting the things spoken by Paul" (Acts 13:45); and Peter speaks of those who "secretly introduce destructive heresies" into the body of Christ (2 Pet. 2:1).

This is why Paul urges the propagation of sound ("healthy") doctrine and teaching. He writes about: (1) sound teaching (1 Tim.1:10); sound words (6:3; 2 Tim. 4:3; Titus 2:8); sound doctrine (1 Tim. 4:6; 2 Tim. 4:3; Titus 1:9; 2:1).

The apostle also reminded the Ephesian elders that, when he was with them, he "did not shrink from declaring to you the whole purpose of God" (Acts 20:27). Purpose is *boulan*, and can best be translated the will, decree, council of God. As a singular word, it gives the thought that Paul taught, as a whole package, the entire Bible, or certainly all the major doctrines and principles found in Scripture.

A Complete Doctrinal Statement

The local church needs to publish a complete and thorough doctrinal statement. It must also be taught and continually explained to the assembly. Cults will always seek an avenue into the congregation. Paul even spoke of this when addressing the Ephesian elders: "After my departure savage wolves will come in among you, not sparing the flock; and from among your own selves (the elder body) men will arise, speaking perverse things, to draw away the disciples after them" (v. 29).

It must be emphasized again, that this doctrinal statement must be complete, dealing with issues of Bible prophecy, the isms, social philosophies, and heresies that are weakening the church.

Recommended Books

Josh McDowell, *A Ready Defense* (Atlanta: Thomas Nelson); *A Handbook of Today's Religions* (Atlanta: Thomas Nelson); Von Baalen, *The Chaos of Cults* (Grand Rapids: Eerdmans).

See **Doctrinal Statement.**

Deacon, Definition of

The Greek lexicon notes that *diakonos* can refer to those who wait on tables. As a participle, it can mean "waiter" (Luke 22:26). The idea is to serve as a helper, one who renders service. The word can refer to one who distributes alms, charity support, or one who helps with a collection for the needy. General service and charity dominate both broad usage and definition. Some have conceptualized the deacon as a "go-between" in word (such as a courier or messenger) and in work (an authorized agent).

In a wide sense, all believers in Christ Jesus are called "servants" or "ministers." In Romans 12:7 Paul says, "On *ministry* (*diakonia*), (let us wait) on (our) ministering." He adds, "Since we have this ministry, as well received mercy, we do not lose heart" (2 Cor. 4:1).

In the more specific sense, there is the "board" of servants who are officially part of the leadership that functions in a "serving" capacity in the local assembly. The first reference to the calling and function of these men is given in Acts 6:1-7.

The office of disciple in the church is not to be a high-minded office, but rather a humble position of getting done some tough jobs in the church. This would seem to include charity, but also would spill over to any task that is needed to foster the work of the propagation of the Word of God in an unhindered manner.

Recommended Books

Mal Couch, *A Biblical Theology of the Church* (Grand Rapids: Kregel).

See Deacon, **Description of; Deacon, Spiritual Qualifications of.**

Deacon, Description of

In Acts 6:1-7 the disciples urged the church fellowship in Jerusalem, "Select from among you, brothers, seven men of good reputation, full of [controlled by] the Spirit and of wisdom, whom we may put in charge of this task [of charity]. But we will devote ourselves to prayer, and to the ministry of the word" (vv. 3-4). Note that these men were "put in charge" of this work of serving (*diakonos*) (v. 1). From this will come the idea of the deacons.

All of this came about because Luke noted, "At this time while the disciples were increasing in number, a complaint arose on the part of the Hellenistic Jews against the native Hebrews, because their widows were overlooked in the daily serving of food. And the twelve [disciples] summoned the congregation of the disciples and said and said, 'It is not desirable for us to neglect the word of God in order to serve tables'" (vv. 1-2).

Were these men "voted" on in the good old American tradition of democracy? Some Bible teachers wrongly think so, but most reject the idea. The apostles were acting as the elders of this assembly. Later, other godly men will come alongside the apostles, learn from them, and in time become the pastor-teachers of the various mushrooming congregations. From the above verses we see:

The division of roles: "We will teach the Word, and they will daily serve." The apostles will "put these men in charge of this [charity] task." In other words, the apostles/elders will give the servants their charge and responsibility. The servants were brought before the apostles for approval (v. 6). They then prayed over them and laid their hands on them (v. 6), thus commissioning them to their tasks.

What then was the role of the congregation? And, how did they respond to what was happening? (1) They "selected" the deacons (v. 3). (2) The deacons found "approval" with the apostles' words (v. 5). And, (3) they "chose" out the seven men (v. 5). Luke says nothing about a casting of lots, which would probably be the method of voting. To choose was not a voting but literally in Greek a calling forth, a form of screening, but not technically a voting. And even this "setting-forth" had to be approved by the apostles who were then acting as elders.

The role of deacon is understood as part of the local church, but in Paul's epistles, little is said about them except their qualifications found in 1 Timothy 3:8-13. However, they are addressed in the church at Philippi by Paul in the plural, along with the elders, in Philippians 1:1: "Paul ... to all the saints in Christ Jesus who are in Philippi, including the overseers and deacons."

Recommended Books

Mal Couch, A *Biblical Theology of the Church* (Grand Rapids: Kregel).

See **Deacons, Definition of; Deacons, Spiritual Qualifications of.**

Deacons, Spiritual Qualifications of

Deacons are to be full of [controlled by] the Holy Spirit and of wisdom (Acts 6:3-4). By using the present tense and the present infinitive in Greek, Paul makes it clear that their qualification should be based on how they are living presently, right now! This allows for the fact that they probably are coming from a pagan society with imperfections in the life, both as a lost person, and even as a believer.

While Paul's qualifications are high, as listed in 1 Timothy 3:8-13, it is impossible to find anyone who walks in perfect maturity. Integrity, wisdom, and a growing maturity should be observed and considered most important.

By using the present tense, Paul is saying:

- They are to be right now men of dignity, or men of honor (v. 8).

- They are to be right now not double-tongued, two-worded (v. 8).

- They are to be right now not addicted to much wine (v. 8).

- They are to be right now not fond of sordid gain (they cannot be bought) (v. 8).

- They are right now holding to the mystery of the faith with a clear conscience (v. 9).

- They are right now to be above reproach (v. 10).

- [Their] wives are right now to be dignified (v. 11).

- [Their] wives are right now not to be malicious gossips (v. 11).

- [Their] wives are right now to be temperate (v. 11).

- [Their] wives are to be right now faithful in all things (v. 11).

- The deacons are right now to be husbands of only one wife (v. 12).

- They are to be right now good managers of their children and their own households (v. 12).

It is clear Paul is saying, "the deacons are to be this way right now." Leadership does not mean that one walked a perfect walk in the past. These men had to learn over a period of time how to walk with Christ. They were sinners and made mistakes but now spiritual maturity must be seen in their walk.

Recommended Books
Mal Couch, *A Biblical Theology of the Church* (Grand Rapids: Kregel).

See **Divorce; Deacon, Definition of; Deacon, Description of.**

Deaconess, Issues of

In church history, only in a few rare times is the idea of a deaconess mentioned, as a specific and formal function in the church. However, women from the time of the apostles have played a major role in the behind-the-scenes critical needs of the local church. They have been the providers of hospitality, charity, and hostesses for a place where the gospel could be presented and taught. Early in church history there was the formal creation of nun centers of charity where hospital functions were carried out for the elderly and the sick.

Women have sensitivity for work with children. No church nursery would function properly without the dedication of the mothers, and their care and knowledge of the infants.

Important

However, it must be noted that the official capacity of a deacon groups is confined by the New Testament to men. The issue focuses on the role of a leadership functional body that officially is responsible for the direction and care of the church—this is to be confined to male leadership. No matter how hard the push is from the feminist agenda upon the church, this doctrinal fact needs to be maintained, otherwise the atmosphere of the church will turn feminine, and this is not what is advocated in the New Testament! Two passages of Scripture stand out for discussion:

Romans 16:1:2. This passage reads:

> *I commend to you our sister Phoebe, who is a servant of the church which is at Cenchrea; that you receive her in the Lord in a manner worthy of the saints, and that you help her in whatever matter she may have need of you; for she herself has also been a helper of many, and of myself as well.*

Servant here is *diakonon*, which is used in the feminine gender. Phoebe was to be received just like one of the many saints of that church, not as an official officer representing the body of believers. She certainly was a generous and hospitable woman that Paul is quick to mention. But she does not represent the deacon leadership group.

In Paul's hall of fame of Christian service (ch. 16), he has much to say about both men and women serving the churches, even endangering their lives to do so. He speaks of this woman Phoebe as a servant and helper (vv. 1-2), of Priscilla and Aquila as fellow workers (v. 3) who risked their lives for his sake. He references "all the churches of the Gentiles" who likewise "risked their own necks" (v. 4). And finally, Paul mentions a Mary who "worked hard" (Greek *kopiao*, "to struggle, strive") in the gospel, along with many others whom he cited as fellow workers.

Despite these important facts, there is no justification to see Phoebe, or any other woman, being a part of the official deacon leadership group of a local church.

1 Timothy 3:11. In his discussion about the qualifications of deacons (vv. 8-13), Paul suddenly writes:

> *Women must likewise be dignified, not malicious gossips, but temperate, faithful in all things.*

Paul then returns to discussing the qualifications of the male deacons. Feminists attempt to say that he just switched his thought in verse 11 to describing the official body in the church of "women deaconesses." The Greek word for woman is *gyne* that is translated either *woman* or *wife*, as determined by the context. The New Englishman's Greek Concordance and Lexicon translates it wives in this verse.

Paul is talking about the wives of the deacons. It would not make sense for him to suddenly break off his thought, quickly in one verse talk about a female category of women leaders, and then jump back to discussing the leadership of the male deacons. Only feminists with an agenda to push even attempt to do so in this passage.

What Paul has done is simply to mention the deportment of how the deacon's wives should carry themselves before the congregation. Though a few of the church fathers such as Pliny thought this was a "board" of women deacons, he and others were the exception.

The great godly commentator of Scripture, John Gill, says about this passage: "It is better to interpret the words of the wives of the deacons, who must be as their husbands, which will reflect honor and credit to their husbands." Ryrie concludes:

> Most likely a reference to the wives of the deacons, rather than to a separate office of deaconess, since the qualifications for deacons are continued in verse 12. If he had a difference group in mind, it would seem more natural for Paul to have finished the qualifications for deacons before introducing the office of deaconess. (*Ryrie Study Bible*)

Recommended Books
Mal Couch, *A Biblical Theology of the Church* (Grand Rapids: Kregel).

Dedication, Ceremony of Children

To dedicate children to the Lord has its origins in the Old Testament. Unfortunately, some today see child dedication as a kind of impartation of grace, with the power of infant baptism as practiced in the High Churches. Infant baptism is not biblical, and child dedication was not an early from of infant baptism!

One of the first dedications in Scripture is for Samuel by his mother Hannah who had waited for years desiring to have a son. When Samuel was born she dedicated him to the Lord, and when he was weaned, she took him to the tabernacle where a bull was slaughtered (1 Sam. 1:25). Hannah said to Eli the priest, "For this boy I prayed, and the Lord has given me my petition which I asked of Him. So I have also dedicated him to the Lord; as long as he lives he is dedicated to the Lord" (vv. 27-28).

Though not called a "dedication," circumcision was a rite performed on the eighth day after the birth of a boy. As with John the Baptist, it seems that at the time of circumcision, the child was named (Luke 1:60). Jesus was also circumcised on the eighth day (2:21), and after Mary's purification period was over, He was taken up to the temple in Jerusalem to be presented to the Lord (v. 22). They did this "to carry out for Him the custom of the Law" (v. 27).

While not under the dispensation of Law, and not as a legal mandate, there is no harm for parents to publicly present their new born child to God. There is no magical dispensing of grace or salvation with this act, but before the Lord, and before others, this becomes a pledge of dedication that the child will be raised under the teaching of the Word of God.

Paul wrote to Timothy that "from childhood you have known the sacred writings which are able to give you the wisdom that leads to salvation through faith which is in Christ Jesus" (2 Tim. 3:15).

At the dedication service then, there is the opportunity to: (1) make sure the audience knows that this is not a form of infant baptism, (2) make the point that the child does not become a Christian through this service, (3) let the audience know that the parents are pledging to raise their child under Christian principles, (4) have the gospel explained in its fullest for those present who may not know Christ.

The dedication service can be formatted as the pastor and the parents wish.

Denominational Issues

The Bible gives no place for denominationalism. By around two hundred AD and later, the early church began associations of churches. The authority of a bishop who held the reigns over several churches would control a region. By the seventh century, the power and authority of the bishop of Rome was controlling to a degree all of the congregations within Christendom.

The history of the development of Roman Catholicism is a lesson in how central power and authority destroys the autonomy over local assemblies. It also dulls the local leadership as to theological and doctrinal issues. Authority is automatically given over to the hierarchy so that the local elders and pastors appear to cease thinking and leading.

If church rules and doctrine are all decided in a central location, you have denominational control. If the church is expected to use only the curriculum of that central authority, you have denominationalism. If the central authority tells the local church who they may hire for a pastor, or what seminary he must graduate from, you have denominational control. If the central authority dictates the Sunday church readings, you have denominational control.

Denominationalism also promotes false unity: "Our denomination right or wrong!" Or, "Fellowship at any cost," "Fellowship is the most important Christian virtue!"

The propagation of biblical truth is the most compelling purpose of the local assembly. There can be no love without truth, writes the apostle John (2 & 3 John).

The history of denominationalism is that denominations ultimately become corrupt and bring down their associated churches with them.

Discipline, Of Children

Unfortunately, because of the influence of liberal educational principles and secular psychology, discipline is being removed from the training of youngsters today, in both the culture in general, and within the Christian home. Many young Christian couples were brainwashed in the state universities, and know little about raising godly and disciplined children.

Many parents have bought the lie of secularism that focuses on self-esteem, self-actualization, and self-fulfillment. They do not understand that children must be directed into practicing what is right, but also must be corporally disciplined when they rebel or sin.

Churches need to conduct ongoing young couples classes that help with biblical directives as to how to raise their children. These couples need to realize that their thinking about child training has been polluted with what they have learned in a public school secular environment.

In the New Testament there are only a few key passages on the discipline of children (Eph. 6:4; Col. 3:20-21). Hebrews 12:5-11 can also be included as a discipline passage, though the author of this book applies child-training habits to the maturing of the believer in the spiritual experience.

Why does the New Testament not have more to say about the discipline of youth and children? It may be because the saints of the New Testament knew to draw upon the principles of the Old Testament book of Proverbs for directing children in discipline. The first seven chapters are aimed at young men who need to look to their fathers as to how to live a godly life with the wisdom from above. The rest of the Proverbs also play a strategic role in how to get through life.

Here are a few key passages on discipline in the book of Proverbs:

- 6:20 - Son, observe the commandment of your father, do not forsake the teaching of your mother.

- 13:1 - A wise son accepts his father's discipline, but a scoffer does not listen to rebuke.

- 15:5 - A fool rejects his father's discipline.

- 22:6 - Train up a child in the way he should go, even when he is old he will not depart from it.

- 22:15 - Foolish is bound up in the heart of a child, the rod of discipline will remove it far from him.

- 23:13 - Do not hold back discipline from the child, although you strike him with the rod, he will not die. You shall strike him with the rod, and deliver his soul from the grave.

- 29:15 - The rod and reproof give wisdom, but a child who gets his own way brings shame to his mother.

- 29:17 - Correct your son, and he will give you comfort; he will also delight your soul.

A church has the responsibility to lead young couples in how to be proper disciplining parents. Secular psychology has blunted the Christian's understanding of biblical discipline. Dr. Tedd Tripp has an excellent book on the subject: *Shepherding a Child's Heart* (Wapwallopen, PA: Shepherd Press). Dr. Tripp writes:

> The serious parent must be prepared to swim upstream, as our culture has lost any semblance of submission to authority. You must be consistent. You must train your children to obey through careful discipline and precise instruction. The rules have to be the same each day. If they must obey, you must challenge disobedience and persevere until the lessons of submission are learned. Victory does not come to the faint hearted. You will rarely witness resolute will power such as you find in a toddler who has determined not to obey.

> The most important lesson for the child to learn is that HE IS AN INDIVIDUAL UNDER AUTHORITY. He has been made by God and has a responsibility to obey God in all things. "Children obey your parents in the Lord, for this is right" (Eph. 6:1).

Recommended Books

Steve Sherboundy, *Changing Your Child's Heart* (Wheaton: Tyndale House); Phyllis Schlafly, *Who Will Rock the Cradle?* (Washington, DC: Eagle Forum); Richard Fugate, *What the Bible Says About Child Training* (Garland, TX: Aletheia Publishers).

Discipline, Of Leadership

The best preventative medicine against failing leadership is found in Paul's injunction, "Do not lay hands upon anyone too hastily and thus share responsibility for the sins of others" (1 Tim. 5:22). (However, there is another view about this verse mentioned below.) Just a few verses above, the apostle has laid out the guideline for disciplining elders. He wrote, "Do not receive an accusation against an elder except on the basis of two or three witness" (v. 19). This means that it takes at least two for an accusation to be counted worthy of following up on. Paul then adds:

> Those who continue in sin, rebuke in the presence of all, so that the rest also may be fearful of sinning (v. 20).

Though Paul never says that leadership must step down in a moral or doctrinal crisis, it would only make sense that this would happen under extreme circumstances. Showing that even an elder must face discipline when needed, will have a positive effect on the entire church. It is always a danger that the elders might be more tolerant of sin in the case of a fellow elder and may overlook things in the elder's life that need to be addressed.

But notice that Paul issues a strong warning against this; "I solemnly charge you in the presence of God and of Christ Jesus and of His chosen angels, to maintain these principles without bias, doing nothing in a spirit of partiality" (v. 21).

From verse 22, many believe Paul is pointing out the need for a period of time when the one who is being disciplined is examined to see if his repentance is genuine. In other words, Paul is warning against immediate restoration, especially since the elders are living examples whom the flock is following. Restoring one who has not repented of his sin may lead to that elder being an example that leads others of the flock into the same sin.

Many hold that elder moral failure can be prevented if there is a rotation of elders every three or four years, though such an idea is not laid out in the Bible. The negative about this approach is (1) it is not biblical; (2) it makes leadership something that is open for many, when actually mature and godly leaders are rare.

The abuse of discipline has often led to a harsh and intolerant spirit, but neglect of it has proved a danger almost as great. When faced with sinning elders a spineless attitude is deplorable!

Recommended Books
Mal Couch, *A Biblical Theology of the Church* (Grand Rapids: Kregel).

Discipline, Congregational Members

Quoting from Proverbs 3:11-12, the writer of Hebrews lays out the principles of discipline (12:5-6). The author encourages the Christian not to "regard lightly" or "neglect" the benefit of the Lord's discipline. The Greek word for discipline is *paideia*, which in the Greek world denoted the upbringing and handling of a minor child. It included direction, teaching, and chastisement.

God disciplines by His providence, but there must also be an earthly discipline in the church for those destroying the peace of the body of Christ, or who are self-destructing with moral waywardness. But such waywardness must be proven by several or more witnesses, based on the directive of

Deuteronomy 19:15: "A single witness shall not rise up against a man on account of any iniquity or any sin which he has committed; on the evidence of two or three witnesses a matter shall be confirmed."

God opens the door for restoration in Galatians 6:1-2. Paul writes, "Brethren, even if a man is caught in any trespass, you who are spiritual restore such a one in a spirit of gentleness; each one looking to yourself, lest you too be tempted."

In Matthew 18, Christ gives the steps of biblical discipline:

- The brother who is in sin must be reproved in private (v. 15).

- If the brother does not listen, two or more witnesses must confront him (v. 16).

- If the brother refuses to listen and repent, his case is to be brought before the whole church (v. 17).

- If the brother refuses to accept godly counsel, he is excluded from the church fellowship (v. 17).

The Objectives of Discipline

- To restore the offender to fellowship with God and the church (2 Cor. 2:5-11).

- To remove the leavening, the corruptive influence, from the presence of the other members of the congregation (i.e., false teaching, immorality, etc.) (1 Cor. 5:6-8; Titus 1:10-16).

- To correct doctrinal error (Titus 1:13).

- To prevent sin from spreading to other members of the assembly and to challenge them unto godliness (Gal. 6:1; 1 Tim. 5:20).

The Examples of Discipline

- An accused elder (1 Tim. 5:19-20).

- A sinning brother (Matt. 18:15-20).

- An overtaken brother (Gal. 6:1).

- An unruly brother (2 Thess. 3:6).

- False teachers (Titus 1:10-16).

- Factious people (Titus 8:8-11).

- The immoral brother (1 Cor. 5).

- An undisciplined brother (2 Thess. 3:7-11).

Discipline is not a public matter to be "voted" on, for or against the person who is under a charge and accusation. Discipline is carried out by the elders and must at first begin as discreet as possible. But if necessary, it must be brought before the church by the elders in order to let the congregation know that the elders are aware of the issues, and if necessary, in order to deal with it properly.

If the repentant decide to remain in the church (which often they do not), they should be placed under the spiritual guidance and care of an elder, so that a learning process can take place. Getting things back on track is the goal of all discipline, not simply punishment.

Recommended Books
Mal Couch, *A Biblical Theology of the Church* (Grand Rapids: Kregel).

Divorce, of Believers

No subject sparks more debate among Christians than the issue of divorce. Generally, believers take sides and move from one extreme view to another. The only consensus that all can agree on is that divorce is without doubt a sin! Often those who hold tightly to a harsh view on the subject do so because they feel the other side is simply going soft on the issue. Those who hold to the tight view fail to acknowledge that "all" sin is wrong! But confession of sin brings restoration. There is no place in the New Testament that would give the impression that there are two classes of Christians: Those who can minister fully, and those who cannot because of past failures, as heavy as these failures may be. While this is hard for some to comprehend, this is the nature of grace as applied to all believers.

Under the old dispensation of the law, Moses allowed divorce if the wife was found with venereal disease. If "it happens [the husband] finds no favor in his eyes because he has found some indecency in [his wife]," he may give her a certificate of divorce (Deut. 24:1). The indecency is *air'rot* in Hebrew and probably refers to disease of the genital area.

Interestingly, Moses without comment mentions the fact that the wife given a writ of divorcement may go on and marry again (vs. 2-4).

Jesus refers to the Deuteronomy passage but there speaks of her unchaste behavior (Mt. 5:32). The way this verse reads in the Greek text, it sounds as if he is really addressing the issue of one who divorces his wife in order to marry another. He could be repeating this thought when He adds, "and whoever marries a divorced woman commits adultery" (v. 32b). The Lord also seems to be addressing the issue of *easy divorce*, the fact that one would divorce so quickly, in order to marry someone else.

The Central Issues

No one argues that divorce is right, and all understand that it is devastating to families and to children. But the issue of God's grace and restitution, because of the forgiveness found at the cross, must not be lost in the discussion.

No One Counsels Divorce

Pastors should never suggest it, but they also realize that, unless there is a miracle of restoration performed by the Holy Spirit, that some marriages are beyond repair. So often, the hardness of heart comes into play, and the offending parties refuse to listen to reason.

Almost all pastors also admit that separation and/or divorce may be necessary because of dangerous physical abuse, or adultery. The apostle Paul too recognizes that divorce is a possibility among believers (1 Cor. 7:10-11). In 1 Corinthians 7, he gives "instructions" that the wife should not leave the husband (v. 10). Often missed is the fact that instructions comes from the Greek word *paraggello*, which means to advise, urge but not necessarily command. The apostle realizes that people cannot be forced to remain together if there is an emotional and spiritual war on the home front. He understands the emotional issues at stake when there are problems in the marriage.

In verses 12-17, Paul gives his opinion about a mixed marriage with a believer and unbeliever. Let the partners remain together, if possible, because the unbeliever is "sanctified" and the children are kept "holy" because they are in an intact family (v. 14). However, the apostle says staying in a dysfunctional family is difficult, and he gives leeway if it becomes intolerable for the believing spouse to try to live with an unbeliever.

This clearly seems to be what he is saying when he writes his conclusion of this matter: "Only, as the Lord has assigned to each one, as God has called each, in this manner let him walk. And thus I direct in all the churches" (v. 17). The idea is that, in many cases, some do not have the gift to be able to put up with the terrible emotional problems that can develop in both marriages of unbelievers, and in mixed marriages between the saved and the unsaved. The great Greek scholar Robertson Nicoll writes on verse 17: "Under this general rule the exceptional and guarded permission of divorce mentioned in verse 15 was to be understood. The exceptional sense is given here."

Again, it must be stressed that at all costs, a marriage is meant to be forever. God's grace can make this happen, but carnality raises its ugly head and divorce follows.

Further Study

Though the context is about the domestic issues of the elder, see the commentary notes on Titus 1:6 in this book.

See **Divorce, Restoration Issues; Divorce, Various Views of.**

Divorce, Restoration Issues

Interpreting the Scriptures means the student must take notice of what the Bible says and does not say! Though divorce certainly is sin, the Word of God never says that remarriage is impossible. Many attempt to enforce such a prohibition, but Christians who have remained unmarried after divorce are almost non-existent. Then they go about carrying a heavy weight of guilt, are often treated as second-class citizens at church, and feel that God is through with them concerning ministering and serving the Lord.

The Bible fails us if restoration found in Galatians 6:1-3 does not include the terrible and debilitating sin of divorce. In this wonderful grace passage, Paul writes:

> Brethren, even if a man is caught in any transgression [lies down by a dead body], you who are spiritual restore such a one in a spirit of gentleness, each one looking to yourself, lest you too be tempted. ... But let each examine his own work, and then he will have reason for boasting about himself alone, and not in regard to another. (Gal. 6:1-4)

Remarriage Issues

Remarriage is possible under some very biblical and practical guidelines. Each case is different and requires wisdom by church leaders and godly counselors. Sound guidelines are spelled out in the Titus commentary section under Titus 1:6 in this book.

See **Divorce, of Believers; Divorce, Various Views of.**

Divorce, Various Views of

Below is a list of views on divorce that have "silently" split the evangelical church. These issues are hush, hush and are rarely discussed, and certainly not biblically analyzed, in local church Bible studies. Everyone has distinct views, or shades of difference, because the subject is kept so quiet. The reason seems to be that those who remain quiet and confused feel that they would be going soft on sin, if they should allow those divorced to be remarried.

There is no question the problem is a difficult one from an emotional standpoint. But if grace works at all, it should also come into focus on the issue of divorce. Below are some of the different views among evangelicals on the subject:

- No one can be remarried who has been divorced. Almost no one seriously advocates this position. This position denies the truths about confession, restoration, forgiveness, and grace.

- If one is the innocent party he/she may remarry. This position makes the Christian community the judge and jury of divorce issues. It also places the "judges" in the bedrooms and living rooms, thinking they can determine who was right, and who was wrong, in the breakup of the marriage.

- One may remarry but can never be used of the Lord again. Their gifts must be put in storage and they become second-class Christian citizens! This is a common view, however, many churches realize that after solid spiritual restoration, and a show of godliness and spiritual growth, those divorced may be used again to serve Christ.

- Church leaders and pastors can never serve again. This probably is the most common position of many churches. The question is never asked, "but maybe his wife was an axe murderer! Does this make a difference?" Usually no answer or discussion is offered. The answer is always a no with little explanation or discussion.

- With proper practical and scriptural guidelines, and with a meaningful passage of restorative time, men may serve in leadership positions again. This is not a softening of the sin issue. It seems to be a proper New Testament position that takes in the entire body of teaching on the subject.

A Re-Examination

See the discussion on Titus 1:6 in the commentary section of this book.

See **Divorce, of Believers; Divorce, Restoration Issues.**

Doctrinal Statement

Paul told the Ephesian elders that he taught them the full counsel of God, "For I did not shrink from declaring to you the whole purpose of God" (Acts 20:27). The Bereans were said to have "received the word with great eagerness, examining the Scriptures daily to see whether those things were so" (17:11).

Such passages tell us that the entire field of the Bible was open to the student of the Word, so that the whole corpus of scriptural truth would be the source for truth.

A doctrinal statement attempts to place before the congregation the guidelines of the major doctrines to help steady the spiritual direction of the local church. Without a "detailed" doctrine statement, the church may have no defense against error when it knocks on the door.

Many reject a doctrinal statement saying, "All we need is the Bible. It is our doctrinal statement!" While this is certainly true, there needs to be some way of setting forth and highlighting the beliefs the leadership says must be defended at all cost. In a foolish frame of mind, some church leaders have argued: "We don't want to be too detailed in our doctrinal beliefs. Love is all we need. And besides, doctrine confuses and brings division. We want people to come to our church simply because of our friendliness!"

Throughout church history, it has been shown that without a firm doctrinal foundation, a church will fall into error, or outright liberalism. Even when a doctrinal statement is detailed and strong, the enemies of error can still find a way to come in and wreck havoc against the spiritual health of the assembly.

A Point of Unity

While many Christians are seeking to set doctrine aside for the sake of unity, the Apostle Paul called for exactly the opposite among the church at Corinth, urging them doctrinally to "say the same thing" (1 Cor. 1:10). He clearly envisioned doctrine as being an essential point of unity among believers in a fellowship. Not only does he urge them to "say the same thing", but even clarifies his intent by saying that there be no divisions among them. A doctrinal statement, then provides a set of doctrinal points under which believers within a fellowship can stand and interact together in a singular set of beliefs and practices, rooted in the content of Scripture (2 Tim. 3:16,17).

A Point of Distinction

As much as a doctrinal statement provides a point of unity, it also provides a point of distinction. Doctrine provides definition to the beliefs and practices of a fellowship, and that definition serves to distinguish that fellowship from others that do not hold to those beliefs and practices. The doctrinal distinction is not to be simply arbitrary or capricious, but is to reflect a carefully studied conviction regarding the essential and critical truths of Scripture (2 Tim. 2:15), expressed in a concise form. Those distinctions stand as a statement that those points of doctrine are true and fundamental, as opposed to that which is biblically false or inconsequential. As a result, the distinctions that are made by the doctrinal statement provide:

- A means of evaluation for those considering joining the fellowship (Acts 17:11).

- Essential points of unity for those maintaining fellowship (1 Thess. 5:21).
- A definition of those who should stand outside the fellowship by reason of their belief, practice, and/or teaching (Rom. 16:17; Eph. 5:11; 2 Tim. 2:5, 19-22, 3:5).

The Content

Since the doctrinal statement is to express that which is true, it should be entirely and substantially referenced to specific Scriptural passages that clearly make those points. Only Scripture can provide the necessary foundation of authority for such a doctrinal statement (2 Pet. 1:20, 21). Further, the doctrinal statement should be sufficiently detailed so that it expresses the breadth of that which is essential in Scripture, and the range of theological, moral and practical issues that are facing, or will soon face, the fellowship. In this sense, the doctrinal statement will be an abbreviated systematic theology. It will also address issues that are current either among those in Christendom or in the society.

In Acts 20:28-31, Paul is speaking to the elders from Ephesus for the last time, and has just told them that he has conveyed to them the whole counsel of God. He then explicitly warns them in rather graphic terms about the "wolves" that would come in even from among them to tear the flock to pieces. The doctrinal statement of the fellowship will serve as a principal means of monitoring, identifying, and guarding against these vicious "wolves". The elders of the fellowship should therefore not only formulate the doctrinal statement with great care, but also check the teaching and practice of the elders and the flock against it regularly (1 Tim. 4:16). It becomes an essential tool for their role in ministry, which includes defending the flock from within and without. The content of the doctrinal statement will not, therefore, be a substitute for the Scriptures, but rather be squarely based upon Scripture, and continually drawing us to the foundational truths of Scripture (John 17:17).

Recommended Books

Mal Couch and Russell Penney, *Doctrines That Cannot be Compromised* (Tyndale Seminary); Lewis Sperry Chafer, revised by John F. Walvoord, *Major Bible Themes* (Zondervan).

Doctrine, Definition of

Didache and its related words refer to a body of objective teaching, truth. The Greek lexicons note: active sense of instruction, exhortation in the form of teaching, teaching with authority. (EDNT)

Paul makes the authoritative teaching of the Word of God the number one responsibility of the elders/pastors. The Word of God gives salvation light, and promotes spiritual growth in the believer. "The Word of God is alive and powerful and sharper than a two-edged sword, even [deeply] piercing as far as the separation [opening up] of soul and spirit, of both joints and marrow, and able to [critically analyze] the thought patterns and plans of the heart" (Heb. 4:12). (Expanded translation)

The elders/pastors should make sure that exegetical verse-by-verse teaching is the mainstay of the churches, but as well, that there is a clear presentation of doctrinal instruction going forth for all ages to absorb.

To the church leadership and elders/pastors the apostle Paul writes:

- *They were astonished at the doctrine of the Lord* (Acts 13:12).

- *The form of doctrine which was delivered* (Rom. 6:17).

- *Teaching every man with wisdom* (Col. 1:28).

- *As you have been taught, teach* ... (2:7).

- *Teaching and admonishing one another* (3:16).

- *[Keeping] the traditions that you have been taught* (2 Thess. 2:15).

- *I suffer not a woman to teach or usurp authority over a man* (1 Thess. 2:12).

- *These things ... teach* (4:11).

- *Who shall be able to teach others also* (2 Tim. 2:2).

- *[Teaching] with all longsuffering and doctrine* (4:2).

- *Hold fast to the faithful word as he has been taught* (Titus 1:9).

Doctrine, Importance of

Theology, when studied systematically, is the ordering of truth from the Scriptures, which deals with all that God reveals about Himself and His universe. It the logical and realistic treatment of those truths which are found in the Bible.

Doctrinal knowledge of God is both factual and personal. To know facts about a person without knowing the person is limiting; to know a person without knowing facts about that one is shallow. God has revealed facts about Himself, all of which are important in making our personal relationship with Him close, intelligent, and useful.

A knowledge about God should deepen our relationship with Him, which in turn increases our desire to know more about Him.

The purpose of biblical knowledge:

- *To lead people to the possession of eternal life* (John 17:3; 1 Tim. 2:4).

- *To foster Christian growth* (2 Pet. 3:18), *with doctrinal knowledge* (John 7:17; Rom. 6:9, 16; Eph. 1:18) *and with a discerning lifestyle* (Phil. 1; 9-10; 2 Pet. 1:5).

- *To warn of judgment to come* (Hos. 4:6; Heb. 10:26-27).

- *To generate true worship of God* (Rom. 11:33-36). (Ryrie)

Regardless of the size of the congregation or the setting in which it must meet, the Word of God must be taught, not simply "preached"! This is the central mandate given to the elders/pastors. But few in contemporary times are giving exegetical teachings from God's Word. Too often, the "pulpit ministry" is given over to shorter devotionals or simply topical messages. Yet for the church to be healthy, doctrinal content cannot be ignored.

Charismatic Churches

It has been heard dozens of times from the charismatic churches that to study Scripture is stifling. "Too much biblical knowledge is dangerous" some say. Though it is true that "knowledge can puff up" (1 Cor. 8:1), spiritual knowledge still needs to come into the mind and heart and then be lived out in the life of the child of God. Paul writes:

> *So that you may walk in a manner worthy of the Lord, to please Him in all respect, bearing fruit in every good work and increasing in the knowledge of God. (Col. 1:10)*

Charismatics are much like ancient Gnostics who separated the mind from the spirit. They argue for "spirit" truth sometimes even over biblical revelation. They are often heard to say, "God told me," or "God showed me," with no objective evidence or biblical support. Because of this, false doctrines and teachings come into their midst, like the "holy laughter movement," "the implanting of gold in the mouth fad," "the prosperity teaching," and "the speak-the-word heresy." Most repudiate doctrinal teaching and are against advanced, higher educational biblical training.

Recommended Books

Charles Ryrie, *Basic Theology* (Chicago: Moody); Mal Couch, *A Biblical Theology of the Church* (Grand Rapids: Kregel).

See **Doctrine, Definition of; Doctrine, How to Teach it.**

Doctrine, How to Teach it

As already mentioned, doctrinal subjects should be presented on a continual basis in the church, even to the youngest of children, on their own level of understanding. The elders/pastors should look at an entire one-year doctrinal curriculum as to what should be taught the flock. But as well, verse-by-verse exegesis of biblical books must not be neglected!

See **Doctrine, Definition of; Doctrine, Importance of.**

Ecumenism

See Ministerial Associations.

Elder, Definition of

In the Hebrew language, the word elder is actually translated as such from a variety of root words. For example:

- *godoul*: great, tall - Gen. 29:2

- *rav*: superior - Gen. 37:1

- *kabbeer*: valiant - Num. 26:5

- *sovayo*: grey from age - Ezra v:6

These ideas about eldership come over into the New Testament. Elders then are the older men who should have a lot of life-experience in order to lead the church with spiritual wisdom.

Elders can lose their direction and go spiritually blind to the truth. Such was the case in the Gospels and in Acts (4:5-12). As the ministry of the apostles progressed, Christian elders began joining them in the decision-making processes for the Jerusalem church, as illustrated in Acts 15.

The New Testament church knows nothing other than elder leadership.

Recommended Books

Mal Couch, *A Biblical Theology of the Church* (Grand Rapids: Kregel).

See **Elder, Description of; Overseer, Definition of; Teacher; Pastor; Elder, Education of; Elder, Spiritual Qualifications of.**

Elder, Description of

According to the New Testament, the only way elders take up their ministry is by an appointment from other elders. McGarvey writes:

> It should be observed that a plurality of elders were appointed in "every church;" and this, so far as we are able to trace the facts, was the universal practice of the apostles. In appointing these, Paul and Barnabas were but following the example of the older apostles, by whom this office was instituted in the churches of Judea. (*A Biblical Theology of the Church*, 194)

The elders-pastors-teachers were to be living examples of good works, "with purity in doctrine, sound in speech which is beyond reproach" (Titus 2:7-8). Though the word doctrine (*didaskalia*) has a basic and simple meaning in Greek, the theological implication as used by Paul is awesome. The lexicon defines the word as "teaching, instruction, to impart."

The elders/pastors were to carry out a "noble process, with a glorious goal." All was to be aimed at nothing short of an accepting community of believers with a mature reliance on the Head, Jesus. In Acts we can feel the pulse, the heartthrob of this great teacher Paul. His aim was to inform the mind, awaken the understanding, stir the reason, and quicken the judgment. Paul expounded (Acts 28:23), exhorted (20:1), disputed (9:29), reasoned (19:8-9), persuaded (28:23), discoursed (20:25), admonished (20:31), commended (20:32), rehearsed (21:19), and made defense of the truth (24:10).

This is the present task of those who are elders as defined and described in the Scriptures.

There is no room for weak pastors who may be unsure in their teaching convictions and leadership!

Recommended Books

Mal Couch, *A Biblical Theology of the Church* (Grand Rapids: Kregel).

See **Elder, Definition of; Overseer; Teacher; Pastor; Elder, Education of; Elder, Spiritual Qualifications of.**

Elder, Education of

Elders/pastors need strong and deep biblical education. Some churches are attempting to train leadership within their own ranks in leadership training courses taught by the head pastor. This may be successful to a point, but it has a limitation.

It is appropriate for elders today to receive solid biblical training by extension courses. But this must take place with caution in view. There are very few schools that are strong in hermeneutics and interpretation, the biblical languages, theology, and exegetical studies through books of the Bible. The school also needs to be evangelical, conservative, teaching the pretribulational rapture of the church, and the premillennial return of Christ.

Any other biblical preparation would be unacceptable!

See **Elder, Definition of; Overseer; Teacher; Pastor; Elder, Spiritual Qualifications of; Elder, Description of.**

Elder, Spiritual Qualifications of

The elder is also the pastor/teacher, and overseer. In other words, there are four descriptions for the men who are the keepers of the truth in the local church.

The qualifications of elder are given in 1 Timothy 3:1-7, and also in Titus 1:5-9. In the Titus passage, Paul uses an alternative description for the role of this leader, and calls him the overseer (*episcopos*) (v. 7). When the elders are mentioned that are always referred to in the plural, i.e., a group of elders who are to lead the local church in its mission. The same group of men can be called "pastors, indeed teachers" (Eph. 4:11), and elders and overseers!

As with the qualifications of the deacons, Paul uses the present tense to describe what the elders are to be like. "They are to be this way right now!" is what the apostle is saying. By using the present tense, he is saying:

- They are to be right now irreproachable, upright, transparent in character (v. 2).

- They are to be right now a one-wife kind of man (v. 2).

- They are to be right now non-addicted to wine (v. 2).

- They are to be right now self-controlled, have mental soundness (v. 2).

- They are to be right now "down to earth" (v. 2).

- They are to be right now hospitable, friendly (v. 2).

- They are to be right now skilled in teaching (v. 2).

- They are to be right now not to be a drunkard (v. 3).

- They are to be right now not like those who strike out, fight (v. 3).

- They are to be right now gracious, gentle, forbearing (v. 3).

- They are to be right now not like those who not go to war, fight (v. 3).

- They are to be right now not a lover of silver (v. 3).

- They are to be right now like those who manage their own house (v. 4).

- They are to be right now those who have their children under control (v. 4).

- Right now he must not be a neophyte (v. 6).

- Presently he must have a good witness toward outsiders (v. 7).

The great Calvinist, Scottish Greek scholar Patrick Fairbairn says of a one-wife kind of man: "Even Jerome, with all of his ascetic rigor, speaks favorably (in his comments on Titus) of the interpretation that this phrase is addressing the issue of polygamy. [Jerome] states that, according to the view of many and worthy divines, it was intended merely to condemn polygamy, and not to exclude from the ministry men who have been twice married." [Patrick Fairbairn, Commentary *on the Pastoral Epistles* (Grand Rapids: Zondervan, 1956),136.]

Paul sees nothing wrong with men pursuing the role of elder. To be a pastor-teacher is the greatest calling. These offices in the local assembly require the most skilled and dedicated leadership. It is not just a position of honor or power. Instead, it is a labor of dedicated service that brings out the best in men.

The one seeking this office to guide the congregation must have the right heart and should set aside carnal and personal ambitions. He must be called to the Lord Himself and seek to serve Him in all things.

Recommended Books
Mal Couch, *A Biblical Theology of the Church* (Grand Rapids: Kregel).

See **Elder, Definition of; Elder, Description of; Elder, Education of.**

Evangelism, Definition of

The word evangelism is not used in the New Testament, and the personal noun evangelist (*euagelistas*) is used only three times (Acts 21:8; Eph. 4:11; 2 Tim. 4:5). The gift of evangelist is given by the Lord Jesus to His Church, as a supportive office "for the equipping of the saints for the work of service ..." (Eph. 4:12).

While Timothy may not have had the gift of evangelism, Paul instructed him "to do the work of an evangelist" (2 Tim. 4:5), and this would support the idea that all have an obligation to share the gospel of Christ, even though this may not be their first gift.

The word for "good news, gospel" (*euagelion*) is used dozens of times in the New Testament, and so is the verb "proclaim the gospel, preach" (*euangelizo*). Paul refers to the teaching of the gospel in many verses in his epistles. He says: he preached the gospel (1 Cor. 15:1); he preached it to the Gentiles (Eph. 3:8); the gospel produces salvation (Eph. 1:13); it is the gospel of Christ (3:6); there is fellowship in the gospel (Phil. 1:5); he wishes the furtherance of the gospel (1:12); he practices the defense of the gospel

(v. 17); he lives for the hope of the gospel (Col. 1:23).

Paul defines the gospel as the prophecies about Christ in the Scriptures, concerning His burial, resurrection, and appearance before the twelve apostles, then even to upwards of five hundred other brothers (1 Cor. 15:1-6).

The central historical fact about the gospel is the resurrection of Jesus. Paul saw personally the resurrected Lord (vs. 7-10), though he is the least of the apostles (v. 9). This gospel, "so we preach and so you believed" (v. 11).

This gospel of Christ must be preached (v. 12), for "if Christ has not been raised, then our preaching is vain" (v. 14).

Collectively, the Church is commissioned to evangelize a lost world with the truth. Individually, each Christian is also mandated to tell those whom they contact about the saving grace of Christ.

See **Evangelism, Guidelines for; Evangelism, Responsibility to.**

Evangelism, Guidelines for

Going into homes with the message of Christ may be the most effective way of witnessing. House evangelism is personal, intimate, and probably more productive than simply passing out tracts on a street corner. Paul practiced home evangelism. He told the Ephesian elders that he was "teaching [them] publicly and from house to house, solemnly testifying to both Jews and Greeks of repentance toward God and faith in our Lord Jesus Christ" (Acts 20:20-21).

Many verses attest to the use of the home for evangelism, for church, and for discussion of theological issues. For example, Paul "came to Caesarea; and entering the house of Philip the evangelist ... stayed with him" (21:8).

Because of today's social climate, many are weary of opening their homes to hearing the gospel. Many claim to be "religious" and turn away those wishing to share the truth. Also because of the fact that the cults go from house to house, many are fearful of opening the door to some strange "new" view.

Some churches are practicing an ongoing neighborhood blitz, reaching homes with a variety of informational pamphlets that invite people to attend specified Bible studies. The first reactions may be non-committal, but in time, this approach may produce results.

Some feel this "soft" approach is deceptive and avoids the great spiritual issues that should be addressed in a more frontal manner. But others feel that, by keeping up a steady stream of pamphlets, letters, tracts, a spiritual curiosity is generated that opens meaningful doors to witness the grace of God found only in Christ Jesus.

Though not simply a small gospel tract, *The Unfolding Plan of the Bible* color booklet (Mal Couch, Tyndale Seminary) helps people follow the "red line" of redemption from the Garden to the cross! Not only is the gospel made clear, but the booklet carries the reader from eternity past to eternity future.

Without a doubt, prayer must go before an evangelistic "campaign" for winning the lost to Christ! Training Christians in sharing their faith and answering spiritual questions may also produce vital fruit for the sake of the Lord.

See **Evangelism, Definition of; Evangelism, Responsibility to.**

Evangelism, Responsibility to

Young pastor Timothy was told to do the work of an evangelist (2 Tim. 4:5), though this may not have been a distinct gift in his ministry. Aquila and Pricilla worked hard to share the truth of the gospel, even having in their own house a church (1 Cor. 16:19). Unbelievers often came into these assemblies and needed to hear the Word of God taught with clarity and simplicity, not with confusion (14:23-25). These hearing the gospel may fall on their faces "and worship God, declaring that God is certainly among you" (v. 25).

Many Christians risked their lives to serve the Lord and share the truth in a hostile environment (Rom. 16:1-16). Peter used the home of Cornelius for giving the gospel to Gentiles (Acts 10:23-48); Paul used the house of the jailer (16) and of Jason (17), and even his place of arrest in Rome to witness to the elders of the Jews (28).

Philip saw the opportunity to share Christ with the Ethiopian on the Gaza road. He saw the man reading from Isaiah 53 needing a word of understanding. After the Ethiopian official had trusted Christ (v. 37), Philip continued his journey, passing through Azotus, he continued preaching "the gospel to all the cities" on his trip (v. 40).

With these and other examples, it is clear that every opportunity should be used to share Christ, to all classes and levels of society. To Saul it was said, "he is a chosen instrument of Mine, to bear My name before the Gentiles and kings and the sons of Israel" (Acts 9:15).

See **Evangelism, Definition of; Evangelism, Guidelines for.**

Expository Teaching

Exposition means to "lay out and make plain a thing or idea." As such the exposition, or "making plain" the meaning and application of the Divine revelation to precious eternal souls is the high calling, duty and privilege of the man of the Word. In this sense when the expositor speaks or writes accurately, his words become a supernatural portal through which mortal man sees and apprehends the heavenly realms and eternal truths. In fact he sees himself as he truly is, and through this the Divine stoops down and impresses His mind and heart into the imagination of temporal creatures. Expository teaching is the *means* by which the veil between the temporal and the eternal is lifted by the agency of the Holy Spirit, so that the creature might gaze momentarily on his Creator, who is forever praised.

Jesus declared to his Father, "Sanctify them by the truth, your Word is truth." *John 17:17.* Jesus declared no other means of sanctification that the Spirit would use.

The Present Desperate Need

Unfortunately, the primacy and efficacy of expository teaching is no longer an undisputable fact in many of today's churches and pulpits. A downward spiral of churches filled with culture saturated congregants who have been trained to and now desire to hear light and easily digested self-validations, pastors who care more to be approved of by man than by God, a pragmatic "what works" mentality, and seminaries that teach "how to" methodologies of ministry rather than equipping pastors to study, absorb and expound the Divine self-revelation of the Word. To be painfully honest, our seminaries can supply any number of men who love Christ, are relational, equipped to lead ministries well, are process oriented, can counsel competently, and as one Eastern Orthodox critic of Western Protestant pastors put it well, "are a quivering mass of availability."

What is needed, now more than ever, is men who will pay the price to study the Scriptures, learn the original languages, avail themselves of the history and culture surrounding the authors and the original recipients, develop the patience and tenacity of a tree farmer, and finally, stand and deliver the exposition to his charges. We need shepherds who care for the *quality* of the food their sheep eat, not just the *quantity*.

Listen carefully to the last cry of the apostle Paul as he was about to face his own earthly end:

> *"I solemnly charge you in the presence of God and of Christ Jesus, who is to judge the living and the dead, and by His appearing and His kingdom: preach the word; be ready in season and out of season; reprove, rebuke, exhort, with great patience and instruction. For the time will come when they will not endure*

> *sound doctrine; but wanting to have their ears tickled, they will*
> *accumulate for themselves teachers in accordance to their own*
> *desires; and will turn away their ears from the truth, and will*
> *turn aside to myths. But you, be sober in all things, endure hard-*
> *ship, do the work of an evangelist, fulfill your ministry." (2*
> *Timothy 4:1-5)*

Paul, and apparently the ascended and heavenly seated Christ, were not impressed with men who were merely capable to make people feel good about their church attendance (not that feeling good about being part of, and participating in, the body of Christ is a bad thing. It well ought to be glorious). What seems to be rewardable to the shepherd and *ultimately* effective in the soul of the listener is the careful exposition of Scripture to the flock.

Expository Teaching – What it Is

Nehemiah makes clear for us the work of expository teaching. The people of Israel had been brought back out of captivity and were rebuilding Jerusalem and its wall. They had been born and raised in a foreign country and were barely familiar with the words of Scripture. Few of them spoke Hebrew as a first language anymore, and they could not easily understand the words of the Book of the Law.

In 8:1, the people gathered and asked Ezra, the scribe, to bring out the Book of the Law and explain it to them. It is worth noting that they asked a scribe, a man learned in studying, in Hebrew, and in the specific systematics of the Mosaic Law.

In verses 4 and 5 we are told that Ezra and his fellow scribes stood on a podium so that people could see and hear him. The people were expected to, and did indeed, show great attention and respect to the Word and to its expositors.

In verse 8 we are told that the expositors read from the Law of God and translated or exposited ("made plain") the sense of the words so that the people understood what was being read.

Verse 10 is not to be missed. The people were told to go and have a feast and a party to celebrate their new understanding of the Word of God. What better reason for us to celebrate joyfully the Lord's Supper than as a response to the Word?

Expository teaching is the careful, interesting, absorbing, illustrating, sometimes humorous, sometimes serious farming of the soil of the Scriptures. It is book by book, line by line, sometimes word by word so that the meaning of the words and sentences are brought to full bloom in the imagination of the listener.

Expository teaching well done soars alone and high above all others forms of spiritual communication in that it uniquely honors the verbal inspiration of the Word. Other forms of "sermonizing" cannot do this because they are removed from the actual text by layers of human thought and wisdom. Although occasionally helpful and motivating, they do not have the same kind of effect as exposition because they are not directly dealing with and from, the *theopneustos*, the God-Breathed text.

The expositor should be careful that his words do not become merely technical commentary *about* what God said or did, but that they *are* the words.

Expository Teaching – What it is Not

Exposition, which is the pastoral function expressed publicly in the pulpit or in writing, is not to be confused with exegesis, which is the hermeneutical/interpretive function that the pastor does in the study. Much harm is done by confusing the two in the pulpit.

Exegesis is the raw study, the practical outworking of the science and art of interpretation. It combines all the elements of the literal, historical grammatical hermeneutic with systematic theology to determine the answer to the following question: "What *did* the author mean *when* he wrote this text and what did his *readers* take it to mean?" Exegesis works as often as possible with the original languages and with historical and cultural data in an attempt to time-travel back to look over the shoulder, as it were, of Paul or Obadiah or Moses as they penned the words. Exegesis is done behind closed doors and should be the bulk of your study time.

Exposition is the refinement of the study results into the presentation to the modern listener or reader to explain those results and to answer the questions, "What did the author mean and how does that translate into modern thought and (if possible) how does it apply to our lives." Good exposition may *occasionally* take the listener behind the study doors to explain a Greek verb tense or word meaning when necessary and appropriate. Too much of this, however, becomes boring, or feels like a "show off" and ultimately indicates that you have not done your expository homework. While appearing to be scholarly it can actually show the laziness of the expositor. Wisdom and sensitivity to the state of the congregation are necessary components. A "behind the scenes" look at a word or verb tense is best done in the context of painting an historical picture for the listeners rather than as a purely technical exercise.

In summary, exposition is to exegesis what flight is to an aircraft. The plane drives the flight and makes it possible. There is no flight without the plane. But no matter how beautiful or cleverly designed the plane is, *flight* is what airplanes are made for. The plane had better fly or the design effort is worthless.

It is beyond the scope of this article to deal with the relationship between exposition and homiletics. Let it suffice to say that in our modern churches perhaps too much emphasis is placed on homiletics and not enough on exegesis and exposition.

> *Resources for Expository Teaching*
> * *Crisis of the Word: A Message To Pastors and Would-Be*
>   *Pastors (2 Timothy 2:15)*
>   www.conservativeonline.org/journals/1_2_journal/Cris
>   is_of_the_word_frm.htm
>
> * *An Introduction to Classical Evangelical Hermeneutics*,
>   Mal Couch – gen. editor
>
> * *New Testament Exegesis*, Gordon Fee
>
> * *To What End Exegesis*, Gordon Fee
>
> * Software: BibleWorks – *Hermeneutica*

Fellowship, Biblical

Koinonia is translated partnership, fellowship, with the personal noun *koinonos* translated partner, sharer.

Unfortunately, when the word is so often used, the thought is simply "fun, food, and fellowship"! But the biblical idea should communicate the thought of, a meaningful relationship whereby the local assembly, and even the broader body of believers everywhere, has a ground zero base of commonality built on trust in the Lord Jesus as Savior.

Churches should broaden the use of the word spiritually so that it is not simply seen as some temporal activity that feeds social enjoyment. However, there is nothing wrong per se with times of friendship and recreation, just the two should not be confused in the thinking of believers.

Too often, people get bent out of shape with one another and are quick to leave the congregation for another church. Their spiritual family ties are really very weak. It is appropriate to change churches: (1) if major moral problems are not addressed, (2) if the teaching of the Word of God is neglected, (3) if the church shifts in its doctrinal integrity, (4) if the polity of the church strays in the wrong direction, i.e., it becomes soft on elder rule and leadership, goes to congregational voting, and places women in elder and deacon positions.

In reference to the Church, the word fellowship is first used in Acts 2:42. The early Jerusalem church was "devoting themselves to the apostles' teaching and to fellowship, to the breaking of bread and to prayer." Paul writes about the believer's call "unto the fellowship of [God's] Son" (1 Cor. 1:9). He also used the word as communion when referring to the Lord's Supper (10:16). He speaks of this fellowship as a mystery (Eph. 3:9), the fellowship in the gospel (Phil. 1:5), the fellowship of (or in relationship with) the Holy Spirit (2:1), and he adds that we have a fellowship in Christ's sufferings (3:10).

Some of the most important passages are in 1 John 1:3, 6, 7. John says our fellowship is with the Father and the Son, and we must be walking in the light, to claim this fellowship, or we are walking about in the darkness and "lie and do not practice the truth" (v. 6). Fellowship is not equal with salvation; it should be the natural result of the salvation experience.

Finances, Handling of

Introduction

It may come as a surprise to some to find that Scripture addresses finances rather extensively. Money and related subjects are mentioned often and broadly in Scripture, and aspects of finances within the church are covered frequently as well. It makes good biblical sense to say that church finances should be handled in a consistent manner with all the other doctrines and affairs of the church. Money is involved in some way with a great many other aspects of the church. These differing aspects will be addressed briefly below.

Who Should Handle the Finances?

Within the church the proper handling of money is important, and yet there are those whose biblical functions are specifically defined so as to exclude the handling of money as a major function. Very importantly, the elders/ pastors within the church have been given charge of the shepherding of the flock, which in practical terms involves teaching, prayer and pastoral care. While they should have a voice in directing the disbursement of funds for the sake of spiritual oversight and meeting spiritual needs, the day-to-day dealing with finances should not be such as to distract the elders/pastors from 00their shepherding role. While the day to day handling of finances is not biblically specified, the role of deacons was initially established in the church for the purpose of allowing the apostles, who were at that time acting in the role of elders, (see also 1 Peter 5:1-4) to focus on the teaching of the word and on prayer (Acts 6:4). It would make sense, then, for deacons to have either a direct, or a supervisory role in the day-to-day handling of finances. This also places the financial responsibility among those who have presumably also met a set of biblical criteria, and have therefore undergone some prior assessment regarding their character, spirituality and demonstrated personal qualifications (1 Tim. 3:8-13).

Counting the gifts to the church offering each Sunday (and at other times, if needed) should be done by responsible, mature individuals. Some churches have established a policy of two people counting the gifts, in order to avoid any temptation or concern over pilfering of church funds, especially since cash amounts can be substantial. Since an individual's giving to the church is to be based on grace and not on the Law or the motivations of the flesh (2 Cor. 9:7), a number of churches have opted to have offerings placed in a box in the back of the church. This approach is also consistent with basing the church operations on faith instead of what can be seen and counted upon in human terms.

Who Should Make Major Financial Decisions?

While ideally the elders/pastors should not get so involved as to put a great deal of their time into money management, there will be a definite need for their input and authority in regard to major directions, significant policy decisions, and any financial matters that will substantially impact the spiritual well being of the church (see Acts 20:28-31; Phil. 1:1; 1 Tim. 3:1; 1 Pet. 5:1-4, regarding the role of overseers and shepherds). Beyond those domains where the elders have specific authority for financial involvement, the deacons should be charged with managing other aspects either fairly directly or in a supervisory capacity.

How Should Spending Authority be Established?

Spending money needs to be such that there is adequate ability to spend funds on things that are needed and authorized, without providing undue potential for abuse or financial surprises. Spending controls should be in place that will avoid spending abuse or fraud. Monitoring income and spending patterns at intervals by a larger group is best in order to avoid a trend from getting out of control before being discovered and corrected. Such monitoring also helps assure that those over the various areas of responsibility are of the same mind regarding the various aspects of the church. This reflects the concept that the church is, by Christ's life within the believers, a living organism (Eph. 4:15,16), rather than just a human organization.

How Does a Church Assure Sound Financial Decisions?

Experience, spiritual maturity (I Tim. 3:1-13), expertise, and good understanding of responsibility and procedures will go a long way toward putting the church on a solid financial footing. Having men in place who also have a mature understanding of their limitations and the abilities of others is critical as well. Biblical founding of the elders and deacons, prayer about financial matters and needs, sound policy, and monitoring are all necessary. If good biblical wisdom is implemented in the area of church finances, money will not be a major issue in the life of the church, but will be a matter of praising God and giving Him the glory (1 Pet. 4:11).

What About Pastoral Compensation?

Regarding the compensation for elders / pastors (1 Tim. 5:17,18), those decisions are best made by other elders, or by a combined group of elders and deacons, especially if the elder group is smaller in size. Compensation, in most churches is understandably going to be significant, and probably the majority of the church's budget, so those kinds of decisions ought to be made by spiritually mature men (1 Tim. 3:1-13) who have an understanding of the overall church financial picture. Some outside consultation or expert assistance may be advisable in the event that specialty expertise is needed in some area, and in that event it would be well to be assured that the outside expert has solid background in the area in which they are providing advice.

Although churches can, and typically do, establish themselves as a tax-exempt organization, there is a great deal about that status that seems to lead churches and/or paid pastors or staff into trouble if they do not observe all the changing laws and regulations that govern their tax standing. These matters can include churches losing their tax-exempt status for reasons other than their financial activities, conflicts with the Internal Revenue Service over pastoral compensation and withholding, housing allowances, and the like. In practice, the greatest number of problems have come from pastoral compensation matters. Most churches should seek varying degrees of outside assistance in these matters, and have a means of monitoring changes in the tax regulations.

See **Giving, Tithing.**

For Resources on Pastoral Tax and Financial Matters*

- Clergy Tax Net, http://www.clergytaxnet.com

- Clergy Financial Planning Service, http://www.clergy-support.com

*Note: these websites are provided in that these contain valuable documents and information resources for paid pastoral staff, but are not necessarily a recommendation of the services offered by these firms. Each church should make a determination of the need for outside services and if so, the best firm to meet those needs.

Foot Washing

The groups that practice the ritual of literal foot washing would be The Catholic Church (only among the leadership), the Eastern Orthodox (only among the leadership), some Pentecostals, and some other minor or splinter groups. Mainstream evangelicals generally do not.

Foot washing is found in the Upper Room Discourse recorded in John 13:4-16 where Jesus washed the disciples' feet during Passover. Mary, the sister of Lazarus, also washed the Lord's feet with costly perfume, and with her hair (12:1-11), as did an unnamed woman simply described by Luke as a sinner (Luke 7:36-50).

Foot washing was common in biblical days for guests coming to a meal. People reclined on couches to eat, and their dirty and dusty feet needed washing.

But to make it an ordinance or a ritual for the Church is wrong. This is to miss the point Jesus was making with His disciples. Because of John 13:14, some believe Jesus commanded foot washing. However, from what the Lord was trying to show the disciples by the context, He did not command them to wash each other's feet, but He said, doing this is "an example that you also should do as I did to you" (John 13:15).

Christ was showing the disciples that "being washed all over" is spiritually like salvation (vs. 8-11), but the washing of the feet is necessary because believers are walking about in a dirty world! Jesus asked His disciples, "Do you know what I have done to you?" (v. 12). Of course they knew that He had just washed their feet physically with water! But He was trying to get across a spiritual point of needing ongoing experiential cleaning of the feet, because they lived in a sinful world.

The Bible should be interpreted with a literal, normal base and understanding, but this must not be wooden-headed or supra-literal so that the message is lost in ceremony or ritual.

Funerals

Funerals should not be extravagant and boastful eulogies that simply praise and glorify the ones who have died. Especially if a pastor does not know if the deceased is a Christian, it would be best to simply preach the gospel for the sake of the living who are present.

Should a pastor indeed preach at a funeral of someone he did not know? Particularly if he knows that individual was not a Christian? The answer is yes because this is a great opportunity to tell those present about eternal life found only in Christ.

What Should be the Order of a Funeral?

This can be determined by the pastor and the family. Even favorite verses or songs can be planned out for a testimony to those attending. Or, from *A Manual of Church Services* purchased from a Christian Book Store, an order of service would be made available.

Below are only a few of the verses of Scripture that should be included in a funeral service:

- *As for me, I shall behold Thy face in righteousness; I will be satisfied when I awake* (Ps. 17:15).

- *It is better to go to a house of mourning than to go to a house of feasting, because that is the end of every man, and the living take it to heart* (Eccl. 7:2).

- *And as for me, I know that my Redeemer lives, and at the last He will take His stand on the earth. Even after my skin is destroyed, yet from my flesh I will see God; whom I myself shall behold, and whom my eyes shall see and not another* (Job 19:25-27).

- *I am the resurrection and the life; he who believes in Me shall live even if he dies, and every one who lives and believes in Me shall never die* (John 11:25-26).

- *For the Lord Himself will descend from heaven with a shout, with the voice of the archangel, and with the trumpet of God; and the dead in Christ shall rise first* (1 Thess. 4:16).

Giving

The Old Testament had a lot to say about generously giving and sharing. Giving to the priests and the care of the tabernacle/temple was done by the command for tithing, the sharing of a ten percent of total income.

Some Illustrations of Giving

Hospitality giving of a meal was first mentioned in regard to Abraham and the angelic visitors (Gen. 18:1-7), the gift of the gleanings in the fields for the poor (Ruth 2), the sharing of food with the widow and orphan (Job 31:17), the giving of clothing (v. 19-20), the general thoughtfulness of sharing a banquet with those less fortunate (James 2:2-5).

Paul writes two chapters on the principle of New Testament giving (2 Cor. 8-9):

- Giving was for the physical needs of those in poverty, such as with the persecuted Jerusalem saints (8:2).

- It was for the support of the Jerusalem saints (v. 4).

- Giving was a gracious work (v. 7), and a proof of Christian love (v. 8).

- Paul did not command giving (v. 8), to give was from his own conviction (v. 10) and based on a man's ability (v. 12).

- What was pledged, Paul says he is coming "to get it," and they should be prepared as they promised (9:4). The Corinthian church was given a reminder that they pledged a gift (v. 5).

- Giving should not be done sparingly (v. 6), but done as one purposes in the heart, because God loves a cheerful giver (v. 7).

- God is able to supply an abundance "for every good work" (v. 8).

- Those provided plenty should give to produce a "harvest of righteousness," not simply to spend their riches on themselves (v. 10-11, 13).

Elders who worked hard "especially those who work hard preaching and teaching" could receive a stipend called "double honor" (1 Tim. 5:17-18), because they are like the ox who receives a reward for grinding the grain. Besides, "the laborer is worthy of his wages (v. 18).

When it comes to financial giving, Christians in America and in a few other countries, may receive a tax-exemption from the Federal or central government. Because financial records must be kept, and reports must be made to revenue offices, many Christians believe they should give their funds to their church without reporting such giving to the government. While tax-exemptions seem to encourage charitable gifts, many believe higher spiritual reasons should drive giving to the Lord.

Today, most church giving goes to charity, missions, support of pastors and staff, and support of the church facilities.

What is Financial Giving?

Giving is fellowship (*koinonia*). It is a financial sharing in common or partnership in God's ministry of the defense and confirmation (establishment) of the Gospel of the Person of Christ (Phil. 1:5-7; Rom. 15:24-26; 2 Cor. 8:4). A critical perspective for the believer is that giving is sharing in common with a ministry of the finances which is already God's. (i.e. God gives us the privilege of allocating His finances).

To What Ministries Should One Give?

Every true ministry (i.e. God's ministry) is begun and is continually performed by God. The distinction is important because there are ministries which are not begun nor performed by God, but by Adam. Likewise, there are ministries begun by God but are no longer being performed by God, but rather are being performed by the Adamic nature. Every believer should therefore seek wisdom and be discerning regarding the ministry he or she is supporting, since it may not be biblical fellowship.

What is the Spiritual Character of Giving?

Giving to God's ministry is durative and consistent for as long as God performs the ministry (Phil. 1:5; 4:10,15,16,18). Due to the lack of financial means a believer may not have the opportunity to give financially – but fellowship (care, concern, love, etc.) continues for the ministry and the ones ministering (Phil. 1:5; 4:10). Giving is the fruit of abiding in Christ and being led by the Holy Spirit (Phil. 4:7). Giving is a grace, i.e. a financial gift is a grace gift - out from God's grace (2 Cor. 8:4,7,19).

What is the Source and Manner in Giving?

The source of giving is from grace. It is from the new man who is created in Christ and led by the Holy Spirit (2 Cor. 8:4, 7, 19) Giving financially is only a portion of the totality of giving, since all that we have and are belong to Him (1 Corinthians 6:19,20; 7:23). The totality of giving includes the following, in order of sequence and priority:

- Giving ourselves to the Lord, that is, making ourselves and everything that He has graciously given us available to Him. In doing so, we are to seek wisdom and guidance from Him on how we should allocate all that is His.

- Giving ourselves to the ministry of the gospel of our Lord Jesus Christ, which includes the exercising our spiritual gifts in the local church for the edification (building up in the faith) of the body. This principle calls us to be participating in God's ministries in the defense & confirmation (establishment) of the gospel of Christ.

- Giving financially, according to the principles set forth in Scripture and presented herein.

What principles are generated from 2 Corinthians 9:7? This verse directs that every man should give. It is common to the character of the Christian, by virtue of who he is in Christ. Further, each one should give as he has purposed, or chosen in his heart. Since the middle voice is used, it means that this choosing is not mandated by others, but by each believer in fellowship with the Lord. That giving is explicitly not to be done grudgingly (out of fleshly resentment), or out of compulsion (under a law system), but rather cheerfully (out of grace), as pleases the Lord. God looks on the heart and not on the financial percentages, formulas, etc.

Believers are exhorted to give from Grace, as shown in the top diagram below, and not from the basis of Law, as shown in the lower diagram. Giving from Grace is consistent with our God-given position. Giving out of any Law-based motivation is based on giving out of the flesh.

See **Tithing.**

Gossip, How to Handle

What Does God's Word say Directly About Gossip?

Gossip is not a subject that one commonly finds in a book on systematic theology, and it is not one that Scripture deals with extensively. But what Scripture states in brevity on this subject, it more than makes up in clarity. An Old Testament passage that stands out most clearly on this matter is Proverbs 20:19:

> He who goes about as a slanderer reveals secrets, Therefore do not associate with a gossip.

Proverbs, of course is providing for us God's wisdom, spoken within a Jewish context. God's wisdom, according to Proverbs, is not to associate with a gossip. Not associating with the gossip will accomplish the following:

- It will avoid your being the subject of the gossip's evil "revelations."

- It will keep you from being tempted to join in the gossip chain.

- It will send a message to the gossip that such behavior is not welcome.

Paul also writes of gossip very directly when he is addressing a list of potential or known problems among the Corinthian church (2 Cor. 12:20-21):

> *For I am afraid that perhaps when I come I may find you to be not what I wish and may be found by you to be not what you wish; that perhaps there will be strife, jealousy, angry tempers, disputes, slanders, gossip, arrogance, disturbances; I am afraid that when I come again my God may humiliate me before you, and I may mourn over many of those who have sinned in the past and not repented of the impurity, immorality and sensuality which they have practiced.*

Notice the other items in the very same list of problems (let us call them sins, as Paul does), and that Paul is not relishing having to deal with these. Gossip is not a trifling matter – a trivial sin! Gossip always stems from the flesh (Gal. 5:19-21, which lists the works of the flesh, has a similar list to that of 2 Cor. 12:20-21). Its motivation is to make the gossiper appear better by means of denigrating the subject of the gossip. It also supposedly implies a sense of importance for the gossiper because of "special information" (sort of a "private gnosticism"). It is a matter of discipline, and hopefully, repentance.

Take note that gossip is among those things that would cause Paul to mourn!

So What Should a Pastor Do?

There are, quite fortunately, several things that can be done to prevent, deal with, and correct gossip problems in the church:

The pastor should not initiate, participate in nor encourage gossip in any way. Perhaps one of the most subtle ways of initiating or participating in gossip is to "share" things with those who are not a part of the problem or a part of the solution. Gossip can even come in the form of "prayer requests", if we are not careful. Even sharing things from the pulpit that ought to be kept private can facilitate gossip.

Gossip can be dealt with in a preventative way by occasional teaching about the biblical teaching on gossip, and its related subjects, as will be addressed shortly.

When gossip shows up as a known instance within the church, there is an identifiable biblical pattern for correcting such things within the church. The hope and intent of such discipline is that repentance and restoration will result. If not, then the biblical procedures must be followed to deal with the problem. Even then, the hope and intent of such discipline is ultimately for restoration. If the matter is one involving a married woman, the leaders should consider that her husband may need to be involved, since he is her head (Eph. 5:23).

Resources on Church Discipline

Church Discipline, J. Hampton Keathley III
http://www.bible.org/studies/theology/eccles/churdisc.htm
Biblical Studies Foundation*

*Note: While this file is recommended regarding church discipline, and there is much that is valuable on this website, there are some files on this site with which the authors do not agree, including the teaching known as Progressive Dispensationalism as well as the inclusion of the Apocrypha in the NET Bible.

See **Discipline, Approach to; Discipline, of Leadership; Discipline, Congregational Members.**

Heresy, How to Handle

The apostle Paul writes about the peril of an apostasy coming (2 Tim.

3:1-9) but that had also arrived in his own day. Heresy opposes the truth, comes from a depraved mind, and rejects biblical truth (v. 8). The answer to heresy, he says, is to follow his teaching, "conduct, purpose, faith, patience, love, perseverance" (v. 10). The apostle does not mind mentioning heretics, such as Alexander the coppersmith, who "did me much harm" (4:14). He urges Timothy to "Be on guard against him yourself, for he vigorously opposed our teaching" (v. 15).

Those who teach error in the assembly "must be silenced because they are upsetting whole families" (Titus 1:11). Paul does not mind labeling those who cause problems: "Beware of the dogs, beware of the evil workers, beware of the false circumcision (Judaizers)" (Phil. 3:2).

A Strong Doctrinal Statement

This is the beginning for keeping the wolves away from the door, but the elders must also work diligently to protect the truth. When heresy begins to raise its head, it must be dealt with quickly. This would begin by the elders calling in anyone in the congregation who is spreading error. The first purpose is to enlighten those who are in error. If they resist, they should be asked to leave the church. When they leave, it would be appropriate for the elders to teach from Scripture exactly where their teaching was biblically wrong.

Elders are also "overseers" who have a responsibility to warn of false teachings that go against the biblical revelation. No doctrine should be ignored. There must be a round-robin of explaining the Word of God on a continual basis.

Recommended Books

Mal Couch, *A Biblical Handbook of the Church* (Kregel).

See **Cults, Protecting the Congregation from.**

Hermeneutics, Importance of

Can and must we know what the Scriptures say? Among those who would call themselves "evangelicals", the great majority would agree that Scriptures are inspired and infallible, as well as the standard for faith and practice. The great difficulty, however, comes in two aspects of the use of Scripture among believers:

Believers are called to "say the same thing", and not have any doctrinal differences (1Cor. 1:10). They are urged to contend for "the faith" (Jude 3), which is an understood and doctrinally stable body of beliefs, and not "the faiths", as if a spectrum of beliefs was normal. Believers are to unite under singular doctrine, not set doctrine aside in order to unite.

Timothy was told to watch his "life and doctrine closely" (1 Tim. 4:16). Each believer, and especially a pastor, is to measure and direct his own life and doctrine according to the word of God.

In order to do either of the above, we must be able to determine the meaning of Scripture.

Furthermore, in today's philosophical environment, there are three epistemological, philosophical questions that must all be answered "yes" in order for the Scriptures to be useful and relevant to us in the biblical sense:

- Is there singular absolute Truth?

- Has the Truth been given?

- Is the (absolute, singular, given) Truth knowable?

If we answer each of the above questions with a "yes" on the basis of a biblical worldview, then we conclude that since the truth is knowable, we must be able to determine the meaning of Scripture.

Knowing exactly what a passage means is directly tied to the adequacy of a pastor. For any given verse or text of Scripture, it is a known fact that among those who call themselves Evangelicals, there is typically more than one, if not several interpretations for that same verse or passage. Based on the two lines of reasoning given above, there is only one intended meaning for each biblical text. That there would be multiple meanings for a single text flies in the face of Truth being knowable, watching our life and doctrine closely, or saying the same thing. Since 'multiple meanings for each passage" cannot be arrived at from the text of Scripture, the problem must lie in how it is interpreted.

That is the reason for establishing and maintaining a sound, consistent hermeneutical approach to Scripture. 2 Timothy 3:16-17 says that, "All Scripture is inspired by God and profitable…" for the purposes of:

- Teaching

- Reproof

- Correction

- Training in righteousness

And the above-given purposes are specifically to the end that, "...the man of God may be adequate, equipped for every good work.." It is critical that we know the single, intended meaning of Scripture in order to be able to teach, correct, etc. If a pastor cannot know the singular, intended meaning of a specific Scripture passage, then it follows that a pastor will not be adequate, nor will that pastor be equipped for every good work.

Since knowing exactly what a passage means is so important, how can we know what a passage means? There is a science of biblical interpretation, known as Hermeneutics, which is related to the science of Hermeneutics that is employed in the legal profession and in literature studies. While the full scope of that science is beyond this text, some references are listed at the end of this article. The first and primary rule of interpretation of Scripture has been well stated by Dr. David L. Cooper, who wrote in *An Exposition of the Book of Revelation* (Los Angeles: Biblical Research Society, 1972), 9:

> "When the plain sense of Scripture makes common sense, seek no other sense; therefore, take every word at its primary, ordinary, usual literal meaning unless the facts of the immediate context, studied in the light of related passages and axiomatic and fundamental truths, indicate clearly otherwise."

Recommended Books and Internet Resources

Roy Zuck, *Basic Bible Interpretation* (Victor Books); Bernard Ramm, *Protestant Biblical Interpretation* (Baker Books); Mal Couch, *Classical Evangelical Hermeneutics* (Kregel).

Hermeneutics, Drew Freeman
http://64.226.87.51/topics/hermeneutics.html
Grace Notes

Foundations: How to Study, Drew Freeman
http://64.226.87.51/equip/equip1.html
Grace Notes

Languages, Biblical, Use of in the Pulpit

What is the value of biblical languages in shepherding a church? Paul, writing in 2 Timothy 3:16-17, tells us that, "All Scripture is inspired by God and profitable for teaching, for reproof, for correction, for training in righteousness; so that the man of God may be adequate, equipped for every good work.." The inspired Scripture, written for the benefit of the body of Christ, was written in the original biblical languages: Hebrew and Greek. Anyone who has studied these languages properly has seen the richness of meaning and the aid to discernment that this understanding of the biblical languages provides. Since Scripture, as inspired by God, is profitable for all the purposes given above, it makes sense that conveying every aspect of what was inspired to the believers in a church body will be optimal for their equipping. Paul considered it critical to have conveyed to the Ephesian Church - especially the elders - the "whole counsel of God" (Acts 20:27).

Should biblical languages be used from the pulpit? It is without question the charge of the shepherd to teach the word (2 Tim. 4:1,2). Since the full conveyance of the truths of God's word is required for the maturity of the believers within a fellowship, and the pulpit is a key point of dissemination of those truths, then teaching the meaning and significance of the biblical languages as they shed light on the biblical text from the pulpit is not optional, but essential. The pastors' aim is to equip believers so that they are capable of exercising clear discernment with a clear understanding of life, doctrine, and their place of usefulness in the body of Christ. They should not be allowed to remain in a state such that they are tossed about by shifting winds of teaching and subject to those who are manipulative and deceptive (Eph. 4:11-16).

How should the biblical languages be used from the pulpit? The answer to this question will depend on the character of the body of believers under the pastors' care. It should be one of the focuses of shepherding to familiarize the believers within the fellowship with the character of the biblical languages. At the same time, there will always be those in the congregation who are new in the faith, or who have little exposure to biblical languages in their prior church experience. The principles for use of biblical languages from the pulpit should therefore be as follows:

Teaching is to disciple believers to maturity (Matt. 28:18-20; Col. 1:28,29). The use of biblical languages should be such as to achieve that end. By stripping the meaning of the biblical text in the original languages from pulpit exposition is falling short of that end. The intent is not to entertain or produce good feelings, but to teach – and that means content and substance. Culturally based inclinations or shifting church practice to the contrary should not guide the shepherds of the church in this regard – Scripture should. Depth of understanding should be our focus rather than catering to increasing numbers of attendees with shallow understanding.

Since there are those who are young in the faith, or simply young at your church, there will be a need to explain things such as what is meant by "passive voice" and to explain its significance. This should be done not just once but each time, if there is any question as to its being understood. The point is that the shepherd is to place understanding in the minds of believers, and complexity above their ability to grasp, even with the best of explanations, is not useful to the end goal. Modern technology (ranging from overheads, handouts, to computer-based presentations) expands the opportunity to convey the truths of Scripture from the original biblical text all the more clearly.

Training in the understanding of biblical languages will prepare the believers to receive the richness of meaning that is in the Scriptures. Weekday evening classes, Sunday morning electives, and correspondence courses can be provided, encouraged, and facilitated in order to achieve this in the local church.

Tools for understanding the biblical text should be made available to the entire congregation, not just a studied few. Greek New Testaments in the pews provide not only a tool for personal reference, but convey a message as well. Additional biblical language reference materials can be made available in areas of general access, such as the church library, website, lobby, etc. These tools can be English language transliterated as well as Hebrew or Greek alphabet based materials.

Legalism

Legalism is a technical description of some of the Pharisees who opposed, first the Lord Jesus, and then later the apostle Paul. A form of salvation by works was advocated by many during the time of Christ, though the Law was never given as a way of salvation in the Old Testament.

In the Jerusalem Council, certain believing Pharisees argued that it was necessary for the Gentiles coming to Christ to keep the Law of Moses (Acts 15:5). But Peter answered, that God made no distinction between Jew and Gentile, and He cleansed their hearts by faith in the gospel of Christ (v. 9).

Finally, a letter went out from the apostles and the Jerusalem elders to the effect that "it seemed good to the Holy Spirit and to us to lay upon you [Gentiles] no greater burden than these essentials: that you abstain from things sacrificed to idols and from blood and from things strangled and from fornication" (vv. 28-29).

The apostle Paul attacks the spirit of legalism in his letter to the Galatians. He argued that legalism, or law keeping, had nothing to do with salvation or a believer's sanctification that follows (3:1-5). "Having begun by the Spirit, you are matured (perfected) by the Spirit."

It seems to be a human egotistical tendency to want to add something to salvation by faith alone. Paul's Galatian audience wanted to return to "weak and worthless elementary things to which you desire to be enslaved all over again" (4:9).

What would be signs of legalism in churches today?

- Adding certain elements to the salvation process, such as baptism, etc.

- Forcing people to dress certain ways.

- Coming down hard with undue demands on the weaker, struggling believer.

- Measuring the other believers' spiritual life by one's own standards.

Recommended Books
Mal Couch, *A Biblical Theology of the Church* (Kregel).

Lord's Supper, Doctrine of

The Lord's Supper is actually a condensed form of Passover that celebrates the substitution of the Lord Jesus for our sins (1 Cor. 11:20-34). Matthew 26:17-30 tells us of the Lord's Passover with His disciples. He told them that Passover was a sign of His death that would initiate the New Covenant (v. 28; Luke 22:20). The cup of wine represented His shed blood, and the bread pictured His sacrificed body, as a lamb substitute under the wrath of God.

The Corinthian church came to the Lord's table drunk and simply using it as a time for eating a meal together. They were coming unworthy, guilty of desecrating the remembrance of His death, and bringing judgment upon their heads. They were to examine their motives, attitudes, and actions as they came together (v. 31). Because of their debauchery, Paul warned them that there was a penalty even of the believer's death ("sleep") that could overtake some of them (v. 30). The behavior of the Corinthians was extreme. What they did is rarely seen in churches today.

The Lord's Supper is meant to be a reminder, a remembrance of what Christ did for us at the cross (Luke 21:19; 1 Cor. 11:24-25). "This cup is the new covenant in My blood; do this, as often as you drink it, in remembrance of Me." This "New Contract" was prophesied in Jeremiah 31:31-on; it would contrast the Law, the Old Contract or Covenant! It would constitute a permanent forgiveness of sins and the indwelling of the Holy Spirit.

See **Lord's Supper, Ceremony of.**

Lord's Supper, Ceremony of

To Roman Catholics, the bread and wine actually become the flesh and the blood of Christ as it enters the throat. This is called Transubstantiation. Other "high" churches see the real "spiritual" presence of Christ in the elements. Others also see the Lord's Table as a true spiritual and efficacious ceremony as imparting some kind of spiritual grace to the partaker.

Evangelicals take the Lord's Supper as simply a reminder, a remembrance as Paul alludes to in 1 Corinthians 11:24-25.

How Often Should the Lord's Supper be Enacted?

Many churches believe every Sunday. However, there is good evidence that when Paul says, "For as often as you eat this bread and drink this cup ..." (v. 26), he is simply saying, "when you do this, do it this way!" Churches may then have the freedom to share the Lord's Table at different times, and are not required to do so every week.

As to how this ceremony or remembrance is carried out, should be left to the individual churches. There seems to be no set formula as to how the elements are presented. It would seem most appropriate that the church elders would officiate at this service. Prayer and scriptural readings should be included.

One of the arguments against doing the Lord's Table every week is that it can quickly become commonplace and lose its meaning. Human nature, such as it is, can soon fall into a ritual that has lost its focus. This must be avoided at all cost. Too, legalism over the Lord's Table should also be noted. People can brag on their taking of the Lord's Supper. Or, they can "feel" more spiritual because they do it a certain way. The Lord is seeking the heart of His people; He is not interested in ritual!

See Lord's **Supper, Doctrine of.**

Marriage

Marriage is a God-given institution and an honorable state. If a pastor senses that a couple is "sleeping around," he must urge that they consummate their relationship. Couples today can be socially or spiritually unequally yoked and imbalanced. Pastors may see this and then face a terrible problem—should they marry the couple or ask them to wait? Unfortunately, many couples today, Christian and otherwise, are going to bed together and risk having illegitimate children. Because of this, it is difficult to counsel the couple to wait in order to get to know the other person better—though this is the prudent thing to do.

Should a pastor marry a couple if he knows one is unsaved? The pastor should first attempt to witness Christ to the one who is not a Christian, and also warn the saved one, of the problems he or she will face. The best choice is that he should not marry the couple, so that the "blood is not on his hands," so to speak. This should be sobering to the Christian and hopefully make him/her rethink their position on the matter.

No matter what the dynamics, pastoral counseling is a must for marriage preparation.

See **Weddings; Marriage, Counseling for; Marriage, Remarriage issues.**

Marriage, Counseling for

Secular psychology should have no part in any counseling. With that said, there is the place for strong emotional, domestic, and spiritual advice for those planning marriage. The ideal would be that the couple would wait for about one year, from the time that they became serious, before tying the knot! But generally speaking, the bite of the love bug does not allow the couple to wait that long. The purpose of a one year courtship is so that the couple can iron out issues and problems before the "I do's."

At least four sessions should be spent in marital counseling. The questions should begin by asking about the couples' conversion experience. They need to face other questions and issues they have not thought about. Often problems arise early on in a marriage because the questions below are not asked. The pair just has not thought about them:

- What church shall we go to?

- Are we balanced spiritually?

- Does the woman really believe the husband is the head of the house?

- But what does this mean to her, and to him?

- Will the wife work?

- Should we have children soon?

- How many children do we want?

- Are there problems they both are concerned about, such as jealousies, angers, etc.?

- Are there in-law issues?

- Are there financial debts that have not been spoken about?

- Does the woman see herself as first and foremost a biblical help-meet to her husband?

- Does the husband see himself as the protector and provider of his wife?

God has Humor!

While these and other issues need to be addressed, the Lord is the author of history and of our lives. No one can cover all the bases and address everything a newly married couple will face. Part of the purpose of marriage is to rub the rough spots off of the other person. Tensions will arise; failures and mistakes made! Problems cause believers to fall on their faces and ask the Lord's help and guidance.

Good Christian books about marriage can be loaned out for those planning for the wedding bells. Homework assignments, and chapter reading assignments, can be made for both the man and woman. They can work through questions together and share their thoughts with the counselor when they come back together.

The elders and their wives make excellent counselors for those engaged. Not only should there be personal counseling, but marriage classes should be held regularly in churches that have a significant singles group facing marriage.

Recommended Books

John Piper and Wayne House, *Recovering Biblical Manhood &*

Womanhood (Crossway); Dennis Rainey, *Staying Close* (Word).

See **Weddings; Marriage, Remarriage Issues; Marriage.**

Marriage, Remarriage Issues

Remarriage was allowed under the Mosaic Law (Deut. 24:1-2). The Sadducees and the Pharisees permitted remarriage. Jesus seems to be addressing easy-divorce in Matthew 5:31-32, but He was also strongly against the divorcing of one partner in order to marry another (Mark 10:11-12). Divorce brings on sin that is destructive to the order of the Christian and even secular home life. No one has ever questioned this, but what to do next, in regard to possible remarriage, has caused strong differences of opinion.

While not wanting to admit it, almost all Evangelical Church leaders allow for remarriage, though some believe those who are remarried may no longer serve the Lord in a spiritual capacity. Generally, if the divorce has taken place many years earlier, they are not so reluctant to give a positive nod for a remarriage!

Many Christians who have remarried have moved on in spiritual growth and maturity, and bring a certain measure of counsel and patience to fellow believers who are struggling in their own domestic life. They appear to be able to give good spiritual advice that saves other marriages. They are counted as faithful witnesses to the Lord's grace and mercies with their restored lives.

See **Divorce; Weddings; Marriage, Counseling for; Marriage.**

Membership, Church

See **Church Membership.**

Ministerial Associations

Any shepherd who has served in a local body for any length of time has been asked to become involved with a local ministerial association. These same shepherds have also found that involvement with a local or regional ministerial association is rarely a neutral matter for conservative evangelical pastors and congregations. Over and over we have heard from pastors that most such associations are either a tremendous blessing or a terrible headache for a man of the Word. The reason for this polarity was apparent to the prophet Amos. As he put it, "Can two walk together, unless they are agreed?" (Amos 3:3)

The Essential Conflict

Ministerial associations (commonly and hereinafter referred to as "Ministerials") are by their nature either ecumenical *or* biblically evangelical. The driving force of the ecumenical mindset is the elevation of organizational, visible and emotional unity and is accompanied by the necessary suppression of doctrinal distinctives and differences as "not Christ-like" and therefore immoral. The driving force of the biblical evangelical mindset is doctrinal, evangelistic and spiritual with organizational unity arising naturally from a commonly held theological framework and shared vision. Because of these opposite drives there will always be tension between the two mindsets and it behooves the local church leadership to recognize this tension in advance for what it is and make their choices accordingly. Wise leadership and decision-making before the fact can save the local church from a host of conflicts, problems and heartaches that can arise from recognizing too late the essential and unbridgeable differences between some congregations.

A Biblical Framework for Unity

The Word has much to say on the topic of unity. First, we are to be "diligent to preserve the unity of the Spirit in the bond of peace." *Eph 4:3.* It is noteworthy that Paul does not tell us to go out and *create* unity, but to diligently *maintain* the unity that is already inherent in being united by the sanctifying ministry of the Holy Spirit, which is organic. There is an implication that there is no organic unity with those who are not sanctified by the Spirit. Further, we are to be peaceable in this diligence. Paul explicitly tells Timothy that he "must not be quarrelsome" especially with those who might disagree with him. (2 Tim 2:24.) Second, the scriptures clearly call us to be in, and operate from, a framework of doctrinal agreement. Paul summons the fractious and divided church at Corinth not to set aside their doctrinal differences, but to resolve them.

> "Now I issue this summons to you all, 'Brothers! (my summons being enforced by Name of the Lord of all of us, Jesus Christ), that you collectively think and speak the one same

thing so that there be no tear in the common fabric, rather the tears in the fabric of your discernment, reasoning and judgment having been perfectly mended.'" (1 Cor 1:10 Author's amplified translation.)

Paul instructs these divisive Christians to settle down and really think about what they believe and he calls them to agree with the one true *corpus* of apostolic doctrine so that the body would not be torn and fractured. He approves of neither selfish individualism and preference nor organizational unity at the expense of doctrine. He tells them to "think and speak the one same thing."

Third, the scriptures tell us to major on the majors and minor on the minors. With regard to disputable matters, Paul tells the Roman church, "Who are you to judge the servant of another? To his own master he stands or falls; and stand he will, for the Lord is able to make him stand." *Romans 14:4* Of course the issue of what is a disputable, non-core, issue and what is core and non-negotiable is a serious topic. But we are instructed here to wrestle with and come to a conclusion on that matter as well. Significant differences are not to be glossed over and minor differences are to be left up to the Lord to judge and correct.

Lastly, the scriptural norm is for genuine Christ centered bodies to cooperate with, encourage one another and work together in various ways. *Acts 18:27, 2 Cor 8:1-7*

It should be noted here that Jesus' oft quoted prayer for unity in John 17 should not be seen as Jesus waiting around anxiously for us 21st century Christians to *create* organizational unity. Rather it is a prayer for ontological unity that was gloriously answered and fulfilled by the giving of the Holy Spirit at Pentecost and was and is realized completely by the believer's union with Christ and by the indwelling of Christ through the Spirit in them. There is nothing for us to *do*. It is a finished work. *"that they may all be one; even as Thou, Father, art in Me, and I in Thee,* that they also may be in Us; that the world may believe that Thou didst send Me." (John 1:21)

A Biblical Mandate for Disunity

While we are clearly called to operate cooperatively where there is doctrinal agreement we are also clearly warned to not compromise doctrinal integrity for the sake of visible, organizational unity. The scriptures call us to maintain organizational, personal and ministry separation from a range of people and their teachings. The following passages adequately demonstrate the principle of separation: Matt 7:15, 22. 2 Cor 6, 11:13, 1 Tim 4:1, 6:3-11, 2 Tim 3:5, 2 Peter 2:1, 2 John 7-11, Jude 4-19, Rev 2:2.

To share a pulpit (except in a debate) or to minister alongside, or to appear to be in agreement with those who preach a different gospel, or who deny the Biblical faith, is to sanction their work, and this is not pleasing to the Lord. In such cases the Bible calls us to deliberate and visible disunity for the sake of Christ.

Suggestions for Ministerials

What a wonderful blessing it is when a ministerial is comprised of men of like precious faith. If you live in such a town or region, you should consider yourself very fortunate. For most biblically oriented shepherds, the local ministerial is at best a worrisome compromise or at worst a religious sham. The following ideas are offered as alternatives or as ways to strengthen or shore up a local ministerial.

First and foremost, count the cost of separating right up front. There will be a social price to pay. There may even be negative repercussion from within your own congregation. Brace yourself and trust wholly in the Lord.

Consider starting a new ministerial comprised only of those shepherds with which you have considerable doctrinal agreement. Expand it to a regional if you cannot find enough local churches that are solid.

Write a ministerial statement of faith that is broad enough to encompass small differences but narrow enough to exclude those who should be biblically excluded.

Network with other pastors who may be in a ministerial but also feel uncomfortable with its ecumenical nature. You may be able to pull them out of the corrupt ministerial to start a new one.

Do not waste your time trying to "reform" an existing ecumenical ministerial. It will never happen and you will only be stirring up trouble and hard feelings.

Do be polite and clear in refusing to cooperate with an ecumenical ministerial. Treat it as an opportunity to make the doctrinal issues clear. Do not be rude or superior in your refusal.

Sometimes a ministerial is comprised of good men but has lost its steam. Consider beefing it up with a regular presentation of theological topics by an outside speaker or the members of the group. Many times theologians are hiding in the wings waiting to be encouraged and brought out. Bring interesting articles from the CTS Journal for your fellow pastors to read and interact with.

Missions, Support of

To send forth missionaries has always been the burning task of churches who have a heart for reaching the world for Christ. The job seems two-fold: (1) Reach the lost for Christ, (2) With the newly saved, establish strong Bible teaching churches in order to gain a toe-hold in a given culture.

Some missionary work moves in to a given area of the world through educational, medical, or agricultural work. While these endeavors are important, they should be but door openers for the Gospel.

Because many seminaries and mission organizations are sliding left in their doctrinal stance, churches must be careful in choosing their missionaries.

Many missionaries struggle to raise support from a group of churches. This has been the traditional way for providing income, but it is burdensome on the missionary and his family that has to move about the country when on furlough, in order to find funding. While this spreads the interest and the support among the churches, it would seem better if a church sent forth fewer missionaries, but supplied almost all of their financial needs from the one source. Arguments continue about this problem among those working in missions.

One of the greatest passages about missions is found in Acts 15:19-35, where Paul,

Barnabas, Barsabbas, and Silas are sent forth from the Jerusalem church armed with a letter from the people, the apostles, and the elders. The First Missionary Journey (13:1-14:28) is also an important study in strategy for what God wants in missions outreach.

Recommended Books
Russell Penney, *Overcoming the World Missions Crisis* (Kregel).

Music, Contemporary

What is it?

While there is a wide variety of styles represented in contemporary Christian music (CCM), generally this broad music category has been developed from the 1970s to the present. CCM is often placed under categories of music according to secular names given to each style of music, such as:

- Alternative

- Ska

- Rap

- Country and Western

- Pop Rock

- Heavy Metal

For those who are unfamiliar with the CCM music scene, they may be asking, "What is it?" even after this introduction.

Is it helpful?

In the final analysis CCM must be evaluated with the same parameters and according to the same principles that apply to any Christian music. Nonetheless, there are some characteristics of CCM for which some general observations can be made:

CCM was developed at a time when the elevation of experience and feelings was on the increase in the general culture and among a great many Christians.

Secular business and marketing entities have seen CCM as simply one of the music business niches, and have purchased some of the primary channels for recording and distribution.

Music styles in CCM in general reflect those styles seen in the secular contemporary music culture. Customers for CCM generally purchase on the basis of preferred style of CCM, and not on the basis of content.

Lyrical content in CCM can at times be very innovative and insightful, even offering fresh perspectives, but also can simply communicate along the lines of secular lyrics. Lyrics that are unclear, vague, obscure, or even profoundly unbiblical are present in much of what is marketed as CCM.

Performers of CCM are often on the concert tour circuit, and it has been observed that some of those performers exhibit lifestyles that are little different from the secular performers of the same style. This is not universally the case, however. There are some CCM artists who, while on tour, are distinctly different from the secular performing culture.

The general observation, as outlined above, is that much of CCM simply reflects the secular culture, most certainly in its music styles, but at times in the words as well. One could also note that there are some in the CCM scene who make it a point to challenge the modes and morays of the existing culture – in ways that are indeed biblical.

So What, if Anything, Should a Pastor do About and with CCM?

CCM will be marketed, offered or suggested to those within the church in the form of:

- Church-sponsored CCM concerts

- CCM at church youth events

- Music to be played or sung to the youth or the greater church congregation

- Music to be sold through Christian bookstores, mail order channels, etc.

- CCM Concerts at public amusements parks

- CCM Festivals and retreats

- Youth within the church forming their own CCM groups

- Youth within the church listening to CCM while traveling, at home, etc.

The CCM scene is not uniform in its lyrical or music message, stage or packaging message, and there is some of it that is worthwhile, while other aspects are to be seriously opposed. Therefore elders within each church should look very carefully at the use of music in the church, providing biblically sound and wise guidelines for its selection and use within the church. Further, there is a need for not only those guidelines, but as in everything, providing teaching regarding biblical principles in music and worship. Teaching will help to bring about the minds and hearts of those in the congregation, so that believers are equipped, and not tossed to and fro by every wind of doctrine (Eph. 4:12-15). Such teaching will allow the believers in the congregation to exercise their own discernment regarding CCM, rather than having the elders seem "out of step" about the music being offered and promoted among the churches. See also other articles herein on the subject of music for important principles that apply as well to CCM.

Music, Place in Worship

What does God's word say? It may come as a surprise to some that the Greek words for worship do not really have anything to do with music.

Worship in the New Testament is often the translation of the Greek word *proskuneo*. In the NT, generally, to do reverence or homage to someone, usually by kneeling or prostrating oneself before him.

Synonyms for *proskuneo* would include:

- *sebomai*: to revere, stressing the feeling of awe or devotion

- *sebazomai*: to honor religiously

- *latreuo*: to worship in the sense of serving

- *eusebeo*: to act piously toward

- *eulabeomai*: to reverence

It is therefore safe to say from a New Testament biblical standpoint that while worship does not exclude music, per se, music is not as essential to worship as much of the church seems to have come to think. It would be well to say that there is worship that does not include music, and there is music that does not include worship. There is also some area of overlap, in which the music does constitute worship, and in which the worship involves music.

- Worship can include words said, and not sung (Rev 4:9-11)

- Worship can include money given or things shared (Heb 13:15)

- Worship can include presenting our bodies as living sacrifices (Rom 12:1, 2)

- Worship can include our bodily position before the Lord (Rev 5:14)

- One should not lose sight of the true character of the biblical words for worship, however, and especially those in the New Testament epistles.

What is True Worship?

Paul tells us in Romans 12:1:

> *Therefore I urge you, brethren, by the mercies of God, to present your bodies a living and holy sacrifice, acceptable to God, which is your spiritual service of worship.*

And again he writes in Philippians 3:3:

> *...for we are the true circumcision, who worship in the Spirit of God and glory in Christ Jesus and put no confidence in the flesh...*

True worship always is directed toward God and extols His character and accomplishments and promises over our character, our accomplishments and our promises. Colossians 2:18 and 2 Thessalonians 2:3-4 make it clear that there is such a thing as false worship as well, so Christians need to be discerning in this regard. Some of the directions of false worship today would include:

- Human beings

- Self

- Feelings

- Musical composition

- Unbiblical spirituality

A key Scripture in the understanding of the biblical application of music to worship is found in Colossians 3:16,17, which is written in the translation by Kenneth Wuest as:

> The word of Christ, let it be continually at home in you in abundance; with every wisdom teaching and admonishing each other by means of psalms, hymns, spiritual songs, with the grace singing in your hearts to God. And all, whatever you do in the sphere of word or deed, do all in the Name of the Lord Jesus, constantly giving thanks to God the Father through Him.

From this set of verses we see that the word of Christ is not incidental to the biblical expression of music.

God's intent is that music is to be expressed from a heart and mind that are deeply immersed in - literally "at home in" - the truths of His word.

Further, all three of the categories of music that Paul the apostle gives here are to have the character of teaching and admonishing.

This is similar to what Paul says in II Timothy 3:16, 17 where he speaks of God's word in terms of correction.

There is a substantial place for songs to be corrective and exhorting.

The content of what is presented in the form of music is therefore not secondary or incidental, but rather an essential part of the whole of worship as it is expressed in music. The location of this singing is not externally focused, but in hearts.

Note the three types of songs that Paul refers to in these verses:

- Psalms: *psalmos* – often used in reference to the Psalms

- Hymns: *humnos* – refers to songs which are sung in praise directed to God

- Spiritual Songs: *odais* – songs which are spiritual in content

These three categories convey a variety of musical expression as to content, but are not exclusive to one another. There will be, then:

- Songs containing lyrics drawn directly from Scripture – even the Psalms.

- Songs which are sung directly to the Lord – in the second person.

- Songs which are of a general spiritual nature.

Scripture makes a place for all three categories of songs, but allowing overlap. This would indicate that though we would not want to break things down to formulas, that a balance of all three kinds of songs is fitting for churches.

Music, Proper Control and Use of

What about discernment in the musical lyrics? Musical lyrics are more readily compared to the revealed content and revealed intent of Scripture than musical composition. It is God's intent, as revealed in I Thessalonians 5:21, 22, that we test everything – holding everything up to the yardstick of Scripture . There are a great many songs and hymns in common use today, some of which conform to the biblical criteria, and some of which fail basic biblical tests. One may even have songs with lyrics which are direct quotes from Scripture – but are applied in the wrong context, and are therefore unbiblical. We will present shortly more explicit criteria for evaluating musical lyrics.

What about discernment in the musical composition? Musical composition – the non-lyrical elements of music - is the aspect of music which is most difficult to define from a biblical standpoint, but that is not to say that there are not biblical tests which can and should be applied. Musical composition is the artistic medium through which the objective lyrical content of the music will be expressed, and the artistic medium most certainly has a message as well, albeit more subjectively. Musical composition, even without words, is capable of conveying a broad spectrum of emotions, and is even effective in telling a story as well as describing events, scenery and personalities.

Examples of this in the secular realm would include classical instrumental musical pieces such as Peter and the Wolf, Grand Canyon Suite, and the Nutcracker Suite.

Emotions, sentiment and even situations are so effectively communicated via music that movies will almost always use music to tell us, without words, that we should feel tense, tragic, frightened, sad, relieved or excited. In really well-done musical scores for movies, the musical score will often be sold separate from the movie itself, because it takes one through the range of emotions and environments that were contained in the movie. What music composition alone does not do as well as written words is to communicate propositional truth, to communicate truth with respect to time, or what ought to be done or could have been done.

So What are the Key Principles About Music and Worship from Scripture?

1) Musical Lyrics are to be Biblical in Doctrine

This may seem obvious, but is often overlooked. A proverb among those in the advertising field is: If you do not have much to say, sing it. Songs are a way to convey something other than real propositional content, or to convey content that the mind might reject if stated as a proposition. On the other hand, Paul has just as clearly communicated to us that songs not only can but should be solidly biblical.

The following principles are doctrinal as well, but are given in order to be clear about the extent of the doctrinal principle with regard to music.

2) Musical Lyrics are to be Biblically Balanced

While a given core of music for worship may be biblical, it may not be biblically balanced in the realm of kinds of doctrine. For instance, one might have a collection of worship music which is focused substantially on thanking the Lord for what He has done, but is lacking in direct worship of who He is, acknowledgment of His glory and majesty, or anticipation of His coming.

3) Musical Lyrics are to be Biblical as to Dispensation

A number of contemporary praise songs, even those which are quoted directly from Scripture, are based outside of the current dispensation, and therefore contain teachings or are founded on theology that is not true of the current dispensation. A number of the newer "praise songs" teach that the Holy Spirit must be felt, and that the Holy Spirit must fall on one repeatedly, only returning with periodic pleadings. These points are not a matter of being picky about theoretical doctrines, but of practices that directly impact how a believer is to live from day to day.

4) Musical Lyrics are to be Biblical in Eschatology

Both recent songs out of the Latter Rain movement and even a number of older hymns written a century or two ago reflect an Amillennial or Postmillennial eschatology. Christ is pictured as the presently reigning King of the church or earthly kingdom, rather than the One who will reign in the Millennial Kingdom. These words are often well established in our church hymnals and even Christmas carols, and they reflect an eschatology that is based more on pagan influence, tradition and the turns of church history than upon Scripture. In parallel with this, some songs reflect an eschatology that flies in the face of multiple warnings about the growing apostasy of this present church dispensation.

5) Musical Lyrics Must Uphold God as the Promise Maker and the Promise Keeper

How far better to sing "Great is Thy Faithfulness" than to sing songs reciting our promises to Him. He is not asking us for our promises to Him, but faith in Him. Faith in Him, not our promises, directs worship toward Him.

6) Musical Lyrics are to be Biblical in Perspective

The Scriptures are given to us to tell about a beginning and an end. According to God's word, human history and God's working in it are described as linear. History is going somewhere. It has a purpose. That is why Genesis starts off with "In the beginning God" That is also why Revelation draws together all the passages about the future and tells us what will happen in the end. Musical composition, of itself, can easily tend to focus on what is now. When believers in church are encouraged to sing songs that are repetitive, it reinforces a cyclical rather than linear world view. It also takes the focus off of content, and places it upon the emotional and other messages of the musical composition. If a caution about vain repetitions is to be taken seriously in prayer, why not consider that same caution in our singing? (Matt. 6:7)

7) Musical Lyrics are to be Biblical in Godly Focus

Certainly we would not want to denigrate the words of the 18th century classic, Amazing Grace, which speaks of saving "a wretch like me" and "When we've been there ten thousand years". That being said, both the lyrics and the musical composition within the church must ultimately place our focus upon the Lord and upon glorifying Him. An overabundance of lyrics which direct our focus on first person experience either individually or corporately and not on the Lord is fundamentally unbiblical. In the extreme, some songs may make claims for first person experience which are simply not true.

8) Musical Composition is to be Biblical in Godly Focus

Even with music that has lyrics which direct us to the Lord, it is still possible to have musical composition that overwhelms the message of the lyrics. This can happen by a message in the music which stirs people to focus on the individual, the subjective and the cyclical. This is not simply a matter of the choice of instruments or musical style, per se. In churches where elders have allowed it, music has taken on the role of entertainment rather than worship and teaching and admonition. This places a human focus on the gathering of believers instead of a godly focus

9) Musical Composition is to be Consistently Biblical in its Message

While it is lyrics which convey propositional truth, the elements of musical composition convey emotion, environment, events, personalities, and circumstances. These are to be done so as to be consistent with and not overwhelm the biblical message and the message in the lyrics of the song.. Because of this it is suggested that when we have instrumental pieces in the church, that we do so either with musical pieces that are familiar so as to call the lyrics to mind, or to place the lyrics on an overhead. That will direct our thoughts toward the inspired content of the word rather than simply emotionally inspiring music

10) Musical Composition is to be Biblical in Helpfulness

This is an issue that requires church elders to be most discerning and observant. Biblically, everything in the dimensions of music and worship may be lawful, but not everything will be helpful (1 Cor. 6:12, 10:23). This is where the role of elders is most challenging but ever so critical. The elders could simply say that the church will not have any of this kind of music or that kind of music. But the real task after we have determined what is objectively and clearly biblical and unbiblical is to ask what is helpful. In this we have to understand that music composition is culturally based. Few if any of us might find music on a Chinese scale to be helpful in worship – but there would be a different answer among elders in a Chinese church. Ultimately, elders in each church need to be thinking these things through and communicating to those in their church about why they are choosing certain lyrics, musical style, and excluding others.

Final Comments

The biblical basis for musical expression among Christians from Colossians 3:16 and 17 needs to be conveyed to those under their care so that:

- Biblical understanding and discernment guides the selection and involvement with church music.

- Discernment regarding both lyrics and musical composition has been exercised by the elders, and conveyed to the church body.

- Those involved in playing instruments, singing and other technical aspects of musical presentation have not only a biblical understanding but have biblical priorities regarding what is most important in music and worship within the church.

Then when we say "*Soli deo gloria*", our musical lyrics and musical composition say the same thing (1 Cor. 1:10). The final appeal must be to the word of God. God revealed truth in His word because we could gain it no other way. Let us not, then, make a final appeal to anywhere or anyone else (2 Tim. 3:16-17).

Overseer, Definition of

Overseer is *episkopos* and means to over look, or to look out for what is coming ahead. In other words, he must be aware of what is coming toward the church that may bring spiritual harm to the believers. It is clear from several passages of Scripture that the elder and pastor is also the overseer in the church. Where such church officers are mentioned, they are always mentioned in the plural, not as singular. Thus, the overseers/pastors/elders/teachers are actually one group of men described with these four nouns.

In Titus 1 Paul tells Titus to appoint elders (plural) in every city (singular) as he directed (v. 5). While describing the qualifications of the elder, Paul suddenly writes, "For the overseer …" In other words, the elder and the overseer are the same. Paul tells the Ephesian elders, "The Holy Spirit has made you overseers to shepherd (to pastor) the church of God …" (Acts 20:28).

An old English word for overseer is bishop. The early church placed bishops over a group of churches, and thus created a hierarchy that is really not biblical. The pastors are the bishops, or overseers, over their own flock.

Recommended Books
Mal Couch, *A Biblical Theology of the Church* (Kregel).

See **Pastor, Definition of; Elder, Definition of; Teacher, Definition of.**

Pastor, Definition of

Surprisingly, the noun for pastor (*poimen*) is used only once in the New Testament in describing the church officer. Paul writes, Christ has given some "as pastors indeed teachers" (Eph. 4:11b). The apostle urged the Ephesian elders to shepherd, pastor the church of God (Acts 20:28). In this passage he also says, "The Holy Spirit has made you overseers to shepherd …" There is the inter-twining of the words elder, overseer, and shepherd in Paul's thinking when he refers to the leadership of the church.

Recommended Books
Mal Couch, *A Biblical Theology of the Church* (Kregel).

See **Elder, Definition of; Teacher, Definition of; Overseer, Definition of.**

Politics and the Pulpit

Any pastor who has discussed politics or politicians from the pulpit has enjoyed that blissful and blistering experience of making half the congregation very happy and the other half very angry. Politics is second only to the selection of the color of the new carpeting in the foyer in its ability to excite the passion of American churchgoers. In all seriousness, the matter of politics and the pulpit has serious spiritual, pastoral and legal implications for your church that are worthy of examination.

Democracy's Blessings, Democracy's Curse

"Remind them to be subject to rulers, to authorities, to be obedient, to be ready for every good deed, to malign no one, to be un-contentious, gentle, showing every consideration for all men. For we also once were foolish ourselves, disobedient, deceived, enslaved to various lusts and pleasures, spending our life in malice and envy, hateful, hating one another." (Titus 3:1-3)

As a people who have enjoyed the blessings of a democratic republic and unprecedented personal and political freedom for over 200 years, we have become complacent, complaining and hedonistic in both our exercise of, and attitude toward our freedoms. Unfortunately, these attitudes have permeated the church and many Christians and entire congregations complain much politically, do little, vote little, demand their "rights," are hedonistic in their behavior, and are a poor example of Christian humility toward God ordained authority when it pinches them.

In the above passage Paul instructs shepherd Titus to regularly remind Christians to consciously exercise a respectful Biblical world-view toward authority in *stark contrast* with their former unregenerate behavior. Pastors would do well to follow in Titus' footsteps, pointing out to Christians that their civic and public duties are a direct reflection of their understanding of God's sovereignty in placing governing officials, even ones they find politically or personally repugnant.

Perfect Offices – Less than Perfect Officers

A point that seems to have been lost on modern Americans is the distinction between respect for an office and the person occupying that office. The current cultural norm is to respect the *person* if we like and approve of them and their policies, and to disrespect the *person* if we disapprove. This, however, is decidedly not the Biblical view of authority, which clearly distinguishes between the office and the person occupying it.

The OT history of David and king Saul is illustrative. Without question Saul was a less than moral man, an irrational politician and insanely obsessed with the elimination of *one citizen* who was innocent of all charges. Yet when presented with the golden opportunity to do away with Saul, David's conscience bothered him for even taking a snip of Saul's royal robe while Saul relieved himself in the cave where David and his men were hiding. "So he said to his men, 'Far be it from me *because of the LORD* that I should do this thing to my lord, the LORD's anointed, to stretch out my hand against him, since he is the *LORD's anointed.*'" (1 Sam 24:6, emphasis mine).

In short, David differentiated between the weak, jealous and incompetent man and the man's office as ordained of God. In David's mind there was a priority of moral imperative and top on that list was obedience to God followed immediately, and evidenced by respect for, the office of the king. This does not, of course, imply that believers should automatically obey everything that any authority orders. David certainly did not, and there are times when obedience to men is disobedience to God. The issue is, however, how many modern Christians have damaged their witness by refusing to conform to the Biblical norm of respect for God ordained offices and "to be ready for every good deed."

Government – Its Biblical Purposes

The scriptures tell us that the purpose of government is to:

- Restrain evil and reward good behavior (1 Peter 2:13-14) including a judicial system and capital punishment for murder (Gen 9:6).

- Provide military protection against invaders or marauders (military defense seen as a general principle in the scriptures).

When governments go far beyond fulfilling these two basic purposes the record, in the Bible, of governments is largely negative. (See 1 Sam 8:11-19 for example). The size, power and resource consumption of government that we experience in the United States, for example, is stratospherically larger than anything recommended by the Bible or approved or imagined by our Founding Fathers. It should be understood that no major party in the US or Canada reflects the wisdom of size and function limitation outlined in the Bible. In addition, the scriptures assume the depravity of man in giving him basic governmental constraints. As Christians we should understand that any political party, politician or law that assumes the "essential goodness of man" is at odds with divine revelation.

That being said, we are called to be "salt and light" and are to "Do all things without grumbling or disputing; that you may prove yourselves to be blameless and innocent, children of God above reproach in the midst of a crooked and perverse generation, among whom you appear as lights in the world," *Phil 2:14-15* We are to do and give our best given the culture, government and politics to participate in a constructive, redemptive and uniquely Christian way in the society and politics of our day. Christians in a representative democracy are uniquely privileged to participate in determining the laws and leaders of our local, state and federal governments. As such they should see themselves as agents of divine sovereignty.

Politics and Pastoral Care

It is beyond the scope of this article to deal with matters of policy. Our concern is local and pastoral. That is, what should the pastor teach on the subject, and what example should he set? A Biblical framework and priorities, a world-view, for making political decisions should be taught, irrespective of political parties and candidates.

Here is an overview of a framework and priorities that are suggested by Scripture:

No form of government will bring in the Kingdom. That awaits the King and the Millennial Kingdom. Past attempts to "Christianize" governments have failed miserably.

No form of government is necessarily "Christian" and that includes democracy and America. (Some countries with benign dictatorships are arguably better off than they would be with a democracy.) With regard to politics Christians need to develop a "principled pragmatism" that acknowledges that compromise on some issues is necessary to attain other good results. Demanding absolute perfection does not acknowledge the reality of a complex and confused world or body politic.

Governments exist to restrain evil and keep enemies from invading. Man is depraved and God uses, among other things, the governing authorities to contain that depravity.

Economic and "labor" interests are of lower priority than direct moral imperatives, such as the protection of innocent life, the right and responsibility of parents to train their children and the right and responsibility to worship God. For example, more Americans are murdered *each year* in abortion clinics than were killed in all the years of the Korean and Vietnam wars *combined*. Christians should be taught that the personal selection of a political party, politician or law should never place personal or group economic or labor precedence over the moral imperative. Any party, politician or law that expressly and deliberately does so is outside the express will of God and so is the Christian that votes for it. Such a party, politician or law is *de-facto* disqualified from consideration no matter what other "benefits" it offers.

There is no free lunch. To the degree that a government is generous and "gives money" to various people through social programs, to that same degree it is taking tax money (by force) from someone else, and to that degree it is disabling and discouraging citizens and Christians from caring themselves for the poor, sick, etc. As a society we have transferred responsibility from the family, church and local town to a faceless bureaucracy, and we think ourselves generous for having done so.

Security and comfort always come at the cost of personal freedom and innovation. Historically those societies who insisted on maximum security and minimal personal risk have become weak.

On balance we are here to contribute to our society and government, and not take from it.

What's Legal – What's Not

The question always arises, "What can I say from the pulpit politically, and legally what can our church do politically." Historically in America the pulpit is what made or broke many a political career. The moral authority of the pulpit and the pastor was very influential, especially in rural areas where most of America lived. With the increasing secularization and urbanization of our society the day when this was true is past. However, it is appropriate for pastors to develop a Biblical framework and to teach it to their church as previously stated.

If your church is *not* a non-profit 501-c.3 corporation then the only limits are, "is it edifying for the church body" and "is it slanderous legally?" However, many churches are 501-c.3 charitable religious corporations and one of the parameters of the non-profit is that such a corporation cannot be overtly political. The IRS is increasingly active in eliminating the non-profit status of churches that they see as overtly political. This used to be defined as explicitly backing a candidate or party. In recent years "overtly political" has been expanded at the urging of secularists to almost anything that touches on public morality. In other words, if you use "hate speech" (condemn homosexuality for example) or participate in an anti-abortion rally, you are being "political".

In short, there is a deliberate crusade to shut the mouth of the moral authority of the local church and pastors. The ACLU and other organizations are using the IRS to "go get 'em" and remove the ability of the pastor to speak on moral issues. Granted, some pastors and churches have truly abused the charitable religious tax exemption for overtly political purposes.

As a shepherd you need to decide what you will tolerate as far as "silencing" goes and balance this with the Biblical mandates on the various moral issues your church faces. Ask yourself if silence is worth the tax exemption.

Here are the things you generally *can* do:

-Host a "candidates night" in which several candidates present their positions to the congregation or to the public.

-Teach a Biblical world-view for making political decisions.

-Register people to vote and urge them to vote (not for a particular party of candidate).

On the Sunday before election day you can deliver a sermon on the general moral issues in the upcoming election, without naming names.

For specific research contact the American Center for Law and Justice (ACLJ) at **www.aclj.org**

Preaching, Defined

The common biblical word for preach is *karusso*. It can be argued that teaching and other related words tell us what should be done within the confines of the local church. A survey of usage shows that "preaching" refers mostly to the proclamation of the Gospel to the lost, while "teaching" is to be carried out for the strengthening and maturing of the sheep.

Many pastors believe they should preach on Sundays, and that teaching is simply confined to the Sunday school hour. Often when pastors say preach, they are referring to a style of delivery that is emotive, energetic, and flamboyant! Yelling and shouting generally accompany this approach. Pastors often try to imitate others they have watched on TV. They believe that part of preaching is to be entertainment.

Most pastors argue that preaching and teaching are the same, but too many passages prove otherwise. Paul writes about honoring elders "who work hard at preaching and teaching" the Word (1 Tim. 5:17); "Teach and preach these principles" (6:2); "They ceased not to teach and preach" (Acts 5:42; 15:35).

That preaching is mainly evangelism is seen clearly in Acts 17. Paul said: "This Jesus whom I am proclaiming to you is the Christ" (v. 3), "The word of God had been proclaimed by Paul in Berea" (v. 13), "He was preaching Jesus and the resurrection" (v. 18), "May we know what this new teaching is which you are proclaiming (v. 19), "The UNKNOWN GOD I proclaim to you" (v. 23).

1 Timothy 4:2 may be an exception to the rule. Paul here uses the word preaching in the sense of teaching: "Preach the word; be ready in season and out of season; reprove, rebuke, exhort with great patience and instruction."

See **Teaching.**

Promotion of Church

It is legitimate for churches to reach out to the community with evangelism promotion, but also promotion about the teaching ministry for the building up of believers. If an assembly is truly a Bible teaching church, it should not be ashamed of telling others of this fact. Promotion should then be for the right reason: "We have a message to tell to the world!"

Madison Avenue techniques should not be employed in setting forth the teaching program of the church. Churches should not use a lot of hot air to gain attention. Entertainment must not be the drawing card for attracting people to the church. Advertisement that caters to the worldly senses must be avoided.

The church may legitimately set forth its teaching ministry and outreach to children by (1) handouts delivered door-to-door in the neighborhood; (2) radio spots; (3) Christian or secular newspaper ads. One strategy would be to promote: a Bible study series; a vacation Bible school; a special speaker; a summer camp program, a prophetic conference, etc.

Good quality material should be produced. Honesty must be reflected in what is written.

Be keeping up a promotional drumbeat, people will begin to see that such a church that is properly enthusiastic about what it is doing. This congregation will begin to receive visitors. Good promotional seed planting may take time to produce fruit.

See **Advertising.**

Prophecy, Importance of Teaching

Is Biblical Prophecy Really Important?

The greatest evidence that can be forwarded regarding the great importance of Bible prophecy is the weight of Scripture that is dedicated to prophecy. If we start with the premise that Scripture itself is important (as every pastor should, of course), then the sheer mass of prophetic Scripture should tell us that biblical prophecy is of primary importance. Some instances of this "weight of prophetic Scripture" and the weighty testimony to its importance would be:

- 28% of the Bible is composed of prophecy

- Some books of the Bible, such as Revelation, are composed of as much as 95% prophecy

- The Old Testament Scriptures were called "the Law and the Prophets" (Matt. 7:12, 22:40; Luke 16:16; Acts 13:15; Rom. 3:21)

- The Lord Jesus Himself was called "a prophet" (John 1:21; Acts 3:22, 7:37)

- One of the major subjects of biblical prophecy in both the Old and New Testaments is the Lord Jesus Christ

- The New Testament frequently quotes the Old Testament prophecies in order to show true and faithful fulfillment

- Note the use of the words "all" and "whole" in Matthew 28:19-20, Acts 20:27, and 2 Timothy 3:16,17. "All" and "whole" include prophecy, among other important biblical subject matter.

Why is Biblical Prophecy Important?

Biblical prophecy provides several important inputs to the life and testimony of the believer. These would include:

Unfulfilled prophecy provides our orientation to things to come, which in turn gives us a present perspective, motivation and confident hope (1 Thess. 5:1-11, 5:23-24; 1 Tim. 6:14; Titus 2:12-14; James 5:7-9; 1 John 2:28, 3:2-3).

Fulfilled prophecy is a significant tool in apologetics for confirmation of the faith of believers, and demonstrating the validity of the faith to unbelievers (e.g., Micah 5:2; Zech. 9:9, etc.). As a tool for believers, it is all about spiritual growth and discipleship. As a tool with unbelievers, it is all about evangelism.

Biblical prophecy shows God's faithfulness, since God's promises made, primarily in the Old Testament, are shown to be fulfilled, primarily in the New Testament. Prophecy is not about satisfying our curiosity about things here on earth, or having mystical knowledge of things to come, but it is all about God's character.

The focus of prophecy is about Jesus Christ, as is especially shown in the book of Revelation. It is His revelation.

Then why is there a tendency to downplay or disregard prophecy in so many churches? Since so many Christians are not using sound

Hermeneutics, and are even using Hermeneutics which are worldly in their source and humanistically subjective, Christendom has come up with a wide variety of viewpoints on prophecy and has spawned massive confusion on the subject. Partly out of seeking to avoid conflict and controversy, and partly out of their own confusion, many pastors have simply steered clear of the subject area altogether. Others have done just as much unnecessary harm by teaching all the views, and asking the congregation to individually pick from among them.

Some have been embarrassed by Christians who have mistakenly set dates for the Lord's return or for specific events they claimed were about to take place. Out of a mistaken understanding of biblical unity others have sought to set aside doctrine (including prophecy) for the sake of unity. The Scriptures, instead, call us to seek unity under doctrine (1 Cor. 1:10), and to contend for "the faith" (that means doctrine), that "was once for all delivered to the saints" (Jude 3).

Psychology

While the word psychology has biblical roots (*pseuche*=soul; *logos*=word, study of), the word has for a long time been used by the secular world, to pretend to be a science about the study of the mind, with no spiritual or biblical connotations.

The psychological field claims more than 250 basic theories and approaches to so-called therapy. Many more "techniques" are propagated in this "profession." Many even in the secular world realize that psychology is a shameful practice and in no way can be called a science. Unfortunately, the field has been professionalized by which most states in the U.S. require licensing in order to be able "to practice." Almost all of the founding theorists were anti-God, anti-Moses, anti-Scripture. Most had horrible upbringings, spoke with demons, hallucinated, heard voices, and were into cults. A secular book that exposes men such as Freud, Rogers, Maslow, Jung, Adler, Erikson as frauds, is entitled An Introduction to Theories of Personality (4th edition), B. R. Hergenhahn (Prentice Hall). Every pastor needs to purchase and read this book!

Many seminaries and Christian colleges are admitting to integrating secular psychology with the Bible. They are pumping raw secular sewage into Evangelical churches. This is why many pastors believe they must present "feel good" messages. They use terms such as: self-esteem, self-actualization, self-fulfillment, hierarchy of needs, etc.

Often large churches hire counselors who have been trained in secular psychology in seminary. They may be born again, but they have absorbed the teaching of the world concerning psychology. Instead of being biblically assertive, they generally simply ask questions, such as "How do you feel about this issue?"

In many churches, university educated young couples are coming in who have been exposed to psychological principles concerning marriage and the raising of children. This is producing a weakened core of young believers who have a "demanding" and self-fulfillment spirit. The young women have bought into the psychology of feminism and want to push for church positions that are biblically reserved for men.

The bottom line is, pastors must resist secular psychology and fervently teach against it often. The brainwashing has already been done to a younger generation. They must see what the Bible says about human nature, and human behavior!

Recommended Books

Dave Hunt, *The New Spirituality* (Harvest House); Jim Owen, *Christian Psychology's War on God's Word* (EastGate); Martin and Deidre Bobgan, *Psycho Heresy* (EastGate); Dave Hunt, *Beyond Seduction* (Harvest House).

See **Counseling.**

Romance, Dating and Marriage

The following is offered as food for thought for pastors responsible to teach wisdom and Biblical parameters to teens and young adults who are in what our culture considers the "dating years" and for those who are looking for a mate. In summary, although the Bible is relatively silent on "dating" its silence should not necessarily be taken as approval. It should better be taken as something simply not considered by the ancients, and for the obvious reasons.

Dating, as is normally practiced, is a recent (20th century) invention and is something that virtually no culture up until that point would have approved of. Physical intimacy of any sort between unmarried people was strongly disapproved of and discouraged. Consider the following: what are the current rates of out of wedlock pregnancies (1 in 3) and STDs (1 in 4 or 5 people)? (Incidentally, they are almost identical rates for Christians and non-Christians.) What would those rates be if dating *never* happened? Of course, this is not a real-world possibility for our society as a whole, but the point should be taken that it is *impossible* for an unmarried woman to get pregnant (outside of the small statistical probability of rape) or for either gender to become infected with an STD if they do not date. We are not even discussing the emotional or relational consequences of dating and breaking up.

To look at it differently, if young *Christians* follow the usual dating pattern (a few dates with a few people and then a series of one or more serious longer term relationships) the probability is well over 50% that they will engage in sex before marriage, with the attending physical, social, relationship and spiritual problems that accompany illicit sex. Accordingly, the following is offered to the pastor to challenge the commonly held modern assumptions of how relationships should progress.

Problems and Pitfalls Associated with the "Normal" Dating Process

- Unprecedented in history, as are our rates of STDs, divorce and out of wedlock pregnancies.

- Removes the couple from their everyday environment and places them in an "ideal," entertaining environment. For example, a woman may seem charming and sweet on a date, but how did she treat her mother and father just before she left the house? A man may seem caring and concerned on a date, but how does he speak to his mother?

- The couple dresses up, primps up, and puts on an artificial attitude, which misleads and delays dealing with the real persons, differences, problems, etc.

- Over-emphasis on early romance actually delays or halts the objective observation of one another's personality, goals, character and morals.

- Throws the couple into intimate situations, away from family and other accountables, which encourages physical intimacy (kissing, backrubs, etc) and sexual temptations far beyond the couple's actual commitment level.

- Physical intimacy beyond the actual commitment level detracts from truly getting to know one another.

- Selfishness and inward focus are the natural environment of dating. The couple becomes preoccupied with being alone and enjoying how the other makes them feel (physically and emotionally) to the exclusion of other healthy and obligatory relationships.

• Because dating only *occasionally* leads to committed marriage, it actually *trains* its participants to divorce! It does this by bringing about a series of relationships where one rapidly grows close to someone, "goes steady" for a while, and then breaks up. This cycle repeats. This actually trains the emotions and mind to break commitments and relationships that become temporarily strained, difficult or boring.

• Younger teens date and take emotional and physical privileges far beyond their ability to commit. This leads to a reduction in the reverence and respect for the institution of marriage.

• Marriage should be honored by all, and the marriage bed kept pure, for God will judge the adulterer and all the sexually immoral.   Hebrews 13:4

• Dating is a recent development (70 years or so) and is associated with the rapid rise in promiscuity, STD's, pregnancy, abortion, etc.

• Causes many relational problems in churches and youth-groups. When couples break up there is always hurt and harm, resulting in resentments between brothers and sisters in Christ, not to mention the ill feelings of the parents! Youth groups can become a great way to meet your next boyfriend or girlfriend, and the next, and the next. This is not appropriate in the body of Christ!

• Our Creator made us to bond permanently with one person. Our emotional, sexual, intellectual and relation-al makeup is designed to bond "till death do us part." Even the smell and feel of the opposite sex is a matter of bonding. The coming together and breaking apart of romantic dating destroys or damages our bonding apparatus. The proof is in all of the family and social problems from which our society is suffering.

May your fountain be blessed, and may you rejoice in the wife of your youth. A loving doe, a graceful deer— may her breasts satisfy you always, may you ever be captivated by her love. (Prov. 5:18-19)

Notice that this verse *does not* say, "sample a bunch of breasts until you find those that satisfy." It also *does not* say to, "be captivated for a while."

- It tends to delay marriage until later. This allows young men and women to develop selfish habits, viewpoints and inflexibility. Dating does this by providing the intimacy privileges (emotional, romantic and sexual) traditionally and Biblically reserved only for married couples. While not all dating is necessarily evil, the overall trend is quite negative. It is a powerful tool in Satan's hand to sidetrack young Christians, to damage their ability to select a proper mate, and to enjoy sex in its rightful place.

- *The Benefits of Courtship – or "Modified" Dating*

Courtship or modified dating is the process of getting to know someone in their own natural environment of family, work and church, and resulting in a committed marriage relationship. It is preceded by careful observation of the other person's character and personality. Ideally it is initiated by the man discussing the potential of the relationship with the woman's father or other responsible person, and obtaining permission to court the woman. The relationship between the man and woman grows naturally and with much less sexual pressure due to the more open and public environment, and the presence of accountables (parents, church members, etc). The intimacy of the couple grows in proper proportion to their level of actual commitment. It is not that the couple never spends time alone, but that their relationship is not focused on exclusive alone-ness. It is focused on shared activities, experiences and times important to both them and their families and churches.

- Is directly Biblical.

- Involves the parents (or other responsible persons) of both parties in the process of selecting the potential mate and in providing safety, prayer and counsel for the couple. In-Law problems are addressed automatically.

- The young woman can be guided, by <u>both</u> mothers or proxies, to meet the domestic, emotional, romantic, and spiritual needs of the young man. She can be taught Godly submission. (Titus 2:1-8)

- The young man can be guided, by <u>both</u> fathers or suitable proxies, to meet the leadership, emotional, financial, romantic and spiritual needs of the young woman. He can be taught Godly authority.

- Allows each person to observe the relationships and structure of the other's family.

- Shows Biblical honor to the parents. (Eph 6:2-3)

- Involves the ministry of the Holy Spirit to work in and through the couple and through the parents, family and church.

- Avoids the confusion of being physically attached to someone who is emotionally or spiritually incompatible.

- Results in a relationship based on truly knowing and loving the person first rather than on physical intimacy as the driving force.

- Encourages care and objectivity in selecting a mate.

- Focuses on character and personality rather than physical, romantic and sexual intimacy.

- Trains the couple to focus on service and helping and relating to others rather than being internally and selfishly focused.

- Requires commitment and vision for the future rather than laziness and hedonism.

- Results in greater emotional and sexual intimacy and

satisfaction in the marriage relationship.

- Leaves more mystery, sexual tension and fun to be discovered during the marriage.

- Provides a more interconnected and stable large family environment for the children.

Problems of Courtship
- Difficult to find a potential mate and family who is committed to the same values and process. People have forgotten how to do this.

- Interfering friends and family who do not understand the process and who pester and tempt to become physically intimate.

- Past patterns of romanticism and hedonism ingrained into one or both partners.

Resources
   I Kissed Dating Goodbye, Joshua Harris
   Boy Meets Girl, Joshua Harris
   www.JoshHarris.com

Sabbath, Keeping of

Sabbath is the Old Testament seventh day of rest, and Sunday is not a duplication of that same day. Traditionally, Christians have mistakenly called Sunday the Sabbath, and used it for a period of resting. In this sense, Sunday has been a blessing in Christian lands, but technically we are not under the Law, and Sunday is not a Sabbath replacement day. Some Christians place a legalistic spin on Sunday that is not warranted by the New Testament. Many argue, "Didn't Christ keep the Sabbath in the Gospels?" Of course He did because He was born under the dispensation of the Law. However, we now live under the dispensation of the Church Age and are not under the Jewish Sabbath.

In the New Testament, all the principles of the Ten Commandments are repeated, but the Sabbath. The writer of Hebrews pictures acceptance of Christ as Savior to be a spiritual Sabbath rest. He writes, "There remains therefore a Sabbath rest for the people of God. For the one who has entered His rest has himself also rested from his works, so God did from His" (Heb. 4:9-10).

See **Sunday.**

Sex, Conflicts in Marriage

Sex problems arise among couples for the following reasons: (1) physical tiredness, (2) after the birth of a child because of hormonal changes of the wife, (3) because of physical issues, (4) and most commonly, because of emotional problems between husband and wife.

Christian couples in the church are often reluctant to come to the pastor with sex issues. Because sex problems can be so embarrassing with someone they know, the couple simply hides the problem, thinking it will go away. A family doctor should also be considered if the problem seems to be outright physical in nature, or has to do with sexual "technique."

However, sexual conflicts seem to arise mostly because of emotional conflicts in the marriage. The couple is hurting or destroying their relationship with arguing, name-calling, or simply coldness or lack of communication. Generally, someone in the marriage has put up walls, lives in anger or stubbornness. All such problems have to do with sin, and/or lack of asking forgiveness when hurting the other partner. But when such wars begin, carnality comes up and creates barriers to marital love.

When these things happen, the sex life is certainly affected, and sometimes so destroyed, it is not repairable. Of course, God can and does perform miracles on hardened hearts!

From time to time, pastors need to hold classes on Christian marriage and be as candid as possible within the setting. He should urge the couples to seek help, especially from spiritual leaders who can be trusted.

Recommended Books
Joseph C. Dillow, *Solomon on Sex* (Thomas Nelson).

See **Sex, Teen Marriage Preparation.**

Sex, Teen Marriage Preparation

Marriage preparation for youngsters should be an ongoing responsibility with the parents. It would not be appropriate for the church to address physical issues about sex. For those youngsters moving into the upper level of schooling, it is appropriate for the church to teach from the Word of God about chastity, conduct in dating, the Godly view of husband and wife, sexual morality in general, and stress the fact that God sees the motives of the heart, and the actions of the physical. He lives within the believer and can be grieved by the sin of the child of God.

Youngsters need to also know about the immoral pressure put on them by the culture. They need to learn to discern how to make spiritual and biblical choices that come from the Word of God.

Churches need to be judicious about how they handle such issues, but must not shrink back from being both wise and candid about sex.

Recommended Books

Josh McDowell, Why Wait? *What You Need to Know About the Teen Sexuality Crisis*; and *The Myths of Sex Education.*

Sunday

The early church met on the first day of the week, not on the Sabbath (Acts 20:7; 1 Cor. 16:2). When the Law ended, Sabbath ended. The Sabbath rest was important to Israel as a day of spiritual contemplation. It also gave physical rest to the people. This practice was unknown among the populations of other nations.

Though some disagree, many believe the apostle John is referring to Sunday when he writes, "I was in the Spirit on the Lord's day, ..." (Rev. 1:10). Another view holds that John was simply saying that he was taken over by the Spirit on a Lord-y, or holy kind of day, that God was using in a special way to speak to him.

From the apostolic period and on into the early church, Sunday replaced Sabbath as the day of meeting. Both the Jehovah Witnesses and the Seventh Day Adventists meet on Sabbath, or Saturday.

Recommended Books

Lewis Sperry Chafer, *Systematic Theology* (Kregel), IV, 102-13; V, 254-57; VII, 109, 270-71.

See **Sabbath, Keeping of.**

Tax-Exemption, of Church

What Does it Mean to be Tax Exempt?

Being tax exempt / nonprofit is a status before the Internal Revenue Service in which the church is not required to pay federal income taxes, plus other benefits and consequences as outlined below. This status typically provides exemption from other state and local taxes as well.

Why do Churches Seek to Establish Tax Exempt (and Nonprofit) Status?

Typically, churches seek tax exempt / nonprofit status for one or more of the following reasons:

- Expenses for the ministry are not subject to federal or state income taxes

- Purchases can be made free from state sales taxes

- The contributions of others to the ministry are deductible on their income taxes, to the extent that contributions are made, received, and handled in accordance with certain requirements

- The church can solicit contributions more easily, including tax deductibility of contributions and lower postal rates, as outlined briefly herein.

- Postal rates for qualified nonprofit entities can be as much as 68 to 87% less than others will pay for qualified mailings.

- There is a limited amount of free radio and television advertising available for qualified nonprofit organizations

- Incorporation of a nonprofit organization provides an increased level of protection from liability

What is Involved in Achieving and Maintaining Tax Exempt / Nonprofit Status?

There are initial filings, setup procedures, and ongoing operational requirements for obtaining and maintaining tax exempt / nonprofit status.

These do or can include:

- Incorporation as a nonprofit entity in your state

- Constitution and bylaws, as facilitates incorporation, the general operating guidelines and overall purpose of the church

- Establishing and maintaining of corporate minutes

- Application for federal tax-exempt status - IRC 501(c)(3)

- Applications for exemption from state income taxes

Churches, unlike other nonprofit entities, are exempt from some federal and state filings and notifications. There are also specific requirements for the solicitation, handling, and acknowledgement of contributions, as well as the application for and handling of nonprofit mailings at special rates. Outside assistance in the obtaining and maintenance of tax exempt / nonprofit status is advisable. Note that there are other requirements for church staff outside of what is described and outlined in this article.

Are There Reasons Not to Seek Tax Exempt / Nonprofit Status?

The size of the ministry might be very small, with expenses that are not high enough to justify the time and expense of seeking and maintaining tax exempt / nonprofit status. This is often true of house churches with no staff. Incorporating the entity might in some cases pose an issue among house churches regarding zoning. Some Christians feel that placing a church in a tax exempt / nonprofit status makes the church subject to the government first, instead of being subject first to God. Tax exempt / nonprofit status does not make the church exempt from Internal Revenue Service and state income tax board audits, nor address separate filings for and tax liability of the church staff. The Roman Empire allowed none of the above advantages to the early church.

Internet Resources on Tax Exempt Status*
Thompson & Thompson
http://www.t-tlaw.com/resource.shtml

El Shaddai Ministries

http://www.elshaddai.com

*Note: these websites are provided in that these contain what are considered to be valuable documents and information resources for churches, but are not necessarily a recommendation of the services offered by these firms. Each church should make a determination of the need for outside services and if so, the best firm to meet those needs.

Teacher

The word teacher is *didaskolos* and is translated master, teacher, and instructor. The word comes from the verb *didasko*. Educationally and theologically, the word implies objective, logical presentation of truth or information. Our English word doctrine comes from this—a body of instruction that is presented in a clear, organized way.

The pastors are designated as teachers, men appointed by Christ for directing and edifying the church (Eph. 4:10-12). The Greek text in Ephesians reads, "[Christ] gave some as apostles, and some as prophets, and some as evangelists, and some as pastors INDEED, THAT IS teachers" (v. 11b).

Besides pastors/teachers, there is the general gift of teaching given to various members of the body of Christ (Rom. 12:7; 1 Cor. 12:28, 29). Others could teach who may not have had the gift of teaching, but they had the desire and they were effective, presenting truth under the supervision of the leaders. The writer of Hebrews speaks broadly about the Jews who in the way they lived and spoke "ought to be teachers" (Heb. 5:12). James warns his audience that, to want to be a teacher, there came a great responsibility to live out what one taught (James 3:1).

It can be shown in the New Testament that the pastor is to be indeed a teacher (Eph. 4:11), and that the pastor/teacher is also called an elder, and an overseer. Four descriptive nouns mark the ministry of the elders in the local church.

Recommended Books
Mal Couch, A *Biblical Theology of the Church* (Kregel).

See **Doctrine.**

Teachers, Sunday School

Some kind of entrance program needs to be set up in appointing Sunday school teachers. A teachers' course should cover (1) a teacher's testimony; (2) a study of the Doctrinal Statement of the church; (3) teaching techniques, (4) having the teacher's heart and spirit for the task. Also, it is appropriate to discuss the teacher's abilities with various age groups. Does the teacher fit better with older, or with younger groups?

Many churches have mandatory teacher training classes that meet in order to go over the material being taught for the month. The curriculum is studied, and sometimes, the pastor teaches the material back to the teachers. The problem with this is overkill! The pastor may help with difficult Bible questions, but if the teacher must simply teach what the pastor dictates, this stifles the work of the Spirit within each instructor.

Sunday school teachers need to care for those in the class. A home visit, a phone call, a special spiritual retreat, etc., are all appropriate to gain confidences. To be a teacher of young minds, concerning spiritual things, is a great opportunity and Godly task.

It is appropriate for teachers to receive a summer break. This is a time to refresh the attitudes and the spirit. Others may fill in for several months.

It is the job of the elders to oversee the curriculum used in Sunday school, though in a church that is focusing on sound doctrine, it would be unusual for the teachers to miss problems found in the material.

Teaching, Topical Messages

Pastors should be giving their people verse-by-verse exegesis from the books of the Bible. But for variety, and for the emphasis on doctrine, topical and theme messages are appropriate from time to time. A doctrinal series is in order so that what the church believes can be reinforced from the pulpit. The Fundamentals for the Twenty-First Century (Kregel), and Major Bible Themes (Zondervan), Basic Theology (Moody), are good volumes to use for such doctrinal studies.

Sometimes it is worthwhile to do an exegetical study through certain thematic passages of Scripture, such as: The Upper Room Discourse, The Olivet Discourse, Romans 9-11, The Sermon on the Mount, 1 Corinthians 12-14, etc.

Pastors need to check themselves as to the depth of their presentations. Many pastors simply give what are called Sermonettes for Christianettes! These are light, little devotionals that are long on emotion, and short on substance. The pastors are equating yelling with preaching, and they are confusing preaching with teaching!

Whether it is with Bible book studies, or topical and doctrinal messages, the pastor should spend no less that ten hours a week in preparation. He should purchase good commentaries, theologies that are trustable and solid.

Tithing

The ten percent giving is first mentioned in Scripture in Genesis 14:20, where Abraham gave to the king-priest Melchizedek a tithe offering as a representative of the Lord. The tithe was incorporated into the dispensation of the Mosaic Law covenant where it is first mentioned as such in Leviticus 27:30. Actually the tithe came out to be more than a simple ten percent. There was the tithe of the land (27:30), the tithe of the grain (Deut. 12:17), the tithe of the yearly produce (14:23), the tithe of workable land for the Levites (Neh. 10:37), the tithe of the produce of the mint, dill, and cumin (Matt. 23:23). Apparently there was also the tithe of all consecrated things (2 Chron. 31:12).

The tithe is not repeated or commanded for the Church Age. However, it is a good bench mark for giving, as long as it is not forced upon the congregation as a legal requirement. Proper giving in this Age of Grace is spelled out by Paul in 2 Corinthians 8-9. The apostle's main criteria is: "Let each one do just as he has purposed in his heart; not grudgingly or under compulsion; for God loves a cheerful giver" (9:7). In contrast to this, the tithe in the Old Testament was commanded!

Many pastors wrongly quote Malachi 3:10 about bringing your tithes and offerings into the storehouse. This was in the temple area, and we have no such central distribution place under the Church Age. Unfortunately, many pastors believe they must insist on tithing by their congregation in order to keep the money flowing in. It is true that if giving is based on what Paul says in 2 Corinthians 8-9, offerings may slack because of the carnality of the people. But the point is that the Lord wants true giving to come from the heart and not from compulsion. When the flock begins to grow spiritually under the teaching of the Word, giving will increase.

What About Tithing?

By definition the word "tithe" comes from the Hebrew word *asar*, which means a tenth part of anything (e.g. a tenth part of seeds, fruit, herds, flocks, etc.).

What does the Old Testament say about tithing? There are 2 instances in Scripture where tithing was voluntarily performed:

- by Abraham to Melchezedek (Gen. 14:20)

- by Jacob to God (Gen. 28:22)

According to the Mosaic Law, the 12 tribes of Israel were mandated to give a tithe to the Levites (Num. 18:20-28; Lev. 27:30-32) because God did not give the Levites any inheritance in the land. The Levites were priests and were to do service in the tabernacle, and later the temple. The tithes, accordingly were one tenth of the yearly increase of seed, fruit, cattle, sheep, etc. of the 12 tribes who had an inheritance in the land and could therefore generate the fruit of the land. The Levites were to take one tenth of the tithes and in turn offer those to the Lord. Every third year the 12 tribes were to offer a tithe for the stranger, fatherless and widow in their land (Deut. 14:28,29).

Is Tithing Mentioned in the N.T?
Tithing is mentioned in the New Testament (Matt. 23:23; Lu. 11:42; 18:12; Heb. 7:5,6,8,9). Every one of these passages either refer to the pre-Mosaic law tithes (i.e. Abraham tithing to Melchezedek) or the Mosaic law tithes. They are references back to the Old Testament, but are not commands nor exhortations to the Church.

Is Tithing Applicable for the Church?
God has revealed the majority of the Church truths, which were a mystery never revealed in the Old Testament or Gospels, through the Epistles of Paul. Tithing is never mentioned in Paul's epistles, and the Church (that is, the Body of Christ) is never commanded nor exhorted to tithe (i.e., give 10 % of either the gross or net). Tithing according to a law principle is diametrically opposed to the New Testament teaching of grace giving. In Christ we have liberty and we are to entrench ourselves in that liberty (Gal. 5:1):

- We are free from our sin (Adamic) nature & the law.

- Tithing is part of a law system.

- Tithing, therefore, is a yoke of bondage with which we are not to be entangled.

Why Then, is Tithing Taught, Encouraged, and Even Demanded by Local Churches?
The primary reason is that the Word of Truth (the Scriptures) is not

being rightly divided by many pastor-teachers (2 Tim. 2:15). They are not teaching Scriptures from a dispensational framework and are thus applying the teachings given to Israel also to the Church.

All Covenant Theology will take the truths that apply only to the dispensation of Israel (e.g. tithing) and apply them to the Church (Body of Christ). Non-dispensational teaching will almost always mix law with grace, though they cannot be mixed, since they are diametrically opposed.

Then How Much Should One Give?

Scripture does not prescribe to the new creature in Christ (the Believer), how much he or she should give.

- There are no percentages given!

- There are no amounts given!

- There are no tithes given!

Whatever amount we give, it is to be on the basis of grace, as the believer purposes in his or her heart, being led by the Holy Spirit (2 Cor. 8:4; 9:7). The Lord is not concerned with the amount but rather He is concerned with the heart and attitude (2 Cor. 8:12). Grace sets no requirements, boundaries, constraints or limits on how much we are to give, since we can never out-give God (Rom. 8:32).

Scripture does, however, give us some examples on the extent of the giving by the early church:

- There may be periods where a believer cannot give due to the lack of financial means or ability (Phil. 4:10).

- The Philippian believers were in deep poverty (beggarly poor) but were generous in their giving, which was based exclusively on grace and the power of God (2 Cor. 8:2,3).

- The Corinthian believers were exhorted to abound in giving (i.e. above & beyond their own power - 2 Cor. 8:3,7).

- One sowing (giving) sparingly will reap sparingly (i.e. spiritual blessings). One sowing (giving) bountifully will reap bountifully (i.e. spiritual blessings, 2 Cor. 9:6)

- God loves a cheerful giver (2 Cor. 9:7).

- As God has prospered us (1 Cor. 16:2).

Recommended Books
Lewis Sperry Chafer, *Systematic Theology* (Kregel), VII.

See **Giving.**

Youth Groups and Life Preparation

Young people passing from childhood into adulthood are among God's most kinetic organisms. Not only are they bursting with energy, they are also learning machines, struggling to translate their increasingly mature feelings, emotions, and experiences from the rudimentary language of childhood into the complex dialect of adulthood.

While teenagers today are physically mature by their mid-teenage years, they are fundamentally no longer given the same level of guided responsibility by their parents and families as they were for millennia prior to the latter twentieth century. As western civilization transformed from agrarian culture to urban society, the traditional moral rudder, the family supported by church and community, was lost. Parents began turning to the church to provide the primary life preparation training for their young people during the early to mid twentieth century. This shift was supported by the formation of national and international youth organizations such as Campus Crusade for Christ and Youth For Christ. For decades these organizations took the place of the family unit in encouraging youth to pursue godliness in preparation to integrate into the body of Christ and the world as adults.

Today nearly every evangelical church boasts a "youth group." Churches and school campuses around the world have a Youth For Christ chapter, Fellowship of Christian Athletes team, some other para-church youth organization, or a youth group of their own design. Typically these youth groups and organizations are segregated into high school and junior high or middle school groups under the assumption that the two maturity levels do not, should not, and will not mix.

Often if you step into a church youth group you will find a thunderous version of the Sunday morning service held at that church, with some rubber chickens and "finger-rockets" thrown into the worship mix. Rock music, a fifteen-minute sermonette, and for dessert, a lively jello fight. Often there are a hundred or more seventh and eighth graders in full energetic contribution, while their high school counterparts are in the next room in an only slightly less disorderly rumble.

Stimulated games and loud music are not necessarily problematic if presented in light of what they actually are...entertainment. Young people need to blow off steam in a safe and somewhat controlled environment. These events can provide the secure setting many teenagers desire, and even double as evangelistic outreach to their peers. Parents are comfortable with having their kids participate in the sanctuary and discipline of these groups, whether they receive the Word or not.

However *teaching* is the meat of making disciples out of these young minds full of mush. It has been said often "the *medium* is the message." If the focal point of the youth night is routinely "contemporary Christian music" it is likely that these young minds will develop with the strong impression that singing the thunderous and repetitive choruses of superficial and emotion-building contemporary Christian music is "worship." If the time revolves around some event such as a tricycle race or marshmallow eating contest every week, it will be difficult to draw their consideration away from silly amusement and toward the deeper truths of doctrine that should be the focal point. If the message presented is video-driven or shallow "feel-good" rhetoric rather than teaching the Word and providing Biblical answers to their tough questions about issues they do not even recognize as theological, then they will assume that "church" is similarly trivial and won't tackle the profound issues of faith their still childlike minds long to embrace.

Today's model of youth ministry emulating the pop-youth culture of this world will magnificently raise up a generation of superficial and self-centered Christians who are unprepared to contend for the faith in an increasingly hostile counter-Christian world, and unequipped to present a tangible and prepared answer for the hope that is within them.

Paul gives Titus a model for teaching youth, which enjoys both Sprit-inspired authority as well as overpowering modern application. Paul begins the second chapter of Titus brusquely exhorting "You must teach what is in accord with sound doctrine." He then gives examples of what should be taught to specific homogenous groups:

> "You must teach what is in accord with sound doctrine. Teach the older men ... "

> "Likewise, [within the framework of presenting sound doctrine,] teach the older women..."

Then Paul gets specific to young people:

> *"Then [when the older women have been trained and are living according to sound doctrine,] they can train the younger women to love their husbands and children, to be self-controlled and pure, to be busy at home, to be kind, and to be subject to their husbands, so that no one will malign the word of God."*

"Similarly, [surrounded by this environment of sound doctrinal teaching,] encourage the young men to be self-controlled. In everything you do set them an example by doing what is good. In your teaching show integrity, seriousness and soundness of speech that cannot be condemned, so that those who oppose you may be ashamed because they have nothing bad to say about us."

Paul's directives are to *teach sound doctrine* and *model the expected behavior.* Those issues peculiar to youth such as gender-roles, dating, marriage preparation, sexuality, suicide, etc., should be taught within a framework of sound doctrine, and presented verbally and through example not as isolated-issues, but rather as life-issues that diminish with spiritual and physical maturity.

Youth ministry *must* be a priority for the elders, and instructing the youth should be entrusted to godly *men* who are able to teach sound doctrine and demonstrate authoritative, godly adult living. This is the time in life when young people are ripe for the transition to sitting under the authority of the Word, of eldership, and of godly men.

At times these now-young women should be taught by the word and deed of the older women of the body. And similarly, the young men can always stand to hear from a godly wife and mother on matters relative to how to treat a wife, sisters in faith, and other women. [In creating and maintaining this secure environment elders should remember to never provide the opportunity for others to question the moral and sexual integrity of the youth workers. A man or woman should never be alone with a lone member of either gender. If private counseling is in order it should be done where others can view the proceedings, never behind closed doors.]

Paul makes no reference to age segregation in his directive to Titus. Blending junior high through early college-age young people together is contrary to the public education model established throughout the twentieth century by the secular humanists. However whether routinely mixed or occasionally joined together, multi-age groups are healthy for everyone involved to observe maturity in action, to provide leadership opportunities, and to challenge young people of all ages to reach beyond the expectations of the age-based programming they have received in the world. Paul commands us not to be conformed to the patterns of this world...

It is not unreasonable to suggest that following a study session the group respond to the Word in worship through singing and prayer. Music presented during this time of response should be appropriately "worshipful" and edifying. After this time before the Lord there can be occasions allowed for the entertainment of boisterous fun and more assertive music.

Providing opportunities for genuine Christian service are an often-overlooked element of youth ministry. Weeklong and summer missions trips around the country and abroad provide hands-on opportunities for young people to actively share their faith, serve others, and experience the response to Christ-likeness. Simply sending the kids out into the neighborhood to perform an evening of "random acts of Christian love" will provide an opportunity for service to others in their own community.

Further, offering activities for unbridled excitement, entertainment, and pure fun are not taboo. As long as teaching the Word is the center of the youth ministry, attending concerts, amusement parks, or a night of bowling extend the secure environment of the youth ministry into the world. A whitewater raft trip can provide the forum for teaching the strength of Christian unity.

Finally, the nucleus of youth ministry is a heart for young people. Those men and women who aspire to help teenagers prepare for leading godly adult lives must have a heartfelt love for this kinetic flock. They must understand the problems facing today's youth, and make opportunities to personally and intimately stand in the gap with each one of these young disciples.

Paul calls the believer not to be conformed to the pattern of the culture, but rather to be transformed by the renewing of his mind. If youth ministry is masked by worldly-based music, all-consuming fun and games, and superficial sermonettes, young people will not be equipped to be transformed spiritually, mentally, and emotionally and make the shift from the milk of childlike faith onto the meat of godly maturity. *Teach sound doctrine and model the expected behavior.*

Visitation, Home

It has been shown effective for increasing church membership, to visit in the homes of visitors. It is appropriate to first ask them if they would desire or allow a visit.

Home visitation is also important as a place for counseling those who are troubled or sick. It is important to phone before arriving at the house. A follow up letter also makes the visit something special and appreciated.

Pastors should not visit single women alone. The pastor's wife should accompany him on such a call. The exception would probably be the older widow of sixty years of age or more. However, it would be workable for just the wife to visit a single woman for a daytime social call or counseling session. Today, visiting in the home is not as popular as in the past. People seem to want to be more private and isolated. Generally, people are willing to come to the pastor's office for counseling or conversation.

Some pastors almost feel a legalistic mandate to visit in the homes. But again, because of the dynamics of our modern times, this may not be necessary.

Hospital visitation by the elders or deacons is certainly in and appropriate in time of illness. Others in the congregation should also visit those sick and in the hospital, but this should be done judiciously in relation as to how sick the individual is.

When church members are sick at home, it seems to still be appreciated for members of the church to bring in food. This is a gesture of help and aid that no one can refuse.

Visitation for evangelism and encouragement of the believers is mentioned in the New Testament (Acts 15:36), as is also the visitation of the poor widows and orphans (James 1:27).

Voting, Congregational

There are only two places in the New Testament where the congregation had an open say on specific issues relating to the direction of the church. However, in both cases this was not a democratic voting as we think of today.

The first is mentioned in Acts 6:1-7 in which the apostles, who were acting as elders in the Jerusalem church, told the congregation to "select from among you, brethren, seven men of good reputation, full of the Spirit and of wisdom, whom we may put in charge of this task" of the daily charity and the care of the widows (v. 3). The Greek word for select is *episkeptomai* and means "look over carefully, examine." In verse 5 we read that the people chose seven men to "serve" (vs. 1, 2) or be deacons to this task, while the apostles (acting as pastor/elders) would devote themselves "to prayer, and to the ministry of the word" (v. 4). The word chose means to call out (*eklego*) and is also not used as a word for voting.

The second mention of congregational involvement in decisions is the choosing of missionaries. From the Jerusalem church "it seemed good to the apostles and the elders with the whole church, to choose men from among them to send to Antioch with Paul and Barnabas—Judas called Barsabbas, and Silas, leading men among the brethren" (15:22). The word here for choose is the same as in 6:3, *eklego*.

In both instances the assemblies had a say about the selection of their deacons and missionaries, but again, this was not a popular vote as we might conceive of today.

There is no question that we have no voting examples in the New Testament church. Elders/pastors/teachers/overseers are the same grouping of leaders who are appointed, not voted into office. Some try to use Acts 14:23 as the example of voting for elders. Here, Paul and Barnabas "appointed elders for them in every church." *Heirotoneo* is here translated as "appointed" though it was the Greek word for voting by the raised hand in the Greek city-states. Why is this word not used here as voting for elders/pastors? Because such choosing was a decision made between two men. It is ludicrous to believe that Paul and Barnabas "raised" their hands with each other in such a selection. In fact, most Greek lexicons point out that this was "an appointment without a vote" [The New Englishman's Greek Concordance and Lexicon (Hendrickson)]. In other words, the context will not allow this word to be used as voting, as implied in its root. The word here takes on another meaning because of context.

The other place this word *heirotoneo* (heir means hand) is 2 Corinthians 8:19 where the brother (probably Trophimus) was "appointed" by the churches to travel with Luke and others for missionary purposes. The congregations had the right to so choose such men.

It is mainly in our American democratic society where the churches feel it is their right to vote on almost every issue, from the selection of the pastor down to the color of the church bus! The sheep are then in charge, and not the leadership and the shepherds that God wants in place in an assembly!

Recommended Books
Mal Couch, *A Biblical Theology of the Church* (Kregel).

Website
See **Church Website.**

Weddings
Wedding services today are often formatted and planned out by the bride and groom, though ceremonies can be found in most Pastor Manuals purchased from local Christian bookstores.

It is enough here to say that, Christ should be lifted up and exalted in whatever is said in the service.

Marriage counseling should be mandatory by the pastor to make sure that both parties have accepted Christ as Savior, and, so that the couple may understand that their home should be a spiritual haven that honors the Lord. Potential problems need to be discussed, with sound advice from the pastor and his wife.

See **Marriage; Marriage, Counseling for.**

Widows, Helping of

In most Western nations today, government-aid programs help pick up the tab for widows. But because of this, churches have lost a sense of care for the women who have lost a spouse. Some in the church feel the husband has taken care of his wife before his death. And many men have provided some life insurance for their wives. But not all. Yet also, many older women want to return, at least in a limited way, to the work force and care for their own needs. However, with all this, the deacons working with the elders should make sure the widow is not neglected.

If financial help is not necessary, there should at least be spiritual and emotional help available. A widow often feels as if she is a fifth wheel and no longer fits in the church family. The church should make sure its widows are not forgotten spiritually. They should be included and invited to all appropriate church social functions.

In Paul's first letter to Timothy he reinforces the fact that the local church has a responsibility to care for the widows in its midst (1 Tim. 5:3-16). Paul commands (Greek, present imperative) Timothy that the church is to, "Honor widows who are widows indeed." At its root, the Greek verb translated "honor" (*timao*) means "to value" or "set a price on." The context of this passage indicates that Paul is using it in the sense of material provision for the widows. He observes three ways to do this, through family, the church, and mutual support.

The bottom line is, widows should not be neglected emotionally, financially, and certainly not spiritually!

Recommended Books

Mal Couch, *A Biblical Theology of the Church* (Kregel).

Women, Counseling of

What principles apply to the counseling of women? The biblical principles of counseling within the body of Christ are given elsewhere in this text, and are applicable to women. There are, in addition to the general principles of counseling, additional principles that apply to the pastoral counseling of women. The pastor-teacher in the role of counseling is called to:

- Flee youthful lusts (2 Timothy 2:22)

- Flee immorality (1 Corinthians 6:18)

- Watch his life and doctrine closely (1 Timothy 4:16)

- Live excellently so unbelievers observe a believer's good deeds (1 Peter 2:11,12)

So What are the Practical Consequences of These Principles?

Since biblically, the pastor-teacher is to be a mature male (Acts 20:30; 1 Timothy 2:11-14; 1 Timothy 3:2; Titus 1:6), the above principles, the experience of centuries, and increasingly church insurance policies make it strongly advisable, if not required, that a man not counsel a woman alone. The pastor-teacher therefore has four options before him in counseling with a woman:

- Counsel with an adult in a nearby room with the door open or similar opportunity for monitoring.

- Counsel with another person present, such as the pastor's spouse, who is perhaps also able to offer counsel (e.g., Titus 2:3-5).

- Counsel with the woman's spouse or other trusted friend or relative present.

- Refer the woman to counsel with another woman (e.g., Titus 2:3-5).

The first option may be more difficult if the discussions are intensely personal or might have significant legal ramifications. The second option is particularly advisable if the pastor-teacher's spouse has biblical counseling training and experience. The third option is viable if the third person will not be such as to interfere or in some way make the counseling process overly complex. The final option – referring the woman to another woman – is viable when there is one or more other women able to counsel, and would be advisable if some aspect of the counseling is better suited for woman-to-woman communication. The greater the risk of temptation on either the pastor-teacher's or counselee's part, the more advisable the third party in the room, or referral to another woman.

What other advice is in order? The counselor should preface the counseling session with a time of focusing one's heart on his position with Christ, and his mind set on things above (Col. 3:1-4). If the life of Christ is lived out in the pastor-teacher, it will not only set the counseling session in the right direction at the outset, but the works of the flesh will not be made manifest. The life of Christ will be expressed in such a way that the counseling time will be spiritually productive and profitable. Should it become apparent that the counseling session is leading any person away from a godly walk with the Lord, it is better to call the session to an end than to continue down a path that encourages problems (2 Tim. 2:22; 1 Cor. 6:18),, possibly even disqualifying the pastor-teacher from ministry, for at least a time (1 Cor. 9:26, 27).

See **Counseling.**

Women, Ministries in the Church

Men and women individually received the gifts of the Holy Spirit as given to all believers for the benefit of the Body of Christ. Gifted men are placed in the Church to take up leadership roles to guide and teach local congregations. Paul writes that Christ "gave some as apostles, and some as prophets, and some as evangelists, and some as pastors THAT IS, INDEED teachers, for the equipping of the saints that they may do the work of the ministry" (Eph. 4:11-12, Greek). Church leadership roles are meant for godly men.

However, the church could not survive without dedicated women who teach younger women (Titus 1), give instruction to the children at home (2 Tim. 3:14-15), take care of charity issues, perform with feminine sensibilities the delicate tasks that make a church a comfortable place to attend, in order to study and worship.

The apostle Paul gives heartfelt commendations to the women active in serving the Lord while under fire! (Rom. 16). He especially mentions Priscilla, Phoebe, and others who risk their necks for Paul himself, and for the churches that are in homes. He adds, "Greet Mary, who has worked hard for you [the Roman believers]" (v. 6). Many other names are mentioned.

The feminists miss the point when Paul says of Phoebe that she is a "servant of the church which is at Cenchrea" (v. 1). Though using the Greek word *diakone,* he is not mentioning her as an official representative of the deacon group at that church, for he goes on and says she is to be received "in a manner worthy of the saints" and that she was "a helper of many, and of myself as well" (v. 2). Phoebe was to be received simply as one of the "saints" of the church and not as one holding the official office, reserved for men, of deacon!

No one can rightly argue that it is appropriate for women "to teach and exercise authority over a man," from 1 Timothy 2:12, on the basis that Paul's instructions were meant to be taken in a cultural sense, and therefore, are not appropriate for our time. Paul argues this prohibition on the basis of doctrine and not culture. He goes on in this passage and says, "For it was Adam who was first created, and then Eve. And it was not Adam who was deceived, but the woman being quite deceived, fell into transgression" (v. 13-14).

Women are emotionally susceptible and can be fooled or led astray more quickly. The Lord wants male leadership in place in the church, to have cool heads in making spiritual decisions. This argument is not "politically" correct today, but never mind, the church must bow to the Scriptures and not what the culture dictates!

Part II

Commentary on Titus

Introduction to the Book of Titus

Introduction to the Pastoral Epistles

These letters from the apostle Paul to his co-workers Timothy and Titus are collectively called the Pastoral Epistles (PE). The term was first applied as far back as 1703.[1] This designation is appropriate because the recipients were two young pastors who needed Paul's encouragement and instruction. Virtually all scholars agree these three books of the NT were penned by the same person within a few years of each other. As such, they can be considered as a unit. An attack on one is an attack on all.

Authorship

An array of documents from the early Church Fathers suggests they not only knew of 1 Timothy, 2 Timothy, and Titus, but also recognized them as part of Holy Writ.[2] About AD 95, Clement of Rome wrote his *Epistle to the Corinthians*. In his letter he alludes to 1 Timothy 1:18 (section xxxvii), 2 Timothy 1:3 (section xlv), and Titus 2:10 (section xxvi). Another ancient saint, Polycarp (c. AD 110), wrote, "But the beginning of all troublesome things is the love of money. Knowing therefore that we brought nothing into the world, but neither have we anything to carry out, let us arm ourselves with the arms of righteousness."[3] His words bear a strong resemblance to 1 Timothy 6:7, 10: "For we have brought nothing into the world, so we cannot take anything out of it either...For the love of money is a root of all sorts of evil, and some by longing for it have wandered away from the faith..." Polycarp's allusions to the PE are frequent in his works. That he was a disciple of the apostle John makes it all the more certain that he considered these three letters to have genuinely come from the hand of Paul.

Clement of Alexandria (c. AD 155-215) quotes 1 Timothy 6:20, 21 and describes them as being from "the apostle."[4] A man contemporaneous with Clement of Alexandria, Tertullian, directly declared that 1 Timothy 1:18; 6:13, 20, and 2 Timothy 1:14 are statements of Paul.[5] Others who cite or allude to the PE include Ignatius, Justin Martyr, Hegesippus, and Irenaeus. Those who rejected the three letters were generally Gnostic heretics.

Date of the Pastorals

Bits of information taken from the PE themselves and from writings of the early Church Fathers supply enough data to ascertain a rather accurate date for the composition of these epistles. Of course this date assumes (safely by all indications; see above) Paul did not die during his first Roman imprisonment as recounted in Acts 28. Conservatives further argue this two-year sentence took place between AD 59 and 63.

Fathers such as Clement of Rome, Eusebius, Gaius, Dionysius, and Origen all concur Paul died in Rome during Nero's reign as Caesar.[6] Eusebius wrote, "It is related that in his [Nero's] time Paul was beheaded in Rome itself, and that Peter likewise was crucified..."[7] Nero himself passed from the scene in AD 68. Armed with this knowledge, conservative scholars teach Paul authored 1 Timothy, Titus, and 2 Timothy (in that order)[8] between AD 63 and 67. 2 Timothy is believed to be the apostle's last inspired letter because 1 Timothy and Titus show him at liberty, whereas in 2 Timothy he writes of his chains (1:16, 17) and impending death (4:6).

Background and Purpose

It is impossible to discern Paul's *exact* itinerary with 100% certainty after he was let go from his first Roman incarceration. He names places that he has visited, but about a dozen routes fit the facts. "It is not a problem of conflicting data, but of insufficient data."[9] Some of the locations listed include Ephesus (1 Tim. 1:3), the island of Crete (Titus 1:5), Nicopolis (3:12), Troas (2 Tim. 4:13), Miletus (4:20), Corinth (possibly; 4:20), and of course Rome (1:16,17). He also set foot in Spain somewhere along his travels.

Even though there is some overlap in Paul's purposes for writing each letter, it is helpful to examine them one book at a time. The factors that motivated the apostle to pen 1 Timothy fall into two classes. His first concern was Timothy's personal well-being. Functioning as Paul's representative, Timothy was left in Ephesus to oversee the churches there (1:3). The presence of aggressive false teachers made his ministry all the more treacherous. Paul had confronted these would-be "teachers of the Law" (1:7) but he was expecting more trouble from them (6:3 – 5).[10] He was not able to return from Macedonia as quickly as he thought (3:14, 15) and therefore sent this letter to his associate to encourage him in the faith. He exhorted Timothy to rebuke them despite his youth (4:12). The letter itself would help Timothy because it would be tangible proof Paul had bestowed his apostolic authority on him.[11] The great missionary even dispensed medical advice (5:23)!

2 Timothy is as personal as 1 Timothy is pastoral. Very little in 2 Timothy has to do with church policies and politics. In all likelihood Timothy knew Paul was dead, or close to death, by the time he received this letter. It must have stirred his heart deeply, as it has many other Christian

workers.[12]

Titus' circumstances are nearly identical to those of Timothy. It seems Paul and Titus had traveled to Crete, a Mediterranean island south of Greece, some time before the letter was written. When Paul departed to other fields of ministry, Titus stayed to "set in order what remains, and appoint elders in every city, as I [Paul] directed you" (1:5). It was Titus' task to finish the work of organizing the Cretan churches. There is no record as to how and when the church was begun. Perhaps some present in Jerusalem on the Day of Pentecost went back and witnessed to their friends and family (Acts 2:11).

A handful of clues within the text gives the reader an idea as to the conditions on the island. The people (at least the false teachers) did not take kindly to the apostle's "substitute," or at least to his teaching, as 2:15 suggests: "Let no one disregard you." The imposters would expend much of their energy on minor matters, and not focus on the more significant aspects of the Law (3:9). The body of Christ was not being edified but was confused and upset (1:11). Titus was not to tolerate them but to muzzle them (1:10, 11). He was therefore instructed to name godly elders, set an example of moral living (3:1 – 3), and make sure only sound doctrine was taught (2:1). It is the opinion of many that this is some of the most beautifully written theology to come from Paul's hand.

This letter would bestow more authority on Titus, and impart some information to him such as Paul's desire to meet him in Nicopolis (3:12) in addition to the matters already noted. The apostle's compassionate encouragement assisted Titus in carrying out his heavy responsibilities.

Biography of Titus

That Timothy and Titus are the recipients of these letters is put beyond doubt by the direct statement of Scripture (1 Tim. 1:2, 2 Timothy 1:2, Titus 1:4). Both of these men were faithful and diligent servants of the Lord Jesus Christ, and two of Paul's ablest co-workers. Since the PE are addressed to individuals and not to congregations, their personal tone is no surprise. Second Timothy especially has numerous verses pertaining to the apostle's relationship with his son in the faith. However, these words were not to stop with Timothy and Titus. All three epistles conclude with a plural *you* ("Grace be with you"). Paul even threw in an *all* at the end of Titus.[13] The PE were expedient for believers in the first century, and on down to us of the 21st century. Biblical truths are not bound by culture or time.

The NT offers no meager amount of information concerning Timothy's background. Acts 16 states he was from Lystra, and that his mother was Jewish but his father was a Gentile. From 2 Tim. 1:5 it is

learned his mother's name is Eunice and his grandmother was Lois. These
devout women must have had a vital hand in his religious upbringing. Even
as a young man he was known as a godly person, the result of being
instructed in the Scriptures from childhood (2 Tim. 3:15). Not only in his
hometown of Lystra but also in the neighboring community of Iconium "he
was well spoken of" (Acts 16:2). Paul likewise noticed him and decided to
bring him along for the rest of the second missionary journey (Acts 16:3f).
Bible students are often curious as to why Paul circumcised Timothy (same
passage). The first Church council had already determined that ritual was
not necessary for salvation (Acts 15), and therefore Paul must have insisted
on it for practical reasons. People knew (or would find out) his father was a
Gentile, and instead of having to explain the situation in every village and
town about it not being a requirement for conversion, the apostle just went
ahead and did it.

Timothy must have enjoyed many hours of conversation and travel with
his mentor for he is mentioned as being with Paul in a score of NT verses.[14]
He is with him in Berea (Acts 17:14), Corinth (18:5; 1 Cor. 4:17), and
Ephesus and Asia (Acts 19:22). Timothy, among others, joined Paul at Troas
at the end of the third missionary journey (20:4). Paul sent him to
Thessalonica to encourage the believers there (1 Thess. 3). This young man
from Lystra was also known in Philippi (Phil. 1:1), Colossae (Col. 1:1), and
Rome (Rom. 16:21). If he is the Timothy of Heb. 13:23 (which is plausible), then it implies he spent some time in jail, too. Surprisingly, his name
is found in all of Paul's letters except Galatians, Ephesians, and Titus.
Because both 1 and 2 Timothy locate him in Ephesus, it is evident he con-
ducted almost his entire latter ministry in that city.

Titus similarly surfaces numerous times in the NT. He is named in
Second Corinthians (2:13; 7:6, 13, 14; 8:6, 16, 23; 12:18), Galatians (2:1,
3), and Second Timothy (4:10). Paul identified him as "my partner and fellow worker" (2 Cor. 8:23). He sent Titus to Corinth to help defuse the troublesome predicament there (7:6, 7; 12:18). The epistle to Titus intimates
the two of them went to the island of Crete, but Titus was left there to
organize and teach the body of Christ (Titus 1:5). From Titus 3:12 we learn
Paul later sent a replacement to Crete so Titus could meet up with Paul in
Nicopolis (3:12). Indeed, Titus is near that area at the end of the apostle's
time on earth (2 Tim. 4:10; Dalmatia was the region north of Nicopolis).
The ancient historian Eusebius advances the tradition Titus returned to
Crete where he served the Lord the rest of his life.[15]

Outline to the Book of Titus

Commentary on the Book of Titus

Chapter One
Elder Leadership in the Church

Paul wanted to make it clear to Titus what was important to the local churches on the island of Crete. Possibly the apostle had left the island earlier and Titus should receive full and permanent instructions as to how to launch the churches there. Paul was writing from past experiences as to how to make churches more effective for Christ. If certain principles were not put into place, the congregations would remain weak.

In this chapter, Paul warns Titus to be alert as to certain moral characteristics of the Cretans (1:12). With this in mind, he shows an understanding about human nature, even about the way some Christians would act because of their cultural backgrounds. The apostle also expressed concerns about Judaizers who were adversely harming the churches (v. 10).

To counter the effect of heretical teaching, it was important to have leaders who were doctrinally sound. The same applies today; without these mature men in place, churches will flounder and fall into the chasm of false teaching. Families will be destroyed and lives ruined spiritually.

Both I Timothy and Titus were written to men acting as elders who presided over congregations in Paul's absence. They were responsible to appoint other qualified elders. The ingredients for these qualifications are nearly the same in both letters.

I. Paul's Greeting To Titus, 1:1-4

1:1 Paul, a bond-servant of God and an apostle of Jesus Christ, for the faith of those chosen of God and the knowledge of the truth which is according to godliness. When Paul was driven to his knees by his encounter with Christ on the Damascus road (Acts 9:1-9), he rose to his feet a humble bond-servant (*doulos*) of God and of Jesus (Rom. 1:1). Other apostles felt the same, such as Peter (2 Pet. 1:1), James (James 1:1), Jude (v. 1), and John (Rev. 1:1). Since the Lord Jesus is very God, Paul had no problem considering his servitude as equal to both the Father and Christ (Rom. 1:1).

Believers in the Lord are not by compulsion the servants of men (1 Cor. 7:23), but they are to be the slaves of Christ first and foremost (Rom. 6:16). However, Christian slaves still had a human responsibility and loyalty to the masters who were over them. They were to remain in that position and be obedient "according to the flesh, with fear and trembling, in the sincerity of ... heart, as to Christ" (Eph. 6:5). But they were to consider their task "not by way of eye service, as men-pleasers, but as slaves of Christ, doing the will of God from the heart" (v. 6). Their servitude was as if "to the Lord, and not men" (v. 7). The promise from God was that whatever they did in good conscience as a slave, they would receive back an honorable reward from the Lord (v. 8).

One of the unique aspects of Christianity is that it has in mind, a higher honor and calling, and a reward that is not simply temporal but eternal. And yet earthly responsibilities are not put aside.

Though Paul refers to God often as Father, his most typical reference in his addresses would be "God." Throughout his writings to Timothy and Titus the apostle refers simply to God (Ritchie):

1. "God's elect" (1:1)
2. "God, that cannot lie" (1:2)
3. "God our Savior" (1:3; 2:10; 3:4)
4. "God the Father" (1:4)
5. "the steward of God" (1:7)
6. "they profess that they know God" (1:16)
7. "the word of God" (2:5)
8. "the grace of God" (2:11)
9. "the great God" (2:13)
10. "they which have believed in God" (3:8)

An apostle of Jesus Christ. The word apostle (*Apostolos*) comes from two words, *apo* ("from, away from") and *stello* ("to stand aloft, put up, make ready"). *Apostolos* came to refer to one sent forth, an envoy, an emissary, or messenger representing a master, mediator, king, teacher, or even philosopher. The stress often falls on the one who gives his authority to the one whom he sends and whom he takes into his service.[16]

In the narrow sense, Paul as an apostle was in the same category as the twelve apostles (2 Cor. 12:11-12). In a wider sense, Silas and Timothy, and other like servants of the apostles, were also called "apostles of Christ" with a certain level of authority (1 Thess. 2:6). Titus also was called an apostle (2 Cor. 8:23).

The chief apostles, including Paul and the twelve, were given special commandments directly from Christ (Acts 1:2). They were responsible for giving forth doctrine (2:42) and of approving certain ones for ministry by the laying on of hands (8:18). To the original apostles Christ revealed Himself after His resurrection (1 Cor. 15:7). As the church developed in Acts, the apostles spent much of their time and energy with training elders to carry on when they were gone (Acts 15).

For the faith of those chosen of God and the knowledge of the truth which is according to godliness.

> *For* (*kata*) is probably *with reference to*; that is, he was appointed to be an apostle *with respect to the faith of* those whom God had chosen, or, *in order* that they might be led to believe the gospel. God had chosen them to salvation, but he intended that it should be in connection with their believing, he had appointed Paul to be an apostle that he might go and make known to them the gospel. (Barnes)

"The rendering should [better] be, 'for (the furtherance of) the faith,' or, in other words, 'the object of my (Paul's) apostleship was, that through my instrumentality the chosen of God should believe.'" (Ellicott)

Those chosen of God. "Those *chosen* or *elect* (*eklektos*) have been sovereignly called of God unto salvation." *Chosen* is a compound word from *ek* (out) and *lego* (to call out). Thus the saved are the *called out ones* by the working of sovereign grace. Paul refers to this great work when he wrote "God has chosen you from the beginning for salvation through sanctification by the Spirit and faith in the truth" (2 Thess. 2:13). This calling is not based on foreseen good works, or even self-generated faith. By good works no one can please God (Isa. 64:6) and faith is a gift from God and not something self produced from within the soul or by the self-will of the individual (Eph. 2:8-10).

Of God is simply the noun (*Theou*) in the genitive/ablative form, with the causal idea. God is the one causing or bringing about their election. "God has His elect whom He Himself chose in eternity (I Pet. 1:2); with their faith and their realization of the truth Paul's whole condition and position are agreed; God and Christ made them so." (Lenski)

God's elect refers to those whom He has chosen and with regard to whom He has a certain purpose. To summarize, Paul is saying that one object of his apostleship was that, through his instrumentality, those chosen of God should believe." (Ritchie) All men are totally depraved (Rom. 1:28) and blinded to the gospel (2 Cor. 4:4). They are given over to believe a lie (v. 3). Only the elect come to faith in Christ (John 6:37, 39).

> The elect are from both the Jews and the Gentiles; some of every kindred, tongue, people, and nation; these were chosen in Christ from eternity, and are the peculiar objects of the affection and care of God, whom He calls, justifies, and glorifies: and there is a special *faith* that belongs to these. (Gill)

And the knowledge of the truth which is according to godliness. The thought is "the knowledge of truth is designed to lead to godliness." It is special knowledge of divine truth. (Fairbairn) The word *knowledge* is *epignosis* and is a compound noun from *epi* ("upon") and *gnosis* ("knowledge"), or, "a special or peculiar knowledge of the truth," in a fuller sense "knowledge intensified." (Fairbairn) In an Old Testament sense it is knowledge as recognition "of (the will of) God that is effective in the conduct of the one who knows God." (EDNT) As Stott writes "*The knowledge of the truth* which issues in *Godliness*, and *the hope of eternal life* which, though still future, has been promised and guaranteed by God."

Godliness (*eusebeia*) is a word that can mean "piety, fear of God, devout, worthy of reverence, venerable." The root *seb* carries the thought of stepping back from something or someone, to maintain a distance. From this, came the metaphorical idea of trepidation, with the intension of shame, wonder to something approaching fear. (Brown, 1:91) This is a strong spiritual word as used in the New Testament. Paul then is writing of "knowledge [of the truth] that has respect to, or tends in the direction of, godliness." (Fairbairn) "The (truth) with a view to godliness." (Robertson) The knowledge of the truth should then promote "godliness, the life of Christian virtue, the spirit of true consecration." (Hendriksen)

In the hope of eternal life, which God, who cannot lie, promised long ages ago. As can be seen, the thought continues and the sentence does not actually end until verse 4. A better translation for *hope* (*elpis*) would be *anticipation*. This is not, "Well, I *hope* I will have eternal life," as if it were a wish, but it is of a certainty and a longing for eternal life promised by the

Lord! The preposition *in* could also have a stronger meaning. It could better read, "'Resting on' ... from the single Greek word *epi*. But it is better to understand this word as 'with a view to,' as in Ephesians 2:10." (BKC)

The believer in Jesus is going forward toward that great day when eternity will begin. This will come either by death or by the rapture of the saints in Christ. A better world in which we see the Lord face to face (1 Thess. 2:19; 3:13) is the glorious promise of old.

What did the apostle have in mind when he wrote of a promise made long ago? He could be referring to the picture of salvation as seen in the animal covering the Lord gave to our first parents in the garden following the Fall. Because of sin, death would be certain. "You are dust, and to dust you shall return" (Gen. 3:19b). But in a cryptic message symbolized in the garments of skin that clothed Adam and Eve, there would also be a covering that would foreshadow a picture of redemption from that terrible penalty of sin (v. 21).

Paul could also have had in mind the words of Job: "I know my Redeemer lives, and at the last He will take His stand on the earth. Even after my skin is destroyed, yet from my flesh I shall see God; whom I myself shall behold" (Job 19:25-27a).

Eternal life is certain also because of the Lord's attribute of Truth. He cannot lie! Our salvation is based on His promise. "This life the God who does not lie..., who never breaks his word and promise, promised, and not just recently, but ages ago, to all the ancient patriarchs as far back as Adam." (Lenski) The statement that God "who cannot lie" is actually an adjective (*apsudees*) from two Greek words, the negative *a*, and the word for lie *psudees*. This best reads, "the unlie-able God!" or "the cannot-lie God!" "We human beings lie, and the Cretans were notorious liars (12), but God never lies. Indeed he cannot, because 'he cannot disown Himself,' that is, contradict his own character." (Stott) (See 2 Tim. 2:13; Num. 23:19; 1 Sam. 15:29; Heb. 6:18)

Long ages ago (*pro chronon ainon*) could read "before times of ages." Aristotle and Plato associated *chronos* (time) with the movement of the all! (EDNT) *Chronos* is generally an expression of the duration of time. Here, it probably does indeed refer as far back as the beginning with the Fall of Adam.

1:3 But at the proper time manifested, even His word, in the proclamation with which I was entrusted according to the commandment of God our Savior. The *but* (*de*) shows the contrast from the past. (Verse 3 actually is a parenthesis.) "He promised then, *but* now He has revealed ..." "At the proper time" (*kairois idiois*, locative) could better [read] "*In His own seasons.*" (Robertson) "Manifested" (*Phaneroo*, aorist active indicative) means "to make visible, to bring to light, make known, reveal." At the right season of time, the gospel was made known. The aorist tense would seem to mark a specific moment at which this truth was brought forth and made evident. God is the author of time and history. He had a plan of redemption that arrived at just the right moment according to His timing. Fairbairn paraphrases: "the eternal life which God promised before eternal times, but in its own seasons manifested through the word."

His Word. With *word* (*logos*, singular), Paul seems to be specifically referring to the message of the gospel. By using the singular noun *logos*, he sums up this good news into a total package of revelation that includes all that is made known about Christ and the redemption He now provides for humanity.

In the proclamation with which I was entrusted according to the commandment of God our Savior. "Proclamation" (*kerygma*) is related to the verb *kerysso* that means "to herald, proclaim, preach." By using the noun singular Paul is emphasizing the message of the gospel as a complete and entire proclamation. "According to Paul, 'proclaiming' is an activity involving both proclaimer and hearer, and this activity is spoken of, as in the case widely in early Christianity. ... the total aspect of Christian existence becomes visible in the unity of obedient faith, confession, and the concrete conduct of life." (EDNT)

Paul alone was given the full understanding of the gospel, in a certain exclusive doctrinal way. Through him the message of the cross of Christ was systematized and placed into a doctrinal formula. The apostle seems to stress this by using the personal pronoun *ego*. I was entrusted ... *entrusted* (*pisteuo*, aorist passive indicative) could be translated "in-faithed," "made faithful," or "seen as being trustable."

The apostle had a unique relationship to the gospel. His ministry was not a matter of his own choosing. He makes it clear that he was set apart from his mother's womb and was called through God's grace to reveal His Son (Gal. 1:15). He added "that I might preach Him among the Gentiles, I did not immediately consult with flesh and blood" (v. 16). Thus he was divinely commissioned to the gospel "which is committed (*pisteuo*) unto me." (Ritchie) This was a trust that he could not escape. He writes of:

> "the glorious gospel ... which was committed to my trust" (1 Tim 1:11) and "whereunto I am appointed a preacher, and an apostle, and a teacher of the Gentiles" (2 Tim 1:11). The responsibility of presenting Christ in the gospel is now entrusted to us. (Ritchie)

Paul's commission came through the commandment from God. *Epitage* ("commandment") is a compound word with the preposition *epi* ("upon") and *tage*. *Tage* is from the word *tasso* which, with the preposition, means to place someone over or in charge of someone or something. (BAG) In secular Greek, the idea is that one of higher rank gives a command on the basis of the authority granted him. By the use of this word in Philemon 8, Paul is given apostolic authority to transmit instructions to a believer as if to a subordinate. (EDNT)

But as *epitage* is used here in Titus, Paul is instructed directly from God to proclaim the gospel. He is ordered by the Lord to speak! "The work was not undertaken by him, from any will or wish of his own." (Ellicott) He is charged with the mission and the message of salvation. Though he has been given strict orders to share the cross of Christ with the world, it is a commission driven by love.

> The glorious fact that the proclamation of the good news concerning life everlasting had actually been entrusted to one so unworthy as Paul, a fact which caused the heart of the apostle to overflow with gratitude, accounts for this interruption [with verse 3] in the steady flow of the sentence. (Hendriksen)

In this verse God is called "our Savior" (*soter*). This word has the thought of: "*Deliverer, Rescuer, Helper, Protector*". Often the Greek gods, such as Zeus, Apollo, Poseidon, and Heracles were called *soters*. Asclepius was the "helper" (*soter*) of the sick. Even philosophers and statesmen were sometimes labeled with the same term. In the Hellenistic world, the word was applied to the ruling Ptolemies and Seleucids. Pompey in Rome was the "Soter and Founder," Caesar was known as the "Soter of the World," and Augustus was called the "Soter of Humankind." (EDNT) What a slap to the world at that time to likewise call the God of Israel, Soter, and His Son as well with the same description (verse 4). The ancient world did not mind passing the word around to supposedly ruling deities and reigning kings, but the New Testament will use the word in an exclusive fashion, proclaiming there is no other way of finding spiritual and eternal deliverance.

The doctrine of the Trinity is clearly in view because of the identical expression "our Savior" applied to both God (v. 3) and to Christ (v. 4). Both the Lord and His Son share the same redemptive office in rescuing humanity.

> "God our Savior" in this place, as in 1 Tim. 1:1, must be understood as "God the Father." The First Person of the blessed Trinity fitly possesses the title of "our Savior," because through the death of His dear Son He redeemed us from death and made us heirs of eternal life. The Second Person of

the Trinity is likewise a possessor of the title, because He shed His blood as the price of our redemption. The epithet of "Savior"—the title just given to the Father, in the very next verse ascribed to the "Son"—is one of the many indications we possess of St. Paul's belief that the Son was equal to the Father as touching His Godhead. (Ellicott)

Soter is used six times in Titus, more than in any other New Testament writing. Three times it is applied to God (1:3; 2:10; 3:4) and three times to Christ (1:4; 2:13; 3:6). "God our Savior" is used also in Jude 25 and "My Savior" is found in Luke 1:47. John uses "Savior of the world" only twice (John 4:42; 1 John 4:14).

There is a dispensational implication in verse 3. Though there are seed thoughts in the Old Testament (such as Isaiah 53) about a coming *Savior* and substitute for sin, the doctrine was certainly not manifested and made clear until after the death, resurrection, and ascension of Jesus. And even then the revelation was not completely understood until it was finally explained by the apostle Paul (Rom. 3).

We are now in the Gospel Age, the Age of Grace, or, the Church Age. The gospel dominates God's present work with the world. Those coming to faith in Christ are placed into the spiritual body of Christ, indwelled in a miraculous way by the Holy Spirit, given unique gifts by Him, and given their marching orders through the instructions in the New Testament.

Through the work of the Spirit, and the witness of the church, Gentiles are brought to Christ by faith. This period of the Church Age will soon end by the rapture of the believers. And the "dispensation" of the tribulation, as some have called it, will begin. For now, the Lord is providentially gathering His elect and bringing them into the fold. To this glorious task the apostle Paul was completely committed.

1:4 To Titus, my true child in a common faith: Grace and peace from God the Father and Christ Jesus our Savior. *Titus* is a Latin name, though he was Greek by birth. He is one of the least known figures in early church history. The first reference to him is found in Galatians 2:1 where Paul mentions that he and Barnabas had brought him to Jerusalem. In this verse 4, Paul makes it clear that he led Titus to the Lord and into the common faith. Titus probably accompanied Paul on his missionary journeys, but this younger man did not come into prominence until his contact with the Corinthian church. In 2 Corinthians he is mentioned nine times and always with much confidence and trust by the apostle Paul. Paul entrusted Titus with the second diplomatic mission to Corinth where he was responsible for the collecting of goods and funds for poorer believers in Jerusalem.

At the end of this letter to Titus, Paul urges him to join the apostle at

Nicopolis for the winter, after Artemas or Tychicus had come to Crete to replace him (3:11). It possibly was from Nicopolis or from Rome that Titus departed for regions to the north along the Adriatic to the coastal area of Dalmatia. At this point the New Testament does not mention Titus again. However, the church Father Eusebius (circa 325 AD) says that Titus went back to Crete, became the island's first bishop and died there of old age.

The expression "true child" in Greek is *gnesio tekno*, or "genuine, legitimate" child. *Gnesios* is related to the verb *gennao* "to beget, give birth." (EDNT) Titus is Paul's genuine child in the fellowship (*koinan*, "to have in common") of the faith. By this he means he gave spiritual birth to this younger man who was added to the fraternity of believers in Christ. As to the details of his conversion, we have no information.

The possessive pronoun "*my*" is not in the Greek text but has been added by translators because of the expression of endearment that Paul uses to describe his spiritual birthing of Titus. By calling Titus his "true" child, Paul means "'legitimately born, or genuine' and acknowledges that Titus was of a parentage that was not physical but spiritual, 'in our common faith.' '"In' (*kata*) indicates that their relationship was in accord with a 'common faith,' a faith mutually shared." (EBC)

Grace and peace from God the Father, and Christ Jesus our Savior. Though *grace* and *peace* were common expressions of greeting in letters in Paul's day, they are not used as empty words of courtesy by the apostle. These are benedictions and blessings, wishes for Titus coming directly from God the Father and the Lord Jesus. This greeting is similar to Paul's words in 1 Timothy 1:2 and 2 Timothy 1:2, except there he adds the word *mercy*.

Grace (*charis*) is related to the noun *charisma* (gift, gift of grace) and the verb *charitoo* (to favor, to bestow favor upon, to bless). Paul desires that the Father bestow favor upon Titus because of the unthankful task he must perform spiritually there on the island of Crete. But theologically speaking, grace is "God's unmerited favor in operation in the heart of his child." (Hendriksen) *Peace* (*eirene*) theologically would have to do with the peace that the believer experiences from becoming reconciled with God through Christ. But experientially, as in this verse, it has to do with an inner calm, an assurance that no matter what comes, God is not far away. The child of the Lord can trust Him regardless of the circumstances.

This grace and peace originate *from* (*apo*) God the Father and His Son Jesus. One preposition (*apo*) governs the source equally which is God and Jesus. The Trinity again is strongly hinted at in this formula. Both persons together are sending forth these spiritual blessings, grace and peace. If Jesus was a mere man he would in no way join in such blessing and gifting, along with God the Father.

On **Jesus our Savior** note again verse 3 and the further significance in regard to the doctrine of the Trinity. Both the Father and Son are called *our Savior*. "Our" again signifies the common testimony of believers. This interchange is not accidental; both [the Father and the Son] are involved in bestowing the same salvation." (EBC) "The Son has brought to us salvation from the Father, and the Father has bestowed it through the Son." (Calvin)

II. Paul's Charge Concerning Elders, 1:5-9

A. Appointment of Elders, 1:5

From what is said next, one gets the idea that Paul was with Titus on Crete for evangelism purposes. Many believe this would have been a journey undertaken after Paul's first Roman imprisonment.

From what follows, one can surmise that the two were successful in evangelizing various cities on the island but did not have time to return and strengthen the believers by setting the churches in order and seeing that elders were elected... Therefore, Paul left Titus to "set in order what remains and appoint elders in every city, as I directed you" (v. 5b). (NIGTC)

1:5 For this reason I left you in Crete, that you would set in order what remains and appoint elders in every city as I directed you. "For this reason" is *toutou charin*. *Charin* is a preposition that carries the thought "*on behalf of, on account of*." This construction is used only here and in Ephesians 3:1, 14. *Charin* is an accusative of the noun *charis* that means "*graciousness, attractiveness*." (BAG) The expression might be translated "For this gracious reason," or "With this kind intention." Or possibly, "In favor of this." (Lenski)

I left (*apoleipo*, aorist active indicative) **you** has a distinct purpose. Titus was thoroughly trusted by Paul. He had the full confidence of the apostle who knew this younger leader could carry out the task of getting the churches on Crete organized.

That you might set in order what remains. *Might set in order* (*epidiorthoo*, aorist middle subjunctive) is used only here in the New Testament. *Epidiorthoo* is a compound verb from *epi* ("upon") and the verb *diorizo* ("to set limits") (BAG) with the further thought of "to make right, improve, set on the right path." With the aorist tense the thought could mean "that you might start setting in order." The subjunctive is almost like an imperative, "this is what you ought to do." With the middle voice the responsibility really comes down on Titus, "this you must do yourself." Knight adds "that you might set right" the things lacking. It is possible that the preposition *epi* as a prefix to the verb is:

To imply that St. Paul had begun the correction of deficiencies

in the Cretan Church, and that Titus was to carry it still further…If we may judge from this letter, Christianity was at this
time in a very disorganized state in Crete. Titus is to ordain
presbyters (elders), as the foundation of a ministry." (Nicoll)

What remains (*leipo*, present active participle) is better translated "the
many things that are left" unfinished. Or, "the things lacking." Titus, acting as a chief elder and under-apostle, had the authority to straighten out a
lot of issues. It must be remembered that many who had come to Christ
were pagan and had no idea of how the churches on the island must be run.
Though where the Gentiles had some contact with the Jewish communities,
they had some conception, even as unbelievers, of who the God of the Old
Testament was. But now the new dispensation of the church was beginning.
The synagogues would be hostile to the new faith found in Christ. A new
era was starting!

Added to his task of clearing up many issues was the job of appointing
elders. Some in the Baptist persuasion think that there would be the
appointment of only one elder in each church. The single pastor would
have almost the sole responsibility for the congregation. But this is not the
case. There were many churches on the island and there would be a plurality of elders in each assembly.

And appoint elders in every city as I directed you. The idea for *elder*
(*Presbyteros*) comes from both the Old Testament rulership of the community and from the practices of even the pagan world. All societies, communities, and villages in the ancient past were elder ruled. Older wise men,
who had much experience in life were brought into the inner circle of leadership. Rarely was this an elective office but an appointment position by
other elders. The elders would be responsible for the teaching ministry and
spiritual health of the congregation.

Appoint (*kathistemi*, aorist active subjunctive) is a compound word
from the preposition *kata* ("down, according to") and the verb *histemi* ("to
place, to stand, to position"). Thus, "*to conduct, install, bring about*"
(EDNT), or "*to according place*" and put in office. This is not a congregational and popular voting proposition. First of all it would be nearly impossible for the average believers in these new church cells to have much spiritual maturity. However, there would be some men who would be more
mature and responsible and these probably were the ones selected by Titus.
Titus had the absolute authority to make these appointments, as is shown
with the subjunctive, "You should start appointing …" When Titus would
someday leave the island, these men would be in absolute charge of what
happened in the assemblies.

Titus was now acting as an apostolic agent (cf. Acts14:23) in Paul's absence. His authority in the Cretan church[es] was an extension of Paul's own. Such authority ended with the close of the Apostolic Age. (BKC)

In every city. Again, the idea of plural appointments was taking place in the many cities and villages on Crete. This had to be done with much care because problems were certainly beginning to grow. Paul would want only the most responsible men appointed. "In Crete the business of organizing the various churches was far from finished, and undue haste in appointing men to office was contrary to Paul's principles (1 Tim. 3:6; 5:22)." (Hendriksen) "Congregations needed an adequate number of elders and more of them as the membership increased. All congregations were to be properly manned." (Lenski)

As I directed you (*diatasso*, aorist, middle indicative) is a compound verb from the preposition *dia* ("through, thoroughly") and the verb *tasso* ("affix, order, appoint, ordain"). It may read, as "I myself specifically appointed" you. Some believe because this construction is so strong, Paul is telling Titus to get on with the completion of this work because, it may be argued, "Titus had been slack" in finishing it. (Lenski) Though this may not have been the case, "Titus is to do this in accord with Paul's command." (NIGTC) The clause with *hos* ("as") shows the manner in which this work should be carried out, "Like this, just as, specifically as." The aorist tense some feel indicates that Paul has said all this before. *You* is actually "*to you*" ("*soi*") and gives Titus "full apostolic authority to carry out this action carefully in compliance with the standards he gives." (NIGTC)

B. Qualifications of Elders, 1:6-9

1:6 Namely, if any man is above reproach, the husband of one wife, having children who believe, not accused of dissipation or rebellion. Now Paul will lay out the qualifications of such men to Titus. This list is almost identical to what the apostle writes to Timothy (2 Tim. 3:1-7). There, he addresses the list specifically to the *overseer* (*episcopos*), or to the one who "over sees." That is, one who guards or watches what is coming, who evaluates and gives approval or warning. It has the meaning of "guardian, watchman, and protector." The word is closely related to the work of a shepherd. "According to 1 Pet 2:25 Christ is the shepherd and *Overseer* of souls." (EDNT) In 1:7 Paul will show that the elder and overseer is the same person but with two descriptions. In the 2 Timothy 3:1-7 qualifications, and here in Titus:

> What is interesting is that, in both lists, the apostle uses a long
> series of present tenses in describing what the elder is to be. In
> essence, Paul is saying, "He is to be right now this way." In

other words, his past may have been one thing, but what is he like presently? Along with the importance of noting Paul's use of the present tense, several vital mistakes are made when examining the apostle's lists of qualifications. The first, is to presume a man has had a perfect, sinless past. Also, to believe that a prospect for elder-pastor perfectly fits all the requirements is non realistic and does not comply with the facts. No one can come up to the standards laid down by Paul. Nevertheless, they are high biblical goals. But too often they have been used against godly men who will indeed walk with imperfections. The lists can be turned into weapons of legalism to judge, condemn, and remove men who need to be corrected but not necessarily replaced.[17]

With the present tense of the *to be* verb *eimi*, "above reproach," the clause could read "*he is to be right now above reproach*" ("*anenkletos*"). Particularly, the word can mean "*above called*." The word is a compound from the preposition *ana* ("up, above") and the noun *kletos* ("to call"). This means the elder-overseer does indeed have a high calling and he is to be "*irreproachable, blameless.*" The word can be translated "*un-accused*" and is used also to describe the qualifications of the deacon (1 Tim. 3:10). (Lenski) The thought is that presently he should be living in such a way that he cannot be called to account. Nothing can be laid to his charge.(Ritchie) He is *called above* present accusations.

The husband of one wife. Or, *he is to be right now the husband of one wife.* (See 1 Timothy 3:2) By context we translate the word *woman* as *wife* (*gunaikos*). Many commentators have translated this phrase rightly as "a one woman kind of guy." That is, in his present marital state, the elder is to remain faithful to one woman only. Many feel Paul is addressing the rampant problem of polygamy that was prevalent in both the pagan and Jewish world.

> It is the most obvious meaning of the language, and it would doubtless be thus understood by those to whom it was addressed. At a time when polygamy was not uncommon, to say that a man should "have but *one wife*" would be naturally understood as prohibiting polygamy. (Barnes)

Looking just at the words themselves, there must be no reason to look beyond the current marital relationship to any that existed in the past. (Fairbairn) "This interpretation would certainly open the door for restoration, no matter what issue led to a past divorce." (Couch, p. 176) Fairbairn goes on quoting other church fathers:

Thus Chrysostom:

He (St. Paul) speaks thus ... to restrain undue license; since among the Jews it was lawful to enter into double marriages, and have two wives at the same time.

So, too, Theodoret:

Concerning that saying, *the husband of one wife*, I think certain men have said well. For of old, both Greeks and Jews were wont to be married to two, three, and more wives at once. And even now, though the Imperial laws forbid men to marry two wives at one time, they have commerce with concubines and harlots. They have said, therefore, that the holy apostle declared that he who dwells in a becoming manner with a single wife is worthy of being ordained to the episcopate.

Theophylact:

"[Paul] said because of the Jews, for to them polygamy was permitted." Even Jerome, with all his ascetic rigor, speaks favorably of this interpretation (in his notes on the passage in Titus); he states that, according to the view of many and worthy divines, it was intended merely to condemn polygamy, and not to exclude from the ministry men who have been twice married. (Fairbairn, Apendix, pp. 418-29)

On this passage, Ed Glasscock further notes:

"First Timothy 3:2 does not say "an elder must be married only once" nor does it say "an elder cannot remarry." Since the phrase is admittedly somewhat ambiguous, to place this type of stern restriction on a godly man because of such an unclear phrase seems quite unjust. One should avoid the Pharisaical error of binding men with unnecessary and oppressive burdens cf. Matt. 23:1-4; Acts 15:10) and should seek to be gracious at every opportunity."[18]

He adds:

"Paul's concern in 1 Timothy 3:1-10 is that if a man desires the office of elder he must be qualified "at that time," not before his conversion. For those concerned with the testimony of the church, let them consider which glorifies God more—that He takes an unworthy, defiled human and makes him pure enough to become His own servant (cf. 1 Tim. 1:12-16)... Even divorced and remarried Christians can trust the great promises of Psalm 103:12-13 and Isaiah 38:17. If God has made a man clean how can the church consider him unworthy to serve God even on the highest levels?[19]

Glasscock concludes:

"As one considers the many facets of the arguments related to the phrase "one-woman man," it must be admitted that there is no simple absolute answer. One may assume Paul meant to prohibit divorced and remarried men from serving as elders, but one should honestly admit that Paul did not say "he cannot have been previously married" or "he cannot have been divorced." What he did say is that he must be a one-wife husband or a one-woman type of man. Paul was clearly concerned with one's character [in the present] when a man is being considered for this high office."[20]

In so many instances, servants of the Lord who have been restored have been a credit to the work of the Lord. They come with a distinct sensitivity and concern about the heaviness of sin. They also feel deeply about those hurting and have a quickness in regard to restoration and mercy for those down and humbled by transgressions. Churches should be sensitive and open to restoration in these admittedly difficult issues. They need to examine all the biblical evidence on restoration and mercy.

When placing leaders who have been divorced back into important roles, a list of guidelines can help. Those guidelines should give great consideration to the biblical standards and also take into account gracious restitution. For example:

1. Has sufficient time passed for proper emotional and spiritual healing?

2. Has the dust settled in regard to the issue so that the person is able to function properly without undue distraction?

3. What is his attitude in regard to the matter? Has he been repentant about his part in the failed marriage? If needed, has he made proper restitution?

4. As far as can be ascertained, has he grown spiritually and morally from the incident? Has it humbled him and is he using the experience to help others who are failing in their marriages?

5. Is there a consensus among those who know him best that he is ready and able to serve and be used of the Lord again?

6. As far as is humanly possible to know, if this is an issue, has he overcome any moral weakness that could trap him again in a compromising situation?[21]

Having children who believe. Or, *He is right now to have children that believe.* The Greek text reads "Children (*tekna*) having belief." The *having* is a present participle of *echo*, thus "children possessing belief." They are characterized as existing in a state of faithfulness. Some in fact translate this as "faithful children." Generally, with *teknon* we think of a young child who has not reached puberty. But this may not be so. The word comes from the Greek verb *tikto* that means "to bear/beget" and focuses on the existing relationship any offspring may have with father and mother. (EDNT)

But to say that the child presently living at home with the overseer at that time would be expected to be living a near-perfect and godly life, may be pushing Paul's intention too far. The great Puritan John Gill thinks so and writes:

> By faithful children cannot be meant converted ones, or true believers in Christ; for it is not in the power of men to make their children such; and their not being so can never be an objection to their being elders, if otherwise qualified; at most the phrase can only intend that they should be brought up in the faith, in the principles, doctrines, and ways of Christianity. (Gill)

Some commentators possibly disagree with Gill and write that the elder should be "having his children under thorough Christian control. His governmental power must be evident in his own household." (PHC) This may not mean that they are believers in Christ. Barnes believes that the word *faithful* "does not necessarily mean that they should be truly pious, but it is descriptive of those who had been well-trained, and were in due subordination." "Having also a religious family, children that are believers, or at least honest in a moral sense." (Poole) Stott writes:

> Although *tekna* ("children") could be used of posterity in general and occasionally of grown adults, it usually refers youngsters who are still in their minority(which of course

varies in different cultures) and are therefore regarded as being still under their parents' authority.

[Children] not accused of dissipation or rebellion. There is no verb here but it is implied. The phrase actually reads "With the accusation (Instrumental case with the preposition EN) [of] *dissipation* or *rebellion*." *Accusation* is *kategoria*, an old plural Greek word from *kata* ("against"), the negative *a* ("not") and *agora* ("assembly, marketplace") that broadly implies "not to bring something against someone openly in the market place." Or, "to not publicly accuse, or bring a charge against someone openly." (L&S)

The elder's children should not be in such moral defiance as to bring negative light on him or the work of Christ. As already mentioned, some commentators do not think the children have to be Christians but they must be under control, relatively ethical, and not in moral or civic rebellion.

Dissipation (*asotias*, "excess") and *rebellion* (*anypotakta*, "unruly, insubordinate, ungoverned") (Barnes) would place the children of the elder in a state of anarchy against both home and civil authorities. This certainly could not be tolerated. But at the same time, it may be too much to expect perfect children. If the offspring are still pagans and acting as such, this would be a "handicap such as that would be too great for an elder." (Lenski)

> *Asotias* in ancient Greek carried the thought of being a "desperate case" or "past recovery," even "unsaveable." It implied also "moral abandonment." (L&S) "It denotes prodigality, an abandoned, dissolute life." (Ritchie)

> *Anyopotakta* describes one who moves up and away from what is prescribed and ordered. It can refer to those who are "unrestrained, not made subject, and certainly insubordinate." (L&S) It is not impossible that there was a unique problem on the island of Crete with unruly teens and young adults. Paul is concerned that such attention would destroy the witness of such young churches. Yet the apostle's injunction stands for guiding all congregations everywhere. "Christian parents whose children go astray in faith or morals experience acute pain." (Stott)

> In today's culture the difficulties with children have become more and more of a problem. Again, the rule of thumb is not to be too legalistic. This is an important standard laid down by inspiration of the Holy Spirit. And yet, few Christian fathers will be found today who are not in a crucial moral

struggle with their teenagers. They may have done everything properly in raising their children, but the hedonistic cultural tug on this generation of young people is awesome.[22]

1:7 For the overseer must be above reproach as God's steward, not self-willed, not quick tempered, not addicted to wine, not pugnacious, not fond of sordid gain. This verse begins with the two Greek words *dei gar* ("*must be for*"). *Dei* is a subjunctive from an impersonal verb that is translated "it is necessary, one must, has to." (BAG) *Gar* is a conjunction used to "express cause, inference, continuation, or to explain." (BAG) This *for* indicates a kind of summary or additional thoughts the apostle feels he needs to get across. Both of these words together help further explain the spiritual qualifications of the elder, but here calling him overseer ("*episcopos*").

Overseer is a compound word with *epi* ("over") and *skopos* (from *skopeo*, "to look, watch out for"). (EDNT) The meaning is that the elder is one who looks out for the assembly; he looks ahead at dangers and is responsible for warning the sheep of what is coming. That the overseer is the same as the elder is clear. For Paul "the author of the Pastorals the terms *elder* and *overseer* indicate the same person." (Hendriksen) "**Overseer** here [is] most plainly identified with the [elder] spoken of before." (Alford) "The switch in v. 7 to 'overseer' shows that 'elder' and 'overseer' or 'bishop' are interchangeable terms, yet with a different connotation." (EBC)

In Acts 20 Paul called the elders of the church of Ephesus together (v. 17) and reminded them that they were made *overseers* (*episkopos*) by the Holy Spirit *to shepherd* (*poimaino*, "to shepherd, pastor, feed") the church (v. 28). In these verses we see the same group of leaders described by two important pastoral nouns, *elder* (sometimes called *presbyter*) and *overseer* (sometimes called *bishop*). They are then responsible "to pastor" the Ephesian congregation. In Ephesians 4:11 *the shepherds* (*poimeen*) are also called *the teachers* (*didaskalos*). Thus, there are four important nouns used to describe the key spiritual leaders of the church: elder, overseer, pastor (shepherd), and teacher. In almost all New Testament passages, these men are seen as a plurality serving in each individual church. In other words, there should be a body of elders for each assembly. The four words above describe their roles and functions. "The title presbyter refers to the gravity and dignity of the office; the title bishop suggests rather the duties which belong to an elder of the church." (Ellicott) "Elder is the title, oversight is the function." (Robertson)

Must be above reproach as God's steward. Or, "*The Overseer [elder] is to be right now above reproach [in regard] to being God's steward.*" The present tenses continue to dominate the verses as the apostle further explains the qualifications needed for the elder/overseer. He is "to be right now."

Reproach (*anegkletos*) means *blameless*. He should live as not to be charged or accused. God (*theou*, Genitive/Ablative case) is emphatic, "*belonging to God, a steward.*" This construction is "suggesting that the steward of such a Lord should conform to the highest ideal of moral and spiritual qualifications." (Nicoll)

Though the standards are high for the men who will spiritually lead the church, Calvin warns that to expect perfection in human flesh is unrealistic. He writes that Paul does not mean one who is exempt from every vice, (for no such person could at any time be found,) but one who is marked by no disgrace that would lessen his authority.

Steward (*oikonomon*) is a compound noun from *oikos* ("*house*") and *nomos* ("*law, rule*") and has the idea of one who rules or manages the house. From this comes also the word "economy" and "dispensation."

> [Steward] showing at once the original identity of elder and *episkopos*, by the substitution here of the one name for the other, and the weighty reason why he should be of irreproachable character, since by the very nature of his office he has to manage the things of God…Presbyters settled over each church, and these presbyters each and all, bearing the name of *bishop*-pastor, or overseer of the flock. (Fairbairn)

Gill adds:

> One appointed by God over His household and family, the church, to give to every one their portion of meat in due season; one that dispenses the manifold grace, or various doctrines of the grace of God, and mysteries of Christ; and of such an one it is required, that he be faithful, both to his Lord and Master.

Paul shows the importance of the stewardship of the apostles when he wrote to the Corinthians: "Let a man regard us in this manner, as servants of Christ, and stewards of the mysteries of God. In this case, moreover, it is required of stewards that one be found trustworthy" (1 Cor. 4:1-2). Pastors have a difficult task of governing and caring for their flock because it is hard to exercise proper oversight without sometimes becoming frustrated with some members in the congregation. It requires divine wisdom and patience to maintain the balance.

Not self willed, not quick tempered. Here Paul begins listing five vices which must not characterize an overseer. (BKC) *Self-willed* (*authada*) can mean "stubborn, arrogant." The word is found only here in the New Testament and often can mean "self-complacent, assuming, imperious." (Barnes) The opposite is the virtue of being "gentle, kind, gracious" (*epieikes*) that is found in 1 Timothy 3:3. (NIGTC)

Quick-tempered (*orgilon*) carries the thought of being inclined to anger. The word is related to *orge* that means "wrath."

> The pastor-teacher cannot be hot-headed. He cannot explode with unjust rage. Caution: Neither should the pastor-teacher be effeminate. He must occasionally stand up in righteous indignation when believers harm each other with gossip and other sins. He must speak out forcefully against heresy and evil. The Reformers displayed proper moments of anger against evil.[23]

Not addicted to wine. This phrase is expressed by one compound word *paroinos* and is found only here and in 1 Timothy 3:3. The word *para* ("*from*") and *oinos* ("*wine*") means "one effected by wine," a drunkard. Wine is a common drink in the Middle East but some in biblical days, as today, became controlled by it and become addicted. One who becomes an alcoholic certainly could not be an overseer. His witness and influence for Christ would be greatly diminished.

Not pugnacious. Pugnacious means one who is a fighter (*plektes*), one who is continually quarrelsome and a bully. (EDNT) This word is also found only in 1 Timothy 3:3. Paul's words indicate:

> One possessed of that prudence and self-control, that upright-ness of character, that kind, generous, disinterested, gracious disposition, which were fitted to command the respect, and secure the confidence and affection of a Christian communi-ty. (Fairbairn)

Since both of these moral problems are also mentioned in 1 Timothy 3:3, the apostle may be tying them together, indicating the addicted person may just as easily also turn out to be a fighter or brawler. Such a spectacle of a church leader seen reeling from too much wine, whether seen in pri-vate or in public, would have terrible consequences on the pure gospel of Christ.

Not fond of sordid gain. This phrase is also expressed simply by one word , *aischrokerdos*. The word is found only in 1 Timothy 3:3, 8, and here in Titus, and can be translated "repulsively greedy." (EDNT) It may also have the meaning of being "greedy of shameful gain." (Robertson) To bribe and cheat in business is a common vice of the world. But one leading the church could not be so accused in a small or even large commercial community. As with other sins already listed, this too would destroy a testimony.

1:8 But hospitable, loving what is good, sensible, just, devout, self-controlled. By using the contrast *but* (*alla*) Paul stresses these virtuous characteristics, such as listed in this verse, over the vices in the last two verses.

Hospitable (*philoxenos*) is used by Paul also in 1 Timothy 3:2 and in 1 Peter 4:9 where Peter urges "Be *hospitable* to one another without grumbling." Peter seems to "warn against murmuring or complaining when the visitors have left!" (Ritchie) The word *hospitable* is related to the verb *phileo* translated "to love, befriend." Some think *phileo* and *agapao* are synonymous in the New Testament. But it seems that *agaopao* is a deeper and more inward kind of love. This does not diminish the importance of *phileo* because it is an important word in Christian virtue. *Philoxenos* is a compound word from *phileo* ("to befriend, love") and *xenos* ("stranger"). "The elder should be one who is fond of offering hospitality, without a thought of receiving a return invitation or other recompense." (Ritchie)

Loving what is good is actually the one word *philagathos* that is also a compound from *phileo* and *agathos* ("the good"). The elder is to love the good. This means he is to support that which is right and just. He should be commending all that is good, in public, in private, and certainly in the assembly of believers.

> [This] may apply to any thing that is good. It may refer to good men, as included under the general term *good*; and there is no more essential qualification of a bishop than this. A man who sustains the office of a minister of the gospel, should love every good object, and be ever ready to promote it. (Barnes)

Gill rightly adds, that if the elder is not caring about all men, "their company will be disagreeable to him, and he will be of no advantage to them." He must be a lover of souls!

Sensible, just, devout, self-controlled. *Sensible* (*sophron*) is a compound word from *sophos* ("wisdom, wise") and *phroneo* ("to think, reflect, set the mind"). *To be sensible* then is to "think wisely, soundly, use common sense." Some see the word referring to self-restraint or expressive of mastery of self. It could refer to "that self-command which wisely regulates pleasures and passions." (Ellicott) (See 1 Timothy 3:2)

Just (*dikaion*) "may refer to his character, that 'he lives a righteous life.' Or it may refer to the way he treats others, that 'He provides justice to everyone.' This man will be fair to all. He will give you an honest hearing and he can be counted on to do what is right." (Ibid., p. 183)

Devout (*hosion*) is related to holiness and sanctification but more. He must be conscious of how he walks with the Lord and pleases Him. He is aware of his piety and spiritual devotion to his God. "He is faithful in all his duties to God." (Barnes)

Self-Controlled (*enkrate*) is a compound word from *en* ("within") and *kratos* ("power, authority, might"). Or, to have inner strength and discipline. Paul is not talking about self human effort as if moral strength is innate. Lasting discipline has a higher purpose and meaning for the Christian in contrast to the world. The apostle is not advocating a form of modern "self-help" as if we are the moral captains of our own ships. He teaches clearly that all spiritual and moral virtue comes from God. Here, he is advocating

> having the inner strength that enables [the elder] to control his bodily appetites and passions, a virtue listed in Galatians 5:23 as one quality of the fruit of the Spirit. (EBC)

> **Self-Control** comes last in this list of Christian virtues, as it does in the fruit of the Spirit. This is an appropriate ending, "covering everything which has preceded it." (Stott)

1:9 Holding fast the faithful word which is in accordance with the teaching, so that he will be able both to exhort in sound doctrine and to refute those who contradict. *Holding fast* (*antechomenon*) is a present active (deponent) participle of *antechomai*. As a deponent verb, the middle or reflexive voice is not heard. In classical Greek, the verb is in an active voice form. It is a compound of two words, *anti* ("against") and *echo* ("to have, hold, possess"). The first meaning is "to hold against." (L&S) The second usage is "to hold out, stand against." Robertson however translates this verb as a middle voice: "to hold oneself face to face with, to cling to." "*Holding to* correctly suggests the notion of withstanding opposition. Having care of it, making it his business." (Nicoll)

Paul is concerned that the elder stand firm doctrinally and not depart from what has been committed to him. He should "constantly be keeping to, and not letting go" of the teaching of biblical truth. (Alford) This will be one of the main tasks of the elders. They are first and foremost responsible for the doctrinal integrity of the congregation. They are in charge of keeping error at bay. The chief purpose of the elder is "principally for the sake of teaching; for the Church cannot be governed in any other way than by the word." (Calvin)

The entire passage in Greek actually reads "*Holding fast* the *according to the teaching* of the faithful word." The prepositional phrase is "*According to (kata) the teaching (didache).* Lenski translates it "the in accord with the doctrine faithful or trustworthy Word."

> The Word whose doctrine makes it so reliable and worthy of confidence and faith. ... The expression is compact and unites in one concept: the Word—its doctrine—its trustworthiness; the Word—its great contents—its supreme quality. Every elder is to be a man who holds solidly to this Word, who knows it, makes it his whole stay. (Lenski)

The **faithful word** *(pistou logou)* may be translated the truthful word. It is a singular concept, so is *teaching.* This probably includes the fact of the inspiration of the entire new revelation of the cross of Christ and the salvation found in Him. Paul envisions this as a whole. Yes, there are thousands of truths revealed with the coming of Jesus. But the apostle here seems to place those truths all into One!

Sound Doctrine. In other letters Paul writes against those who may advocate "a different doctrine," not agreeing with sound (healthy) words, "those of our Lord Jesus Christ" (1 Tim. 6:3). But he also writes of the *word* as a single unit. He speaks about the "word of the Lord (2 Thess. 3:1), of those who are sanctified by the word of God (1 Tim. 4:5). He urges Timothy to "preach the word" (2 Tim. 4:2) and praises those who labor in the word (1 Tim. 5:17). As well, Paul ties what he as an apostle taught the Thessalonians, not as the word of men, but what it truly was, the word of God (1 Thess. 2:13). He makes exhortation to faith and Christian living, "the teaching" that he connects with the substance, "the doctrine." (Lenski)

Paul continues and uses a *hina* final present active subjunctive clause (Robertson) and writes that the elder "*might be empowered (dunatos)* to be exhorting *(parakaleo,* present infinitive) ...*" All through this section Paul has used the present tense. He may be implying that such vigilance, teaching and exhorting is continual and must never cease. The word *empowered* or "'able' here means equipped, in terms of knowledge and commitment, to carry out one's responsibility as an elder/overseer." (NIGTC) Evil forces constantly come against the truth. The elder will be empowered by holding fast the faithful Word. This is the means God uses to create strong elders who then have power from above because they are standing on what God has said and not on their own devices. If the elder fails to obey in teaching what the Lord has laid down, he becomes an "airy, uncertain man." (Poole) The elder "must himself be sound in doctrine, and fully persuaded of the supreme claims of the truth." (PHC)

When the apostle writes "*sound doctrine,*" he uses the present participle of *hygiano* ("to be healthy"). It is from this we derive the English word "hygiene." By using a participle Paul is saying that this doctrine, by its very nature, is healthy and produces healing results. With the participle "The emphasis is upon sound (*hugiaino*) doctrine; the word signifies 'to be healthy' ... and is to be contrasted with the sickly, unpractical teaching of false teachers." (Ritchie) Here, doctrine is characterized by its very nature as healthy! (See 2 Timothy 2:2.)

To refute those who contradict. (*elencho*, present active infinitive) has a wide range of meaning. The noun can be translated as "rebuke, censure, conviction, correction." (EDNT) In the majority of passages used in the New Testament the word "designates fatherly or divine correction and punishment for the purpose of improvement. ... The intellectual aspect of refutation appears in Titus 1:9." (EDNT)

> In the context, this refutation must be applied apparently against Jewish converts ("the circumcision," v. 10) who are confused and mislead believers. They must be reproved "severely that they may be sound in faith" (v. 13). These are "Jewish church-members (cf. Acts 10:45; Gal. 2:12), [who] belong to the class of futile talkers and mind-deceivers. They probably regarded their circumcision as a mark of superior excellence, entitling them to be heard and looked up to by others." (Hendriksen)

These Jewish members are said to be "those who *contradict*" (*antilego*, present active participle). The word is a compound verb from *anti* ("against") and *lego* ("to speak"). These are continually going about speaking against what Paul and others are teaching that is sound and trustworthy. The apostle goes on and writes strong words against them in verses 10-11.

The task of teaching truth is unending. The church cannot let its guard down. Paul warned the Ephesian elders that: after his departure, "savage wolves will come in among you, not sparing the flock" (Acts 20:29). He added that from their own company men would arise who would "draw away the disciples after them" (v. 30). Such a doctrinal war would never cease. He urged the elders to "be on the alert" (v. 31a) and he reminds them that he spent three years warning and urging. He did not stop in admonishing them, even with tears, to be awake for trouble (v. 31b). "Christian truth needs not only defense against attacks, but also clear exposition. Effective presentation of the truth is a powerful antidote to error." (EBC)

> The pastor ought to have two voices: one, for gathering the sheep; and another, for warding off and driving away wolves and thieves. The Scripture supplies him with the means of

doing both; for he who is deeply skilled in it will be able both to govern those who are teachable, and to refute the enemies of the truth. (Calvin)

III. Problems in the Local Church, 1:10-16

In these verses Paul will be more specific as to what is happening there on the island of Crete. He will prepare Titus in some detail as to what he is to expect. The apostle apparently heard reports and speaks justifiably with righteous indignation, because he sees many being turned away from the truth (v. 14). He reserves some of his strongest language for verses 15-16. He argues that their consciences are defiled (v. 15b) and says they are detestable, disobedient, and worthless for any good deed (v. 16).

1:10 For there are many rebellious men, empty talkers and deceivers, especially those of the circumcision. Paul here uses three very unflattering descriptions of those bringing trouble to the churches. By what he says in the rest of the verse, he notes that they are Jews who probably boast in their knowledge of the Old Testament and continually contradict New Testament truth. The apostle calls them "rebellious," a word he used in verse 6 to describe wayward children of potential elders.

The second word Paul uses is *anupotaktos* ("not made subject, independent, undisciplined, disobedient"). (BAG) The word can mean "spoiled" as with the youngsters mentioned in verse 6. They want to be heard and try to have their way in the congregation. They would rather talk than practice their Christianity. (Barnes) Every church has these kinds in its midst. They seem to never settle down. They act contrary to what others readily accept.

The third word is *phrenapates* and means "seducer, deceiver." (EDNT) The only other place the word is used is in Galatians 6:3 where Paul uses it as a verb and writes of those who deceive even themselves. It carries the thought of "mind-deceivers." (Robertson)

The apostle has little patience with those who are "*of the circumcision*" because they should have more spiritual common sense. Robertson adds "Jews are mentioned in Crete in Acts 2:11. Apparently Jewish Christians of the Pharisaic type tinged with Gnosticism."

Rebuke is especially needful with Cretan heretics, in whom the Jewish strain is disagreeably prominent. Alike in their new-fangled philosophy of purity, and in their pretensions to orthodoxy, they ring false. Purity of life can only spring from a pure mind; and knowledge is alleged in vain, if it is contradicted by practice. (Nicoll)

1:11 Who must be silenced because they are upsetting whole families. This sentence begins with *dei* meaning "It is necessary." See verse 7. "*To silence*" is a present infinitive of *epistomizo* and is used only here in the New Testament. The word is a compound verb from *epi* ("over") and *stoma* ("mouth"). Thus, "*over the mouth*," or "*to stop the mouth*." Originally the word meant "'to put something into the mouth', as a bit in a horse's mouth, and hence to bridle or to muzzle." (Ritchie) This will not happen simply by external means but ultimately only through the power of the Holy Spirit!

The reason Paul is so concerned is that they are upsetting *whole families* or *households* ("*oikos*"). *Upsetting* is a present participle of *anatrepo*, a compound verb from *ana* ("up, over") and *trepo* ("to turn"). Whole families were being turned upside down doctrinally and spiritually. The churches on the island of Crete were in terrible turmoil, and Paul wants it stopped! The faith of entire families was being undermined by poisonous doctrine. "There was, indeed, grave cause why these men should be put to silence; the mischief they were doing in Crete to the Christian cause was incalculable." (Ellicott) Pastors today are often afraid to confront error. They believe they have but a passive role, or they think they might be "unspiritual" to show righteous indignation toward those causing trouble. Too, many leaders are simply fearful of the congregation. "What would happen if church members left and we lost numbers if they are confronted?" they reason.

Teaching things they should not teach, for the sake of sordid gain. Paul gets to the heart of the problem. Money or compensation must have somehow been part of the motive of the Jewish Christians who were causing problems. *Sordid* ("*aischros*") means "repulsive, shameful." The word is in three other places (1 Cor. 11:6; 14:35; Eph. 5:12). It is a word that implies the lowest of motives. *Gain* ("*kerdos* ") means "to win" or "to gain" as with earning finances. These Jewish Christians were in some way making money on giving contrary opinions to the religious teachings of Paul. They were being subsidized through giving spiritual advice. Avarice is a destructive plague in those who teach. (Calvin)

> The majority of deceivers would soon stop if their evil work produced no financial profit. Modern history has some notorious examples where great sums were secured by the leaders and shared with their lieutenants. The Cretans had a bad reputation for heeding itinerating prophets who worked for profit. (Lenski)

1:12 One of themselves, a prophet of their own, said, "Cretans are always liars, evil beasts, lazy gluttons." By saying prophet ("*prophetes*"), Paul is not implying that this is a prophet in the biblical sense but simply a philosopher or wise man in the Greek religion or culture. *Liar* ("*pseustes*") is easy enough to understand. *Evil beasts* (*"kakos therion"*) means the Cretans were untamable, uncontrollable, and unpredictable. *Therion* ("animal, beast") in this context refers to a wild animal or to have bestial characteristics. *Lazy gluttons* (*"gasteres argai"*) actually can be translated *idle stomachs*, referring to those who are given over to luxurious feasting and who do no work.

The prophet Paul refers to is Callimachus, or even more probable to Epimenides, as some of the church Fathers ascribe, a native of Phaestus or Cnossus on Crete. Epimenides lived around six hundred years before Christ. He gave a strong indictment against his own people, saying they were full of lies and were ferocious in character. To deceive and lie became known as "playing the Cretan." The "characteristic was so notorious, that it was the subject of frequent remark; the very expression here used of it is also found in a hymn to Zeus by Callimachus." (Fairbairn) Though the charge may not fit all Cretans, it was an accepted general description of how the population behaved. Because the description became "a kind of byword and reproach to the island, it was to be expected that the noxious qualities would not be long in making their appearance in the Christian church." (Fairbairn)

The apostle will not tolerate such behavior in the new churches developing on Crete. He will instruct Titus to "reprove them severely" in order to turn things around (v. 13).

1:13 This testimony is true. *Testimony* (*"marturia"*) is that which can be seen and not doubted. What Paul is saying cannot be challenged. Everyone could see the fact of it. A testimony becomes an outward demonstration of what is actual. The generalization about the Cretans was true, no matter how much pain was caused expressing the fact. Titus had to face this and so did the people. Paul is applying this ugly but truthful description to the Jewish believers who were living out such a wasted life. They were using the habits of the island to feed off of their own Gentile and Jewish brethren in the faith who were apparently terribly gullible as new believers.

> But Paul knew God could change things, if even progressively and by sound rebuke. Cretans were in Jerusalem and accepted Jesus when the gospel was presented by Peter (Acts 2:11). They were born again by the transforming power of the Holy Spirit. "The elders Titus was to appoint (5-9) were themselves Cretans, who were certainly not liars, but teachers of the truth." (Stott)

It still must be recognized, however, that all sins that are part of the old nature, are not always eradicated at the moment of conversion. That could certainly be said of the Jewish believers Paul refers to. They carried into their

Christian experience sins that were part of their culture, but that would also harm others.

For this cause reprove them severely that they may be sound in the faith . *For this cause* (*di'han aitias*) is a phrase used eight times in the New Testament. It is stating the grounds for what follows. "Since matters stand this way, something has to be done."

> "Therefore," or "for which cause," introduces the action demanded by this situation. Titus must continue to "rebuke them sharply," dealing pungently and incisively with the danger, like a surgeon cutting away cancerous tissue. (EBC)

Reprove (*elencho*, "to rebuke, censure," See verse 9) is a present imperative that may imply that this correcting may have to take awhile and be ongoing. In other words, their change of habit may not come instantly. Though they may not improve quickly, the rebuke should be sharp and certain. *Severely* (*apotomos*) is a compound noun from *apo* ("from, away from") and *tomos* ("to cut sharply"). Titus is to act decisively! He is to "cut off, be abrupt, rugged, and sharp" with his words and actions. (Alford) This word is used only here and in 2 Corinthians 13:10. "It is necessary to appear rude sometimes for safety, if the house is on fire and life is in danger." (Robertson)

That they may be is a final clause with *hina* and present active subjunctive of *hugiaino*, which means "to be healthy." See verse 9. Note that Paul says "healthy *in the faith*." They are already believers in the Lord. But *within* that faith, the apostle wished that they would be free from the disease of sin!

> We note the positive purpose of all truly Christian rebuke. Paul's aim was not to humiliate the Cretans for being gullible, but to rescue them from error in order to establish them in the truth. (Stott)

1:14 Not paying attention to Jewish myths and commandments of men who turn away from the truth. Paul is trying to break the cycle of the Jews who paid more attention to tradition than they did to biblical truth, both Old and New Testaments. *Pay attention* is *prosecho* which is a compound verb of *pros* ("for, toward, reference to") and *echo* ("to have"). The meaning then is to possess something in a positive way, preoccupy oneself with something. To be "holding to," implying the giving of one's assent as well as one's attention. (Ritchie)

The **Jewish myths** (*mythos*, "poetic narrative, fable") probably are references to the books written between the testaments, such as the Jewish Apocrypha scrolls, some of which may go back to 300 BC. Though the fourteen most well known apocryphal works certainly have historical, cultural, and religious value because of their antiquity, for the most part they were not to be considered part of inspired scripture. Some of them, such as Bel and the Dragon, The History of Susanna, were simply fiction, or at the least contained historical inaccuracies and fictional portions. The writings of Tobit and Judith are tales of pure fiction filled with historical errors and questionable morality.

By for many Jews who did not know better, these books were admired, read, quoted, and considered of religious value to the genre of the literature of Jewish faith. Many Jews probably quoted them more than they did the Old Testament. The stories in these scrolls may have formed the basis for much tradition. And the belief in salvation by works, which some of them seem to have set forth, influenced the average Jew to strive for eternal blessings by Law keeping.

Then there was the Talmud, that great body of commentary literature that went back to Babylon. With the Mishna and Midrash, it was an encyclopedia of Jewish knowledge that sometimes granted ancient exegesis to understanding the Old Testament. But in time, it became by some to be more honored than the inspired Scripture. It would be more quoted than Isaiah or Moses. It formed the backbone of Rabbinical Judaism that could be terribly harsh and legalistic. The letter of the Law would in time overshadow true biblical knowledge and smother both godly righteousness and faith. Paul was raised on all of this material. After his conversion he realized how the Apocrypha and possibly the Talmud had distorted God's original message in the Old Testament. He was determined to cut through this body of literature and return to the pure message of the Old Testament, but as well, proclaim the new revelation that centered around the Lord Jesus Christ.

Commandments. More than likely the traditions the Lord referred to when encountering the Pharisees and scribes, encompassed these human elements, *the commandments of men.* For example, the Pharisees always washed before eating, "thus observing the traditions of the elders" (Mk. 7:3). They badgered the Lord and asked Him why His disciples did not follow the traditions they observed (v. 5). Christ answered and called them hypocrites and quoted Isaiah 29:13: "In vain do they worship Me, teaching as doctrines the precepts of men" (v. 7). The Lord then accused them of setting aside the commandment of God "in order to keep your tradition" (v. 9) and noted they also invalidated the word of God "by your tradition which you have handed down" (v. 13). He added, "you [also] do many things such as that." Turning to the crowd he urged them "Listen to Me, all of you, and understand" (v. 14b). This was in reference to the fact that the Pharisees were living by tradition and unbiblical ritual that they thought made them holy. Christ urged His audience to see through such religious practices that were not from God!

In Paul's great personal testimony given in Galatians 1, he admits before being born again, he was well known for his "former manner of life in Judaism" (v. 13) and as well was "extremely zealous for my ancestral traditions" (v. 14). But by the time he began to pen his New Testament letters, the great apostle saw the dangers of following what was not true.

These human regulations caused the new Christians on Crete to *turn away from the truth*. By this Paul meant away from the simple message and truth of the new life in Christ. *Turn away* (*apostrepho*, present middle participle) is a compound verb from *apo* ("from") and *strepho* ("turn, turn around"). With the middle voice it is translated "*Turn themselves away from* the truth." (Wuest) They consciously moved away from the truth. By the present participle Paul could be saying that this is still going on and must be stopped. In identical language Paul wrote to Timothy not "to pay attention to myths and endless genealogies, which give rise to mere speculation rather than furthering the administration of God which is by faith" (1 Tim. 1:4). MacArthur adds:

> Hebrew numerology was applied not only to the Hebrew Scriptures but also to the Talmud, a collection of authorized rabbinical interpretations of Scripture, especially the Mosaic Law, that began during the time of Ezra (ca. 450 B.C.) and continued until about A.D. 500. By New Testament times, many rabbis and other learned Jews, especially those who lived in areas where Greek philosophy was still dominant (as it was on Crete), mixed ideas from Hebrew and Greek numerology and added their own allegorical fancies, making the resulting interpretations more bizarre than ever.

1:15 To the pure, all thins are pure; but to those who are defiled and unbelieving, nothing is pure. *Pure* (*katharos*) basically means hygienically "*clean*," referring to disease. Most references in the gospels allude to the purification from leprosy. Leprosy was a serious illness in the Old Testament that caused those inflicted to be isolated from the camp (Lev. 13-14). A leper was as one dead (Num. 12:12). (EDNT) But as often used in the New Testament outside of the gospels, the thought spills over to spiritual or moral cleanliness or lack of the same.

By *positional* sanctification, Paul writes how the Lord Jesus has cleansed His bride the Church "by the washing of water with the word" (Eph. 5:26).

By this, He presents to Himself, positionally speaking cleansed by His blood, having no spot or wrinkle (v. 27). In the ongoing timeless *experience* of Christians in their walk on earth, they must grow into a sanctification that shows forth more spiritual purity.

Because God promised to be a Father to His children (2 Cor. 6:18), the son and daughter of the Lord should then be careful of the daily walk. "Having these promises, beloved, let us cleanse ourselves from all defilement of flesh and spirit, perfecting holiness in [with] the fear of God" (7:1). Notice that the apostle points to both the outward walk ("the flesh") and the inner spiritual relationship as well. The apostle James is very straightforward on this subject and writes "Cleanse your hands, you sinners; and purify your hearts, you double-minded" (Ja. 4:8).

Here in 1:15 Paul lays down an abiding principle when he writes "*To the pure, all things are pure*" Those who have been made pure within should walk about in their Christian life transparent and clean. Paul is applying this to the Judaizing Christians in the context, though he sets this forth as a principle applicable to everyone. This should be those

> whose hearts are purified by faith, and have true principles of grace and holiness formed in them; whose graces are pure and genuine, their faith is unfeigned, their love is without dissimulation, and their hope without hypocrisy. (Gill)

> The problem with the false teachers was that on the inside, in their *minds and consciences*, they were impure. As a result, even though they claimed to know and follow God, their corrupt actions belied their true natures (cf. 1 John 2:4). (BKC)

To those who are defiled and unbelieving, nothing is pure, but both their mind and their conscience are defiled. *Defiled* ("*maino*") carries the idea of being impure and stained. It is an old word that is used to describe coloring or staining in the dyeing of cloth. It is used only five times in the New Testament. John 18:28 gives a perfect illustration as to how the Jews used the word. For example, as the Jews led Christ from the hearing with Caiaphas to Pilate's headquarters, it is said they refused to enter the Praetorium "in order that they might not be defiled, but might eat the Passover." They were concerned about ceremony and ritual. Morally, they were unclean and devious. But Paul goes further when considering defilement. He is concerned about genuine spiritual defilement not simply some ritualistic and religious display of outward false piety.

Paul uses *maino* as a perfect passive participle. The perfect tense generally means the action began in the past and impacts even in the present. The ones he is referring to have gone through an ongoing living and growing defilement. Besides, they are unbelieving ("*apistos*"). But specifically, their mind ("*nous*") and conscience ("*syneidesis*") are defiled and filthy. *Mind* refers to the thinking and calculating aspect of humans. *Conscience* is a compound noun from *sun* ("together") and *eidesis* ("knowledge"). The conscience is an accumulation or gathering of knowledge that should bring about right action. But because of sin, there is a problem. The conscience can be evil (Heb. 10:22) and it may justify itself and languish in dead works (9:14), and it certainly can be weak (1 Cor. 8:10). Though the conscience may be seared or burned and no longer calculate what is right (1 Tim. 4:2), it still bears a witness (Rom. 2:15).

The believer in Christ may have the conscience sprinkled from evil, and may have faith and a good conscience (1 Tim. 1:19; 1 Pet. 3:16). What we do shows forth a testimony of the conscience at work (2 Cor. 1:12). "Pure men are those who have been cleansed from their guilt by the blood of Christ and, having been regenerated by the Holy Spirit, are being constantly cleansed by that same Spirit from the pollution of their sins." (NTC) (See 1 Cor. 6:11; Eph. 1:7; 5:26, 27; 1 John 1:7, 9)

> Finally, because uncleanness [is] tainting their rational acts and their reflective self-recognitions, nothing can be pure to them; every occasion becomes to them an occasion of sin. (Alford)

1:16 They profess to know God, but by their deeds they deny Him. *God* is in the emphatic position. "We know God, they are loudly claiming!" *Profess* is a compound verb from *homo* ("like") and *lego* ("to speak"). To *like-word* something is to call it what it is, to authenticate, to affirm, to acknowledge, or confess to it. By using a present tense, the apostle emphasizes that these people are long on speech, are good religious talkers, and continually profess that they indeed know God!

To know is a perfect active infinitive of the verb *oida*. With the perfect tense, they profess to have known God in the past and are still walking with Him. Though *oida* and *ginosko* may sometimes be synonymous, there is a classical distinction between the two. *Ginosko* "denotes the theoretical possession of knowledge." It refers to the practical faculty of knowing. ... based on observation." On the other hand, *oida* seems to refer to an intuitive, specific knowledge, an awareness, a perception or personal comprehension. (EDNT)

By their deeds they deny Him. Paul says these people outwardly make a claim to knowing God. They are so self-deceived they fail to recognize that those around them observe their actions and do not believe their testimony. *Deeds* ("*ergos*") refer to what they produce or what can be measured in terms of their religious and moral activities. *Deny* ("*arneomai*") can be translated "refuse, decline, reject, renounce." (EDNT) By using the present tense, the apostle is saying they continually go on and deny Him by what they do. They act as if God was "a metaphysical abstraction, out of all moral relation to human life." (Nicoll) It seems to never cease.

> The false teachers also stand condemned by the test of conduct. They publicly confess that they "know God," are fully informed about him, and stand in intimate relations with him. ... The claim may be pride in assumed Jewish religious privilege or an expression of the Gnostic claim to an esoteric knowledge of God. Perhaps both elements are involved. But their vaunted claim is belied by their evil conduct. Moral quality of life is the determinative test of religious profession (1 John 2:4) and by it true character is exposed. (EBC)

Ellicot rightly comments:

> These bitter foes to the truth, Titus must remember, will present themselves under the guise of friends. They will rank themselves in the Christian company openly, with their lips confessing God, but in their way of life, in their acts, practically denying the very things they were so careful to affirm with their lips; in other words, taking back, withdrawing, the solemn declaration of faith they had been making.

Being detestable and disobedient, and worthless for any good deed. In these final words, the apostle is full of righteous indignation at these false teachers, who are by their acts, and by their teachings, destroying the work of the gospel on Crete. On one hand, they put forth such piety. On the other, they are liars, fakes, and deceivers. No doubt they had to continually contradict what Paul had taught. Here, he uses the strongest, most cutting words against them.

Being ("*ontes*") is a present participle of the "to be" verb *eimi*. Paul is saying they "are existing, are characterized" by these harsh descriptives. With the participle he is saying "these words really describe their very nature." The one participle also substantiates and amplifies the nouns. (Lenski) "Being detestable ... being disobedient ... being worthless."

Detestable ("*bdelyktos*," "horrid, abominable") is an adjective related to the Greek corresponding noun *bdelygma* that is translated "nausea, sickness, filth, nastiness." (L&S) The apostle is reaching for the most harsh word he can use. In fact, the word is used only here in the New Testament. However, the noun is used in Matthew 24:15 and Mark 14:14 to describe the image of the beast that will be set up in the temple. "If in character these false teachers are abominable, i.e. vile and detestable before God." (Ritchie)

Disobedient is *peitho* with the attributive or negative *a*. Thus, "to be unpersuaded, unconvinced, not induced." Paul is virtually saying that these false prophets have no intention of being convinced and obeying the truth.

Chapter Two
Caring For Those in the Local Assembly

IV. Teaching of Doctrine in the Local Church, 2:1-3:11

A. Speaking Sound Doctrine, 2:1-10

In this chapter we gain a glimpse of how Paul gives instructions to the flock. His own way of teaching is revealed and it is both doctrinal and practical. The apostle believed in instructing the aged, both men and women. He wanted instruction to filter down to young women with children and to young men. This included exhortations also to Christian servants. Paul placed the responsibility of this happening directly on the shoulders of Titus who was left in charge of the newly formed churches. The words "encourage," "teaching," and "doctrine" are used frequently in these verses. Other verbs are used as well to impress Titus that the believers must "adorn the doctrine of God our Savior in every respect" (v. 10).

2:1 But as for you, speak the things which are fitting for sound doctrine. With *but* (*de*), Paul introduces the contrast with what has gone before at the end of chapter 1. (Ritchie) This charge is aimed directly at Titus. Paul uses the emphatic personal pronoun *su* to get his attention. He knows this younger man is up to the task and he lays the responsibility to mature these assemblies right in his lap. "But as for you, in contradistinction to those I have just mentioned." (Wuest)

Titus was Paul's brother in the ministry (2 Cor. 2:13), who comforted both the apostle and the church at Corinth (7:6) by his refreshing words (v. 13) and his affection (v. 15). Titus was trusted to collect offerings for the suffering saints (8:6), and was also considered a general messenger of the churches throughout Macedonia (8). As well, Paul earlier had called him his "true child in a common faith" (1:4).

Speaking. By using *speak* (*laleo*), with the present active indicative, the apostle indicates that this is to be an ongoing process. Titus will have to continue to do this in order to gain results. "Titus was to be as active in teaching positive truth as the heretics were in teaching evil." (Nicoll)

Paul adds "things which are fitting" or "suitable." By using the relative pronoun "things" (*a*) he broadens the doctrinal spectrum to include a variety of teachings and instruction. This is in contrast to the deceivers' teachings of "things which they ought not" (1:11) to be proclaiming. His goal is to bring about maturity and change in the lives of the congregations. The

Cretans were deep in paganism and their journey out of it would be long and difficult. *Fitting* is the Greek word *prepo* that can better be translated "suitable." Originally, the word meant "to stand out, be conspicuous" or to be "conspicuously fit" to do a task. (Wuest)

Sound Doctrine. The apostle desires to hear that *sound doctrine* is going forth. He uses almost the same phrase in 1:9, and in 1 Timothy 1:10 and 2 Timothy 4:3. Here in the Pastorals, he uses *sound* (hygiano, present active participle, "to be healthy") "in the metaphorical sense in reference to Christian doctrine. ... Christian teaching is thus characterized as correct or reasonable in contrast to false teachings, which deviate from received doctrine." (EDNT) *Doctrine* (*didache*) often emphasized military regulations or discipline, specific directives and instructions. (L&S) It came to represent logical and clear instruction, objective presentation of fact. Paul incorporates the word into his lexicon of important words as to how truth should be presented. Accordingly, it should not represent simply cold facts without application. The apostle sees God's Word in doctrinal form reshaping lives and creating spiritual maturity. "The idea is, that [Titus] was to adapt his instructions to the peculiar character of different classes of his hearers." (Barnes)

> False doctrinal teaching was bringing forth already its sure fruit, in the form of a life utterly unlike the pattern life of the Master. In contrast to this erroneous and misleading teaching, Titus is directed to exhort the varied ages, the different sexes, the bond and the free, to live lives which will bring no dishonor upon their Christian profession. The strictly practical nature of these charges is remarkable. (Ellicott)

2:2 Older men are to be temperate, dignified , sensible, sound in faith, in love, in perseverance. Apparently, the more mature men (*presbutas*) in the church had many things to learn in the way they lived. Paul uses this same word about himself when he was probably around sixty (Philem. 9). The word is also used of Zecharias, the father of John the Baptist, who questioned the angel about his becoming a father. He said, "I am an old man, and my wife is advanced in years" (Lu. 1:18). "In ancient Greek literature the word sometimes was used of men as young as 50." (MacArthur) It must be remembered that these believers are coming out of a pagan society. They had lived as they pleased in an immoral lifestyle. Paul tells Titus these older believers are "to be right now" (*eimi*, "to be," present infinitive) those who are temperate. Temperate (*nephalios*) should better be translated *sober*. It is an adjective that warns against abusing wine. "Live as *sober* older men." The verb is often used in the sense of sober watchfulness in regard to spiritual issues and in having sound judgment (1 Thess. 5:8; 1 Pet. 1:13). 2 Timothy 4:5 reads, "you however, show *soberness* in all things."

Dignified (*"semnos"*) describes how the old men are to carry themselves. In a pagan society there was a lot of rawness, pushing and shoving in order to survive. But Paul wants these men to live above the way the culture acts. The word can mean "august, venerable, reverent," or mean that one has "integrity, dignity." (EDNT) The older men are to rise above the circumstances of living in a rough society. They should not cave in and live as others who have no guidelines.

Sensible (*"sophronos"*) carries the thought of "being of sound mind," walking "disciplined, reasonable." Often we forget that Christianity is meant to help the believer in areas that even go beyond morality, though biblical morality is also certainly in view. The apostle wants the same thing for younger women (v. 4) and the younger men as well (v. 6). Some have seen in the word "the renunciation of worldly passions." (EDNT)

Sound in Faith. *Sound* (*hyugaino*, "healthy") is a verb (present active participle). Their faith should be continually (present participle) robust, active in the faith. "Healthy as regards the faith." (Lenski) As older men they are to be leading, setting the pace of trust toward God. See also 1:9, 13; 2:1. The Word of God is virile and strong, and if presented as such, should speak to the needs of men. If men are godly, the women and children are blessed. Their relationship with God is made easier. When men, especially supposedly older men, fail, women and children suffer. When the Word of God is taught with strength men often respond with the results that families are strengthened.

[Sound] In love, in perseverance. Paul uses three dative cases articulated ("in") with the three nouns "faith, love, perseverance." *Perseverance* (*"upomeno"*) is two Greek words, *upo* ("under") and *meno* ("to abide, remain") and is better translated *to be patient.* The thought is that one is to shoulder up, and remain secure even though under persecution or pressure.

> In respect to these "three" they must be healthy, sound. The faith must not be adulterated with superstitions—the love must be chivalrous, not sentimental. ... The patience must be no mere tame acquiescence in what seems to be the inevitable, but must be brave, enduring, suffering—if suffering comes—for the Lord's sake with a smile on the lips. (Ellicott)

2:3 Older women likewise are to be reverent in their behavior, not malicious gossips, nor enslaved to much wine, teaching what is good. The apostle wants the teaching of sound doctrine to spill over to the older women (*"presbutas"*) as well. Though men are to be the head of their wives in position within the family (Eph. 5:22-24), in terms of the spiritual relationship before God, all stand as equal. All have their individual and personal walk with the Lord. Therefore Paul wants the older women to mature under the teaching authority of the Word as well. He stresses this by using the word *hostautos* that can be translated "likewise also, just as, do the same, in the same way." The verb "to be" ("*eimi*," present infinitive) from verse two carries over.

Reverent ("*hieroprepes*") is a compound from *hieros* ("holy") and *prepo* ("to stand out, to be conspicuous, to be fit"). (Thayer) The women are to carry themselves and be seen as godly women. They are not to conform to what the other women in the culture are doing. Calvin believes that women often want to hold their youth and dress like young women. They demean their own maturity and attempt to dress culturally fashionable or even flirtatious. Though there is nothing wrong with a woman adorning herself with pretty clothes (Prov. 31:22), there is a line that may be crossed that signals sensuality. Lemuel, the writer of Proverbs 31 reminds the godly woman "Charm is deceitful and beauty is vain, but a woman who fears the Lord, she shall be praised" (v. 30). Paul may have had the entire section (vv. 10-31) of this chapter in mind when he penned his words here in Titus.

Behavior ("*katastema*") is also a compound word from *kata* ("*according to*") *stema* is from the verb *histemi* ("*to stand, position oneself*"). Here *kata* as part of this word could mean "according to anything as a standard, agreeably to." (Thayer) Thus, to be reverent may be translated "to stand, take a position according to an accepted standard." Or, "to be honorable in conduct." (EDNT) Calvin believes this could also refer to the way they dress. They should "give evidence, by their very dress, that they are holy and godly women." (Calvin)

Not malicious gossips. Paul uses *diabolos* for the expression *malicious gossips*. It is sometimes used to describe the devil. It is a compound from *dia* ("*through, thoroughly*") *and balos* from the verb "to throw." A gossip is one who throws accusations against someone. The believer is not to give place to *diabolos* (Eph. 4:27) but instead is to stand against his cunning (6:11). In the coming apostasy, people will be *false accusers* or *diabolical* (2 Tim. 3:3). Though men can certainly gossip, Paul twice uses this word *diabolos* to describe a specific sin of women (1 Tim. 3:11; Titus 2:3). Paul may have the same fear in mind when in the next clause it says "*nor enslaved to much wine*". *Enslaved* is a perfect passive participle from *didomi* ("*to give*") with the idea "to be given over to." "To have been entrapped" or "to have been overcome by" would be an accurate translation. In the Cretan culture, men, as well as women, could be addicted, but it seems to have been a sin that especially gripped females.

That a slavish addictedness to [this] evil was not uncommon among the female population of Crete, and that even a rational freedom from such slavery would be no small or unimportant testimony to the power of the gospel. Both of these exhortations ["not to be gossips"] are in substance pressed, though in different terms, at 1 Tim. iii. 8, 11, the first on females, the second on deacons. (Fairbairn)

Teaching what is good (*kalodidaskalous*) is probably a made-up word by Paul and is used only here in the New Testament. It is a compound from *kalos* (good) and from *didaskalos* (teaching). Thus "good-teachers" or "teachers of what is good." Women have tremendous power in the home setting in which they are able to impart to the children what is good and right. By being homemakers (v. 5) women mold and shape their children in godly ways and attitudes. In modern times, many children are shipped off to day care centers where they are herded through the activities of the day. Very little moral instruction is given in a quiet and peaceful environment. The loss of motherhood in the modern generation cannot be recaptured. But not only in reference to motherhood but with the younger women, the older should be a good teacher. "Aged women should be an example to younger women in the teaching and practice of all that is pure and good. It is impossible to exaggerate the value of the influence of one good woman." (PHC)

2:4 That they may encourage the young women to love their husbands, to love their children. The older women are to be so molded by sound doctrine that they can turn around and teach the younger women. Paul here is describing a trickle-down effect from the older to the younger. The older woman has had rich experiences as a mother and wife. But now the practical lessons she has learned are tempered and shaped by the power of biblical truth not simply by human trial and error. *May shape* is a purpose clause with the *hina* and present active subjunctive of *sophronzino*. The word is used only here in the New Testament and means "to make sane, to restore to one's senses, to discipline." (Robertson) The force of the subjunctive indicates that this is a distinct purpose of the Christian older woman. She is to help form the domestic and spiritual direction of the younger woman. The word *encourage* is not strong enough to convey what the apostle has in mind.

Younger women here is *tas neos* and had the idea of fresh dough, or anything that is fresh or youthful. Paul may even have in mind that these are young married girls who are naive and unsophisticated in the ways of marriage. "'Younger' is a positive adjective literally meaning 'new' or 'fresh' and probably suggests a reference to the newly married." (EBC) Younger men also come into this new relationship with attitudes and sins fostered by the culture. Both sexes will struggle to make a binding relation. It will not be easy, and Paul knows this. But more than likely before their conversion, the young couple had strained relations that were torn and buffeted about by the world. But now submitting themselves to God's ways, there is hope for a meaningful and satisfying marriage, as the Lord intended.

To love their husbands. Paul gets specific in where he wants this instruction to go. He desires that younger women are "brought to their senses" in learning how to get along with their husbands. He does not use *agape* which would indicate a deep form of love. It may be that the apostle knows that many marriages start with burning love but must be sustained by another form of affection and caring. The apostle uses a present infinitive of *eimi* and the noun *philandrous*. The word is a compound from *philos* ("affection, befriend, caring"), and *aner* ("man" or "husband"). It is used only here in the New Testament, though there is a similar word in classical Greek (*philandor*). (L&S) With the present infinitive, Paul is saying the young girl is to "be learning how to care for her husband." This is an ongoing process and experience.

> Love is the first and foremost basis of marriage, not so much the love of emotion and romance, still less of criticism, but rather of sacrifice and service. The young wives are to be "trained" in this, which implies that it can be brought under their control. (Stott)

To love their children. The present infinitive is still in effect with the word *philoteknous*. The word is a compound that is not used elsewhere in the New Testament, though the verb is found in classical Greek (*philotekneo*). (L&S) *Teknos* is the Greek word for child. To have the deepest love (*agape*) for her child is natural for a mother. But by using *philos* Paul seems to be stressing cultivating an understanding of the child, or how to properly take care of one's offspring. He could certainly be going beyond what is natural and be referring to developing qualities that go farther than what is normal. "'To love their husbands and children' renders two separate adjectives, 'devoted to husbands, devoted to children.'" (EBC)

> It may seem strange for older women to be called upon to teach younger women to love their husbands and children. But this is put into perspective when we realize that Christians are constantly being taught in the NT to love, whether it be God or fellow Christians and neighbors (here the closest neighbor). (NIGTC)

With a bit of humor A. T. Robertson remarks, "This exhortation is still needed when some married women prefer poodle-dogs to children."

2:5 To be sensible, pure, workers at home, kind, being subject to their own husbands, that the word of God may not be dishonored. Paul is still writing about what he wants to happen in the lives of younger married women. The list continues and it is meant to be extremely practical.

The apostle wants them to be *sensible*. See verse 2. Being sensible or discreet signifies "an ability to govern all our affections and passions. Discretion is but one piece of the fruit." (Poole) Then he adds *pure* ("*hagnos*") which is related to the word *hagios* ("*holy*"). The apostle uses *hagnos* five times in his epistles. He writes of *pure* things (Phil. 4:8), and keeping oneself *pure* (1 Tim. 5:22). John writes of the purifying effect of seeing Christ when He comes. "We know that, when He appears, we shall be like Him, because we shall see Him just as He is. And everyone who has this hope fixed on Him purifies himself, just as He is pure" (1 John 3:2a-3).

Workers at home in Greek is simply the one word *oikourgous*, which is a compound noun from *oikos* ("*house*") and *ergon* ("*work, task*"). The woman is to expend her energy at home, maintaining a nest and a safe haven for both her husband and children. This is culturally not correct in modern times. Nevertheless, most husbands want to see their home and children protected and taken care of by the loving nurturing that only wives can give. "Mothers who work at home usually find it a more absorbing pleasure than 'going about from house to house' (1 Tim. v. 13)." (Nicoll)

> Their attention, moreover, must be concentrated on their own families. Hence, not only must they be *chaste* but also *workers at home* (see on 1 Tim. 2:10 and especially on 1 Tim. 5:13). The two virtues quite obviously are related. Now, while performing their tasks in the family, these young women must take care that the constant strain of domestic duties does not make them irritable or cruel. (Hendriksen)

Kind is actually the Greek word *agathas* which is better translated *good*. Paul does not dwell on the full implication of this word in the context. The range of what is considered as good is broad, and, as all the virtues he has enumerated, it comes from the sound teaching of doctrine (v. 1). With heavy cares at home, it may be difficult for young women to show forth patience. Yet, "her goodness (or kindness) should shine through." (Ritchie)

Being subject to their own husbands. The verb *hupotasso* is a compound from *hupo* ("*under*") and *tasso* ("*to attach*") and is a present middle participle. It may read "being continually submitting themselves" to their own husbands. Or, "placing themselves under the authority" of their own husbands. Wuest translates the word as "obedient" as used "in a military connection of a general arranging soldiers under him in subjection to himself."

That the word of God may not be dishonored. *Dishonored* is the stronger word *blasphemo* ("*blasphemed*"). It can also be translated "to be slandered, accused wrongfully." What the believer does can cause a reviling or disparagement to the Word of God. Though the Scriptures are "not at fault," the enemies of the Lord would love to cast blame at biblical Christianity itself. "So she's a Christian" they would love to spit out in a mocking voice. The verb is used as a present passive subjunctive with a negative *hina* purpose clause. (See also 1 Timothy 6:1) Carried away by their new found faith, some young wives may have thought home making was no longer important. "Such failure in every-day tasks would, of course, be bitterly charged on the religion of Christ, and the gospel would run the danger of being "evil-spoken" of, even in other than purely Pagan circles." (Ellicott) If the home is neglected, practical Christian doctrine is spoiled and wasted. Truth must find its way down to the lowest level of living.

2:6 Likewise urge young men to be sensible. It is possible that "in all things" in verse 7 may go with this clause, but more than likely it does not. It has been asked, "why does Paul have only this one line of command to give to young men"? At first glance, the answer seems to be difficult to find. One suggestion is that in New Testament times, young men were bound by a cultural code to listen to, obey, and not go beyond the boundaries set for them by the elders of either the church or the village. For them to live and act *sensible* covers a multitude of instructions already given by Paul. In other words, they would be expected to follow the examples of the older men as given in verse 2. The word *sophronos* is used in noun and verb forms by the apostle extensively in the Pastoral letters (1 Tim. 2:9, 15, 3:2; 2 Tim. 2:12; Titus 1:8; 2:2, 4, 5, 6). Here in verse 6 it is used as a present infinitive. "They are to be [living] with common sense."

Urge is a present active indicative of *parakaleo*, a compound from *para* ("*alongside*") and *kaleo* ("*to call*"). One called alongside is done so in order to give advice or counsel. With the present tense here, "continue to admonish." (Lenski) Young Christian men are in need of direction. In Paul's day they were conditioned to listen and follow the directives of their elders.

The young[er] men is the plural masculine adjective of *neoteros*, meaning the younger men (or boys). The word comes from *neos* that carries the idea of "new, fresh." (BAG) It is possible that Paul is referring to older teenagers. Lenski believes the word is describing any man under the age of sixty. But this seems unlikely. As used here, it may imply that they are still formable and pliable. They are not yet hardened spiritually and morally. They are ready to listen and follow instructions.

These young men should have well-governed minds, be steady in their behavior. They are at the age when they should discover personal self-control and learn to avoid temptations. They need to heed the words of their elders and learn how not to indulge, and ultimately ruin, both body and soul. "As a young man, ... [Titus's] age was an advantage in dealing directly with the young men. ... Since young men are inclined to be somewhat impetuous and unrestrained in conduct, their basic need is to be 'self-controlled,' cultivating balance and self-restraint in daily practice." (EBC)

Peter adds that young men are to "be subject to your elders; and all of you, clothe yourselves with humility toward one another, for God is opposed to the proud, but gives grace to the humble" (1 Pet. 5:5).

2:7 In all things show yourself to be an example of good deeds, with purity in doctrine, dignified. The verse begins with *in all things* ("*peri panta*"). Does this prepositional phrase go with the end of verse six or does in begin verse 7. It seems as if the argument is evenly balanced as to where the phrase should go. "Whichever direction the phrase is taken the significance of vv. 6-8 as a whole is about the same." (NIGTC)

In all things. In Greek the opening phrase reads "*in regard to all things.*" Better, "*concerning all things.*" (Wuest) Or better still, "*in all respects.*" (NIGTC) To what is the apostle referring? It seems as if he is summarizing how Titus is to behave before the new believers on Crete. Paul's lists of qualities in the verses above could be extended with additional spiritual examples of how he wants the people to live. But what is more important, he seems to be saying here, is that Titus can show the people how they are to walk before the Lord and before each other. A living example is worth a thousand words. "Doctrine will otherwise carry little authority, if its power and majesty do not shine in the life of the bishop [such as with Titus], as in a mirror. [Paul] wishes, therefore, that the teacher may be a pattern, which his scholars may copy." (Calvin)

Show yourself to be an example. The participle *show* ("*parecho*," present middle participle) in its first definition means, "*to grant, present, cause.*" But in the middle voice, as it is here, it is translated "*show oneself to be.*" (EDNT) Besides the middle voice as part of the participle, Paul also adds the reflexive pronoun *yourself* ("*seauton*"), doubling the middle and reflexive idea. Robertson calls it a redundant middle voice. It might read, "*yourself, be continually showing yourself...*" This grammatical construction gives great "distinctness and emphasis." (Fairbairn) Titus could not miss the point! "Here ... the spotlight is turned upon Titus' actions." (Ritchie) In all that was true, Titus set an example to the rest; in peaceful times, as in times of danger and threatening, he must set the pattern as to how a believer should act. (Ellicott)

Titus was to confront them not only with spiritual words but with a spiritual life that corresponded to those words. Even the most forceful and compelling counsel will fall on deaf ears if the one who gives it fails to live by it. (MacArthur)

Example ("*tupos*") might better be translated *type*. This is a prefigure, model, impression, copy.

A reflection on the Church itself in Titus 2:7 also includes instructions to the Church leader: "Show yourself in all respects a MODEL of good deeds." Even more clearly than in 1 Tim 4:12 the point of the exhortation [is] to be a model both of saintly seriousness as regards doctrine and of moral and ecclesiastical integrity. (EDNT)

With purity in doctrine. Despite what the challenge, the doctrine and teaching were not to change or to bend to the circumstances. Used only here, *aphthoria* ("*purity*") means "imperishability, soundness," or even "integrity." (EDNT) It may even have in mind the teaching that is "correct." Often *doctrine* ("*didaskalia*") in the Pastorals refers to the apostolic Christian teaching as an entire body of spiritual information (1 Tim. 1:10; 4:6, 16; 6:1, 3; 2 Tim. 3:10; 4:3). It is the doctrine which is in accordance with true religion, as Paul speaks of the new revelation (1 Tim. 6:3) and contrasts the false teaching put forth by demonic powers (1 Tim. 4:1). To Paul, doctrine is to be sound (1 Tim. 1:10), good (4:6). "The image of the storm or wind in Eph 4:14 (cf. also Jude 12f.; Heb 13:9) is intended to portray the unreliability of human teaching in contrast to the truth of faith (v. 15)." (EDNT)

Dignified. *Semnotes* ("*Respectfulness*") is related to the noun *Semnos* ("*honorable, respectful*"). In classical Greek it pictures someone who is worthy of respect or who carries himself with stateliness or composure. (L&S) In the Pastorals it refers to respectful behavior. An overseer is to see to it that his children have respectful behavior (1 Tim. 3:4), and the wives of deacons are to present themselves in the same manner (v. 11). The same is expected of elderly men (Titus 2:2) and of the whole Christian community (1 Tim. 2:2). Here in verse 7 the word is probably applied directly as to how Titus is to teach doctrine. It has to do with the manner of his instruction. He was "to combine purity of motive, soundness of matter and seriousness of manner" in his delivery. (Stott) His teaching of truth to these new congregations was not to be taken lightly.

2:8 Sound in speech which is beyond reproach, in order that the opponent may be put to shame, having nothing bad to say about us.

Calvin believes the apostle has just shifted his emphasis to how Titus will relate to the average person in ordinary life and familiar conversation. On a daily basis, Titus was to still carry a certain representation of his position in Christ. He still represented the Master during ordinary conversation during the normal transactions of living.

Sound in speech. By using *logos* in the singular for the word *speech*, the implication is that his presentation is a whole, a unit of expression. It is not simply words plural but one's entire deportment that others hear, and see! Others, such as Fairbairn disagree, and believe Paul is still talking about how Titus is to present himself as he teaches. *Sound* ("*hygies*") is used figuratively, and as used by the apostle before, implies that the speaking (or teaching) is to healthy. (See 1 Tim. 1:10; 2 Tim. 4:3; Titus 1:9; 2:1)

Paul adds that the *speech* is to be *beyond reproach*. *Beyond reproach* is a noun used only here in the New Testament. It is made up of three words: *a*, the Greek negative, *kata* which is normally translated "*according to*," and *gnostos* that means "*known, knowledgeable*." The word could be translated "not according to that which is known." In other words, something is "incontestable" in that there is nothing known against it! It is "not condemned." (NIGTC) Titus should so speak that no one could find anything for which to blame him. He must therefore choose his words carefully and watch the manner of what he says and what he does.

> In his public ministry of teaching Titus must show an integrity, seriousness, and soundness of speech that cannot be condemned. Paul was always concerned lest those who oppose be provided ammunition for their attacks. (BKC)

In order that the opponent may be put to shame. *Opponent* is the word *enantios* that comes from an adverb *enanti* that means "opposite." Here in Titus, Paul uses the word in the sense of the one who is hostile, contrary, and coming against the believer and what he is teaching. The world hates the gospel and detests also those who put forth spiritual truth. The lost are always finding fault and seeking cause to show the weaknesses of Christianity. The minister of the Word must be sure of not only his doctrine but his style and even the verbal "phrases" he uses in speech. Those contrary love to condemn! (Poole)

Put to shame is from *entrepo* and is used as an aorist passive subjunctive. The word is often translated "to be made ashamed." (BAG) The word comes from *trepo* that means "*to turn*." By using the subjunctive mood, Paul is saying that this will be the natural result of being careful as to how Titus delivers truth. In this sense, Paul is saying that the opponents will have to change their minds in regard to what they thought about Christianity. They are going to have to rethink their opinions. The opponent will be "either feeling personally ashamed of his own conduct or made to look foolish because he is shown to have no case." (EBC) The charges against Titus will miscarry. "The irreproachable conduct of Paul's representative completely disproves the insinuations and accusations that were aimed against him." (Hendriksen)

Having nothing bad to say about us. In Greek *bad* is *phaulos* that can be translated *evil*. The English *foul* as in *foul smell* probably comes from this word, as well as the word *fault*. Notice that Paul does not say the evil speaking would be against Titus but against *us*. "The antagonism is directed not against Titus as an individual but against him as a disciple of Christ; hence, really against Christ Himself and all his messengers." (NTC)

> Concerning teachers of the Scriptures, their purity and sincerity of motive and aim must be apparent in their teaching; and their speech in public and private must be pervaded by a dignified seriousness, that the adversary of the truth may be put to confusion by the power of the word and the evident sincerity and enthusiasm of the preacher. (PHC)

2:9 Urge bondslaves to be subject to their masters in everything, to be well pleasing, not argumentative. Because Paul dedicates two verses (also v. 10) to the subject of bondslaves ("*doulos*"), there may have come about a spirit of rebellion by some Christian slaves. They may have reasoned that, since Christ was their new Master, they owed no loyalty to another. These bondslaves were probably household servants and not slave-captives from other nations who lived a miserable existence. Whichever, as new believers in Christ, they had a responsibility to not resist and to serve honorably in the position they found themselves.

Though the apostle does not deal with the issue of a rebellious spirit in his discussion of slaves in Ephesians 6:5-8, he writes on the issues of attitude and heart service rather than simply giving to the master eye service (v. 6a). They need to consider themselves "as slaves of Christ, doing the will of God from the heart (v. 6b). Servants are "to be satisfied and contented with such things as they have, and in their state and condition as servants, and cheerfully abide in the calling wherein they are called." (Gill)

To be subject ("*hupotasso*") is a present middle infinitive that, with the middle voice, puts the spotlight on the subjects, the bondslaves. "They are to themselves continually be underattached." On the word *subject*, see verse 5. This is one of Paul's most important words. He uses it to remind believers they are subject: to government authorities (Rom. 13:1), to those laboring for the gospel (1 Cor. 16:16), to one another (Eph. 5:21), wives to husbands in the domestic order (v. 22), to Christ (v. 24). Peter continues with the theme of subjection and says believers are to be subject or submit: to every human ordinance (1 Pet. 2:13), servants to masters (v. 18), younger to the elder (5:5), and, to one another (5:5). He adds that angels, authorities, and powers are also made subject to Christ (3:22).

To their own masters in everything. Or, "In every respect." But better, "In (with) all things" ("*en pasin*," neuter dative plural). In 1 Timothy Paul distinguishes between those slaves who had Christian masters and those who did not (1 Tim. 6:1-2). Here, he does not make that distinction. Paul balances the issues of human respect with the issues of obedience. Care, honor, and reputation play a key role in all he says on the issue. "Had all masters and slaves everywhere taken to heart the inspired words of Paul [concerning] slavery, this institution would have perished from the earth without blood-baths." (Hendriksen)

> From morning until evening and in every category of work the slave must be submissive to his master. It is hardly necessary to add that this phrase "in every aspect" must not be taken in the absolute sense, as if the apostle meant to say that even then when the master demanded of the slave that he tell a lie or commit thievery, adultery, or murder, the latter must obey. (Hendriksen)

Leviticus 25 gives sound rules for the treatment of slaves. If he is a countryman who has had to sell himself into slavery in order to survive economically, he is to be treated with respect as a stranger or traveler, with kindness. He is not to be subjected to a common "slave's service" (v. 39). He is to be treated simply as a hired hand (v. 40) and released at the fiftieth year of Jubilee, if it comes while he is in the service of the Jewish master (v. 41).

The overall general rule is that a fellow Israelite must not be sold as a slave (v. 42), and, "You shall not rule over him with severity, but are to revere your God" (v. 43). Though Moses' arguments in the same chapter are not the same for the treatment of slaves taken from "pagan nations," he in no way advocates cruelty to them because they were not Israelites. In fact a good case could be made from the context that they were to be treated with equal consideration and kindness.

Masters. After addressing the issue of slaves and their conduct, Paul flips the coin over and writes equally important guidelines for those who are masters and have slaves (Eph. 6:9; Col. 4:1). He reminds them they have a Master in heaven who shows no partiality. They are to render good to those in their keeping and give up threatening words. "Grant your slaves justice and fairness" (Col. 4:1).

In two little often forgotten verses in Philemon, the apostle laid the ground work for the end of slavery, at least within the Christian community. He wrote to the slaveholder Philemon about his runaway slave Onesimus who came to Christ through Paul's witness. The apostle urged Philemon to take Onesimus back without penalty. He asked him to receive him "no longer as a slave, but more than a slave, a beloved brother, especially to me, but how much more to you, both in the flesh and in the Lord. If then you regard me a partner [in the faith], accept him as you would me" (vv. 16-17).

Masters here is the Greek word *despotos* from which we get the English word *despot*. The word "denotes that as owners they had complete authority over their slaves." (EBC)

To be well pleasing. The slave is to always be ("*eimi*," present infinitive) pleasant ("*euarestos*"). This is a compound word with *eu* ("*good*") and *arestos* ("pleasant, pleasing"). The slave is to be "good-pleasing" to his master. The word comes from the verb *aresko* that may be translated "to accommodate, be agreeable, to satisfy." The focus is on the conduct and behavior. They are to give satisfaction to their masters with good will rendering service. (NIGTC) They are to "please them well in all things." (Fairbairn)

Not argumentative. The Christian slave is not to talk back ("*antilego*"). This is a compound word from *anti* ("*against*") and *lego* ("*to talk, speak*"). By using a participle (present active), the apostle is writing that he is not to be characterized as one who goes about challenging and defying his master. He is not to be contradicting. (Fairbairn) This should not be his way of acting. Paul seems to be concerned about the Christian slave witness to the non-Christian world. He will be viewed as a new spiritual creature, whose circumstances may be the same, but whose way of relating has drastically been altered. Or, he may reflect the same bitter attitude, though claiming to be a follower of Christ. Though difficult, the apostle wants slaves, who may be physically mistreated, to show a new heart and mind to his owner.

> So either we give no evidence of salvation, in which case the
> gospel-jewel is tarnished, or we give good evidence of salvation
> by living a manifestly saved life, in which case the gospel-jewel
> shines with extra luster. Our lives can bring either adornment
> or discredit to the gospel. (Stott)

2:10 Not pilfering, but showing all good faith that they may adorn the doctrine of God our Savior in every respect. Paul continues his instructions to slaves. As slaves, they must see themselves in a better light since they now have a higher spiritual calling in Christ. In this sense, the apostle is lifting them above the way they see their station in life. They have a calling to serve the One True God and His Son, the Lord Jesus Christ.

"Even slaves should not think their example a matter of indifference: their religion exalts and beautifies them." (PHC) People do not ennoble Christianity, but Christianity ennobles them.

Not pilfering. The verb is a present middle participle from *nosphizo.* The word means to "set apart, "separate," but in the bad sense "to embezzle" or covertly misuse for one's self. (Thayer) With the middle voice it may be translated "stop stealing [from your master] for your own use." Household slaves in New Testament times were often business managers who had the opportunity to take money, food, jewelry, or other valuables with which they were entrusted. "When Christians do such things, their actions not only are unethical and damage their employer financially but also are unspiritual and do damage to the Lord's name and to their testimony." (MacArthur)

But showing all good faith. The *but* ("*alla*") brings out the contrast in how the slave is to act now as a believer, in opposition as to how he may have behaved. *Showing* is from *endeiknymai* (present middle participle) and means "to prove, demonstrate." (EDNT) "Be yourselves constantly demonstrating, as a way of living" *all good faith* ("*pasan pistin ... agathen*"). *Faith* is here used in the sense of *faithfulness* or *reliability.* (NIGTC) This "good faithfulness" must extend to all areas of the slave's living and serving.

> *Faith* or *fidelity* is here not to be taken in the active sense as a confidence that the slaves place in their masters but in the passive sense as a confidence which their masters may have in the slaves. ... Christian slaves are always to show themselves worthy of being fully trusted by their masters in everything that serves their masters' interests. (Lenski)

That they may adorn the doctrine of God our Savior in every respect. Paul uses a result or final clause with the *hina* and the present active subjunctive of the verb *kosmeo. Kosmeo* here means to "put in order" or "decorate." It may also imply "to make attractive" or "do credit to." (BAG) The apostle is expressing what he wants to see come out of the way these slaves are relating as Christians to their masters. In secular Greek *kosmeo* is often used to speak of the arrangement of jewels in a manner to set off their full beauty. (Ritchie) "God deigns to receive an 'ornament' from slaves, whose condition was so low and mean that they were wont to be scarcely accounted men." (Calvin)

The doctrine of God our Savior is an unusual expression in the New Testament Epistles. In using it, Paul seems to be placing all Christian truth under this entire phrase. He is not simply writing about the teaching ("*didaskalia*") in regard to God, but also about salvation. "He is our Savior!"

Note also the similarity of what the apostle says here with 1:3, where he says he was entrusted according to the commandment "of God our Savior." "*God our Savior*" is not a Trinitarian formula. See 1 Timothy 1:1 where Paul uses the same expression but separates it from "and of Christ Jesus." "Not Christ, but the Father is meant: in that place (1 Timothy 1:1) the distinction is clearly made." (Alford)

In a very real sense, however, the Father is our Savior as well as the Lord Jesus. Many verses attest to this (1 Tim. 2:3; 4:10; Titus 1:3; 2:13; 3:4; 2 Pet. 1:1; Jude 25). The Father planned our salvation and Christ was obedient unto death to secure its blessings for us (Phil. 2:8). "The Father has sent the Son to be the Savior of the world" (1 Jo. 4:14).

The slave then is to be an ornament "in all things, as remembering that it is the doctrine of God our great Preserver, and of Jesus Christ our blessed Savior." (Poole) Though Paul's statement does not have a Trinitarian concept in view, Gill still writes:

> Christ is our alone Savior, and He is truly and properly God, and so fit and able to be a Savior; and the Gospel is His doctrine, not only what He Himself preached, when on earth, but it is a doctrine concerning Him; concerning His Deity, and the dignity of His Person, and concerning His office as Mediator, and the great salvation [comes] by Him.

B. Living Sound Doctrine, 2:11-15

2:11 For the grace of God has appeared, bringing salvation to all men. The *for* ("*gar*") is indicating a conclusion and a summary. *For* "connects vv.11-14 with what has been brought before us already in this chapter; all the pillars of exhortation in vv.2-10 are based upon these concluding verses." (Ritchie) All the moral injunctions Paul has so far discussed come from the fact that God has revealed His matchless grace in the salvation provided by the Lord Jesus. Such a giving of favor is found in no other religion on earth. It is certainly a fact not experienced in Greek or Roman theology. "This summary of 'the teaching' presents the salvation purchased and won for all men, but as one that changes their whole lives from ungodliness to good works. ... 'For' reaches back through the whole chapter." (Lenski) This summary does not only speak to slaves but to all levels and classes of Christians. This grace admonishes all to practice good works.

The **grace** ("*charis*") **of God** brings about the salvation through Jesus. But the apostle's point may also be pointing out that it is that which equally promotes a new way of living. "The grace of God is His unmerited favor toward men expressing itself in active history." (Ritchie)

There is the necessity for right conduct [in] the all-embracing scope of the saving grace of God, which has visibly appeared as a call to repentance, a help to amendment of life, and a stimulus to hope. Christ's gift of Himself constrains us to give ourselves wholly to Him. (Nicoll)

Has appeared ("*epiphano*," aorist passive indicative) is a compound word from *epi* ("*over*") and *phaino* ("*to shine, appear*"). From this word comes the English word Epiphany. The meaning is "*to shine over, to appear over.*" The aorist indicates that this has taken place; this grace has already been given and has arrived. "The illumination of God's gracious work is complete." "Become visible, to become clearly known." (Wuest) "It means that the plan of salvation has been revealed to all classes of men; that is, that it is *announced* or *revealed* to all the race that they may be saved." (Barnes)

Bring salvation to all men. The word *bringing* is not in the text but it is implied in the next word. *Salvation* ("*soterios*") is an adjective modifying and qualifying *grace*. It may read "*saving grace has appeared to all men*" (*pasan anthropois*). The question is raised, "Is this salvation being offered to all men or simply all classes of men?" Or, "Is salvation provided for all classes of men and applied to only the few who are elect?" Good expositors have wrestled over this passage for generations without completely reconciling the meaning.

One's theology comes into play here and causes the reader to fall on one side or the other. Some argue that since Paul focuses on different age groups and the different sexes in the previous verses, and then slaves, he is addressing the fact that Christ died for all kinds of people. If this is so, the apostle is not making a universal statement but he is pressing his point concerning types of people.

The doctrines of predestination and election are absolute truths in Scripture. There is nothing innate in any one that commends that person to God, not even foreseen faith, as some attempt to argue. The depravity of the human race is absolute. No one can come to God unless that man or woman is awakened by the work of the Holy Spirit. It therefore seems to be no violation of these teachings if the provision of salvation is sufficient for all but applied only to the elect.

There is no violation of these points if Paul argues for the provision of salvation for all. By the fact that salvation is provided for all simply adds to the culpability of people. They cannot argue with God, "But I was not of the elect! There was no way I could be saved since I was not chosen!" Instead the lost will stand before God in which all the thoughts will be revealed. "Though not chosen, I did not want You. My heart was hardened and I only wished to run from You."

Some strict Calvinists will object and still argue for a limited atonement or salvation that is applied only to the elect and is in no way available for the non-elect. But able scholars present both sides; or some argue that the issue is not clearly stated in this verse: "Whichever interpretation be adopted, the sense here will not be essentially varied." (Barnes) God "'is God our Savior, who will have all men to be saved' (1 Tim 2:3-4). Sadly not all men will be saved, 'for all men have not faith' (2 Thess 3:2)," and, "God's grace has not in fact yet appeared to all men, but it is laden with salvation for all." (Ritchie)

Paul "does not mean individual men, but rather describes individual classes, or various ranks of life." (Calvin) "In a word, the salvation-bringing grace of God is without respect of persons; it is unfolded to men indiscriminately, or to sinners of every name." (Fairbairn) "Aged men, aged women, young women, young(er) men, and even slaves ..., *for* the grace of God has appeared bringing salvation to men of *all* these various groups or classes." (Hendriksen) "This is to be understood of all sorts of men, of every nation, of every age and sex, of every state, and condition, high and low, rich and poor, bond and free, masters and servants; which sense well agrees with the context." (Gill) Paul is prompted to affirm the universal availability of salvation through Christ." (BKC)

Some teach the doctrines of double predestination. God elected to salvation, they say, but He also predestined to damnation. The Scriptures do not teach this. In fact, Romans 9:22-23 make it clear that God waits patiently for the "vessels of wrath prepared for destruction," but they will not come to Him. But He has made "known the riches of His glory upon vessels of mercy, which He *prepared beforehand for glory*." (Italics mine) Salvation and judgment of course are inscrutable and difficult doctrines, and are beyond our comprehension. However, the Bible clearly states that God chose His own before the foundation of the world (Eph. 1:4). Yet "Scripture makes equally clear that those who do not believe are responsible and guilty for their rejection of Christ (cf. John 3:17-20).

Paul and Peter also concur that God "desires all men to be saved and to come to the knowledge of the truth" (1 Tim. 2:4), and that the Lord is patient, "not wishing for any to perish, but for all to come to repentance" (2 Pet. 3:9b). As taught by Calvin and the Reformers, depravity, predestination and election are scripturally verifiable. However, by examining all the biblical evidence in context, it is doubtful that double predestination and limited atonement are defendable. Concerning the atonement, or the application of salvation grace, it is not that people are actively excluded by God. (MacArthur) As John makes clear in his second letter, Jesus "is the propitiation for our sins; and not for ours only, but also for those of the whole world" (1 Jo. 2:2).

2:12 Instructing us to deny ungodliness and worldly desires and to live sensibly, righteously and godly in the present age. *Instructing* ("*paideuo*," present active participle) is the word from which we get *pedagogy, pedagogue.* The word is also related to the Greek noun *paidion* meaning small child. The overall idea carries the connotation of "teaching like done with a small child." The noun *paideia* can also mean "*reprimand, discipline*" with the thought of teaching that reins in a wayward person, brings about inner control of a rebellious offspring. God disciplines us as sons (Prov. 3:11) and it produces the "peaceful fruit of righteousness" (v. 11). "As in [the Old Testament] wisdom literature, sonship and discipline are 'viewed as a divinely ordained training process.'" (EDNT) With the present participle, Paul is implying that this is an ongoing happening that causes us to reach a stage of denying ungodliness. This teaching personifies *grace* as guiding believers in the things that come from sound doctrine (v. 1). "It comprehends the entire training process—teaching, encouragement, correction, discipline." (EBC) *instructing* qualifies *grace* "and further indicates the purpose accomplished by the appearance of [that] "grace." (NIGTC)

To deny actually reads *in order that [we] might deny.* This is the word *arneomai* and is used as an aorist active participle, with the aorist participial force of a past tense, *having denied.* Though Alford sees the aorist participial idea making the action contemporary with *to live* in the rest of the verse. *Arneomai* is a strong word meaning "*to refuse, to renounce.*" "We act as those who *renounce* while we *should live ...*" "*to deny*" sounds rather weak, limited, and not very assertive. In classical Greek it carries the thought of *to disown, to decline, to cast aside,* and say *no!* (L&S)

The negative pedagogical purpose of grace is to train us "to say 'No' to ungodliness and worldly passions." The aorist participle indicates that grace aims to lead the believer to the place where as a definite act he will voluntarily make a double renunciation of the past. ... Such an act of renunciation, standing at the beginning of a life of Christian victory, must be maintained in daily self-denial. (EBC)

Ungodliness, worldly desires. *Ungodliness* ("*asabeian*") is a compound noun from the negative *a* and the word *sebeian.* The word is used to describe all forms of atheism and even false religion that is dead. It refers to "living without regard to any Divine Being, or according to our own erroneous and superstitious conceits and opinions of Him." (Poole) It must be remembered that believers in Christ may live like atheists and even in their actions look like the lost. Paul said this of the Corinthians when he wrote "for you are still fleshly. For since there is jealousy and strife among you, are you not fleshly, and are you not walking *like mere men*?" (1 Cor. 3:3). (Italics mine) The apostle warned the Ephesians, "do not participate in the unfruitful deeds of darkness, ... for it is disgraceful even to speak of the things which are done in secret" (Eph. 5:11-12).

Worldly desires ("*kosmikas epithumias*") actually means *lusts spawned by the world*, or the popular culture. "'Worldly' means that the desires are connected only with life in this cosmos and seek their satisfaction in nothing higher." (Lenski) By using the plural, Paul indicates that these may be many and varied temptations that the believer in the Lord may fall for and embrace. *Desires* ("*epithusias*") conjures up the idea of the lowest form of tugs and temptations that draw people into dark, forbidden, and heinous activities. These lusts trap the body and soul and are difficult to overcome. The apostle John writes "For all that is in the world, the lust of the flesh and the lust of the eyes and the boastful pride of live, is not from the Father, but is from the world" (1 Jo. 2:16). Here in the Pastoral epistles Paul continues his discourse on *lust* and speaks of "foolish and harmful lusts" (1 Tim. 6:9), "youthful lusts" (2 Tim. 2:22), from which believers are to flee and deny. Only by the gospel, and by the grace it dispenses, can a child of God have victory. "Grace disciplines us to 'renounce' our old life and to live a new one, to turn from ungodliness to godliness, from self-centeredness to self-control, from the world's devious ways to fair dealing with each other." (Stott)

> The gospel insists upon the inseparable connection between creed and character, doctrine and life. It is a discipline, enforcing self-restraint in a world where sin is the normal state of things, and enabling us to live soberly, righteously, and godly, as a constant reproof to the world's sin, and an example and stimulus to all who are striving to conquer the world-spirit. (PHC)

To live sensibly, righteously, godly. *To live* (*zao*) is better translated "*that we might, ought live ...*" (aorist active subjunctive). "Believers should be carrying out their physical existence in this manner ..." For the child of God who faces terrible temptations, grace must be living and active in his experiences. (Fairbairn) The positive side to all this is that we should "live (effective aorist) sober-mindedly and righteously and godly in the present eon." (Lenski) *Sensibly* (*sophronos*) can be translated "*soberly, self-controlled*, with *reasonableness*, or *self-discipline*." (EDNT) The word and its various forms is used sixteen times in the Pastorals. It is one of Paul's favorite concepts. In this verse, such self-control and reasonableness "do not mean mere accommodation to one's civic environment, but are coupled rather with anticipation of the parousia." (EDNT) The *parousia* ("*the coming*") can refer in context to the rapture of the church or the second coming of the Lord to reign in the Davidic Millennial kingdom. Here, the verse that follows is referring to the rapture.

Righteously (*dikaios*) in a popular sense may mean "to live right." But there is more involved in the word in the New Testament. *Righteousness* (*dikaiosyne*) theologically refers to being "legally acquitted." Christ's substitutionary sacrifice affects this work and the redeemed are "declared righteous." This means to be more than simply without sin. Imputed or reckoned to us is the very righteousness of the Son of God! Believers are "justified (made righteous) by faith apart from works of the Law" (Rom. 3:28). And, "to the one who does not work, but believes in Him who justifies the ungodly, his faith is reckoned as righteousness" (4:5). Peter writes that Jesus "died for sins once for all, the just for the unjust, in order that He might bring us to God" (1 Pet. 3:18a).

In 2:12 Paul is referring to living righteously, an extension, a living-out of the new position the believers have in Christ. In their experience, Christians are to live righteously, justly, as those who have been declared positionally justified through faith in Christ. "God's grace requires of us a life of truth and strict justice in all our dealings with our fellow men." (Ritchie)

Godly (*eusebos*) is the opposite of *ungodliness* (*asebeian*) mentioned here in the same verse. (See above.) From the positive perspective, living *godly* means to live with a devotion for the Lord, to have true piety, reverence and respect for Him alone who "is the proper Object of worship." (Hendriksen) Paul wants the believers to have godliness as a genuine attitude of the heart and mind toward God.

Sometimes Christians treat Him with a certain "lightness" and familiarity that fails to show proper respect. This is not to say the child of God should move in the other direction that promotes a stiff formalism. The Lord is after our hearts. He desires communication and fellowship with His own. But He still should be given a proper worship that is not false nor rote. *Godly* refers to "a godly manner, according to the word of God, and agreeably to the will of God: and in all godly exercises, both public and private, and to the glory of God." (Gill)

In the present age (*en to nun aioni*) literally reads "*in the now eon.*" Or, "in the present course of things." (Ellicott) The apostle is speaking of his times, his generation, and his era. Each generation of Christians must live godly in the period of history God has placed them. The evils of today may be a little different than the past, but the child of God must walk according to the Word of God and the injunctions set forth in it. Some generations are destined to suffer greatly. Others face waves of error and false doctrine. But these words of Paul remain firm, and are as applicable to us today as when the apostle wrote them. "The Lord has appointed the present life for the trial of our faith." (Calvin) And, "These are the duties which we owe in the present life." (Barnes)

2:13 Looking for that blessed hope and the appearing of the glory of our great God and Savior, Jesus Christ. This verse clearly seems to be a rapture verse. Paul wants us to be looking for His coming in glory. Since the rapture of the church is the next event on the divine timetable, this is more than likely the meaning.

The doctrine of the rapture of the church is not necessarily proven by any one passage of Scripture. It is built on the evidence built up in many references. For example, Paul commended the Thessalonians because they were both serving the "living and true God" (1 Thess. 1:9b) and waiting "for His Son from heaven" (v. 10a). He adds that Jesus is coming "who delivers us from the wrath to come" (v. 10b) which would of course be the great tribulation. In this letter Paul writes of the "*we*" and "*us*" who may be around "until the coming of the Lord" (4:15). The Lord Himself will descend from heaven with a shout (v. 16) "and the dead in Christ shall rise first. Then we who are alive and remain shall be caught up together with them in the clouds to meet the Lord in the air" (v. 16b-17). He adds "For God has not destined us for wrath but for obtaining salvation through our Lord Jesus Christ" (5:9).

Looking for. *Looking* is the present active participle of *prosdechomai* that has the force of *looking for* in the sense of expecting or waiting with great anticipation. It is a compound word from *pros* ("*with reference to*") and *dechomai* ("*to receive*"). Usually *pros* refers to the location toward which something is moving. (EDNT) The New Testament usage is, "to take up, receive, welcome, wait for, expect." (BAG) Also, "to receive favorably, to admit to, receive hospitably." (L&S) Here with the present participle, the word means "an ongoing welcoming and expectation." "Primarily," it can mean "to receive to one's self" something. (Vincent) This *looking for* then is "an ongoing process of greatly anticipating and welcoming to one's self the appearing" of the Lord. The idea of expectation is strong in the word, "*with reference to receiving* something." Simeon was *waiting expectantly* for Israel's consolation (Luke 2:25); Anna was *looking for* Jerusalem's redemption (2:38). And Joseph of Arimathea was *looking for* the kingdom of God (Mark 15:43). Christ urged His disciples to be ready like servants *waiting for* their master (Luke 12:36; Jude exhorts his readers to persevere in the love of God and *wait for* the mercy of Jesus Christ unto eternal life (v. 21).

The two participles *instructing* in verse twelve and *looking* here are working together, and may read, along with verse 11, "The grace of God has appeared ... *instructing* us [that we might live sensibly] ... [as we are] *looking for* the blessed hope ..." With the present tense, "This expectation being [then] an abiding state and posture." (Alford) This "describes the glad expectancy which is the ruling and prevailing thought in the lives of men looking for their Lord's return." (Nicoll)

Blessed hope. *Blessed hope* (*makaria elpida*) is better translated the *joyous anticipation*. *Elpia* means the "*expectation, anticipation, prospect.*" There is no question about this anticipation. It *is* going to come about, and it produces within the believer a great joyousness that looks forward to ultimate redemption. "Those now being trained by God's grace eagerly anticipate the eschatological future. Having renounced their sinful past, they live disciplined lives in the present and look eagerly to the future (cf. 1 Thess 1:9, 10)." (EBC) This "*waiting for*" in verse 10 shows they are looking for this blessed hope, and the personal return of Jesus. *Waiting for* is a present infinitive in Greek and shows that this waiting as the proper attitude of believers, "ever ready to welcome the returning Lord." (EBC)

And the appearing of [the] glory of God ... For *appearing*, which is often translated *brightness*, see verse 11. *Glory* is the Greek word *doxa* and can mean "reputation, honor, radiance, even reputation." (EDNT) Some versions render the passage *glorious appearing*, but literally "*appearing of the glory*" is better and points to Christ's glorification now in heaven. "His glory shall appear!" The article *the* is not in the Greek text. But the Greek actually places "*the blessed hope and the appearing of the glory*" under one article. Thus, it should read "*The blessed hope, even the appearing of the glory...*" Or, "*The joyous anticipation, that is, the glorious appearance!*" This implies that the reference is to one event viewed from two aspects. "For believers, it is indeed the blessed hope and the longed-for consummation of that hope." (EBC)

Our great God and Savior, Jesus Christ. This is a remarkable phrase in Paul's letter. It strongly supports the fact that Christ is *very* God, and it is an outstanding and important testimony to the doctrine of the Trinity. However, getting to this truth in this passage is complicated, and the process must be explained. It has to be noted that there are many orthodox Evangelical scholars who do not think the phrase is a strong Trinitarian witness. They simply believe God and Christ are seen as separate in the phrase. Others argue that the construction of the phrase is such that the doctrine of the Trinity is in view. Either is grammatically possible.

Before addressing the issue whether the phrase is referring to just one person, it is important to note the complete grammatical construction. "*We who are looking for*" is the subject in the nominative case. There are two accusatives or objects, "*the blessed hope* even *appearing.*" A lengthy genitive phrase follows: "*the glory of the great God and Savior of us.*" Before *great God* is the genitive *the* but it is omitted before *Savior*. "The two expressions [are] as attributive of one and the same person. ... The other consideration is, that nearly all the [Church] Fathers—Greek, as well as Latin—who refer to this passage, understood it simply of Christ." (Fairbairn)

Will God the Father make an appearance? No, He is Spirit and cannot be seen. It will be the Son who will be visible, and He is the great God. The deity of Christ is indisputable by the grammar of many passages but some verses are so direct on the issue that they cannot be questioned. For example, Christ existed in the past as the Word, and the Word was also God (John 1:1); Thomas was never challenged when he said, "My Lord and my God!" (20:28); Paul writes, "Christ according to the flesh, who is over all, God blessed forever" (Rom. 9:5); the writer of Hebrews says, Christ "is the radiance of His (God's) glory and the exact representation of His nature" (1:3); and, "But of the Son He says, 'Thy throne, O God, is forever and ever, ... therefore God, Thy God, hath anointed Thee'" (vv. 8, 9); and Peter adds, "the righteousness of our God and Savior, Jesus Christ" (2 Peter 1:1). Nicoll writes concerning the verse:

> But the proofs that St. Paul held Christ to be God Incarnate
> do not lie in a few disputable texts, but in the whole attitude
> of his soul towards Christ, and in the doctrine of the relation
> of Christ to mankind which is set forth in his epistles.

Other respected scholars add weight to this argument: "Paul, having spoken of the revelation of the glory of 'the great God,' immediately added 'Christ,' in order to inform us, that that revelation of glory will be in His person; as if he had said that, when Christ shall appear, the greatness of the divine glory shall then be revealed to us." (Calvin) "Although the Old Testament makes countless references to God the Father as *great*, in the New Testament that description is used only of God the Son (see, e.g., Matt. 5:35; Luke 1:32; 7:16; Heb. 10:21; 13:20). Perhaps most importantly, the New Testament nowhere speaks of *the appearing* or Second Coming of God the Father but only of the Son." (MacArthur) This passage "furnishes an important proof of the divinity of Christ." (Barnes)

> The appearing or epiphany of the glory of Jesus Christ, shall
> at last arrive. Then he who in his own person is 'our God and
> Savior' ... will come in all his glory, ... which shall transcend
> all that we are able to imagine. (Lenski)

Wuest concludes by pointing out that the grammatical construction "*that blessed hope, even the appearing...*" is also applied on the phrase "*glory of our great God, even Savior, Jesus Christ.*" He further argues that the god and savior of the Roman empire was the Emperor himself, who was seen as the savior of the world and the state. He also was worshipped as the god in the state religion. The Christian's God and Savior in Jesus Christ. Paul was making a protest against emperor worship. Wuest adds, "Both expressions refer to the same individual. The deity of the Lord Jesus is brought out here by a rule of Greek syntax."

2:14 Who gave Himself for us, that He might redeem us from every lawless deed and purify for Himself a people for His own possession, zealous for good deeds. *Who* is the relative pronoun *hos* and its antecedent would have to be the both names seen as a single unit in verse 13.

> The relative clause 'who gave himself' evidently refers to Christ alone, but the construction leads us to take the whole preceding expression 'our great God and Savior Jesus Christ' as its antecedent; this confirms that one and not two Persons are referred to in the previous verse. (Ritchie)

Who gave. *Gave* is the same verb *didomi* used in John 3:16: "God *gave* His only begotten Son." The form is the same, aorist active indicative. "God *gave* His Son; Christ *gave* Himself." *Himself* is the reflexive pronoun *heautou*. The same action, expressed the same way, is the work of the Father as well as the Son. They acted in concert, as with one action, and that of giving. This thought is another block in the building of the doctrine of the deity of Christ and the mysterious teaching of the Trinity. The Father and Son are both doing the same work.

For us. *For* ("*huper*") here carries the thought of "*on behalf of, in place of, for the sake of, instead of.*" "Jesus gave Himself on the cross and *took our place* under the wrath of God." The apostle has in mind the great substitionary atonement passage Isaiah 53 in which the prophet writes prophetically of the coming death of the Messiah: "He was pierced through for *our* transgressions, He was crushed for *our* iniquities" (v. 5). (Italics added) Was He not taken to judgment "For the transgression of my people to whom the stroke was due?" (v. 8b). He further writes, "The Lord was pleased to crush Him, ... He would render Himself as a guilt offering" (v. 10), and, "My Servant will justify the many, as He will bear their iniquities" (v. 11b), "Yet He Himself bore the sin of many, and interceded for the transgressors" (v. 12b).

Paul repeats this idea of substitution often: Christ "who gave Himself for our sins" (Gal. 1:4); "The Son of God who loved me, and delivered Himself up for me" (2:20b); "Christ also loved the church and gave Himself up for her" (Eph. 5:25); and, Christ "gave Himself as a ransom for all" (1 Tim. 2:6).

That He might redeem us. *Redeem* ("*lutroo*") is the word that refers to giving a ransom, especially for the release of prisoners of war, slaves, and debtors. *Lutron* is the "price of release" for the liberation of a prisoner. Generally, the release is determined by law or the "right of the sovereign." (EDNT) Jesus actually gave Himself as the ransom price. He was willing to pay the debt of our sins before the sovereign God.

Christ made it clear to His disciples that "the Son of Man did not come to be served, but to serve, and to give His life a *ransom* for many" (Matt. 20:28; Mark 10:45). (Italics added) Peter also alludes to Isaiah 53 and adds that the Lord's *redemption* of us was not "with perishable things like silver or gold ... but with precious blood, as of a lamb unblemished and spotless, the blood of Christ" (1 Peter 1:18-19). The writer of Hebrews concludes that Christ "entered the holy place once for all, having obtained eternal redemption...who through the eternal Spirit offered Himself without blemish to God" (9:12, 14).

This verse is filled with a reflective and a middle voice reading. "He gave *Himself* (reflexive pronoun), ... that He might *Himself redeem* (middle voice) ... and purify for *Himself* (reflexive pronoun) a people for *His own posses-sion.*" *His won possession* is actually from one word, *periousios*, which is an unusual Greek compound word from *peri* ("*concerning, belonging to*") and *ousios*.

The entire word is a participle from the verb *perieimi* that is roughly translated "concerning what belongs to me." *His own possession* then is translated "*That which is one's own, belongs to one's possession.*" (Thayer) But the word, used only here in this verse in the New Testament, carries the force of "*chosen, elect.*" (EDNT) Or, "a selected people." (Lenski) "A people over and above, occupying a position separate and peculiar, like one's...spe-cial treasure." (Fairbairn) The redeemed then are Christ's special property, chosen and elect, and belonging to Him.

Purify for Himself. Jesus would not only redeem His own "*from every lawless deed,*" but He would *purify* this redeemed people. *Purify* is an aorist active subjunctive from the verb *katharizo*, that means "*to cleanse, make pure or whole*". The word is used as a subjunctive with the *hina* particle and reads as a result clause: "*that He might purify ...*" *Purify* is used figuratively by the apostle (2 Cor. 7:1; Eph. 5:26; also Heb. 9:14) of moral and religious cleansing "and therefore means 'cleanse or purify' from sin." (NIGTC) *Redeem* has to do with the removal of the Christians from the power or con-trol of sin.

Zealous of good deeds. *To be zealous* ("*zeloo*") means to have zeal, show a passionate commitment, in this case, for good works. This concept is strongly influenced and affected by Hellenistic piety and moral philos-ophy. (EDNT) The Jews are said to have a zeal for the law (Gal. 1:14). Paul mentions also the many thousands of Jews "who have believed, and they are all zealous for the Law" (Acts 21:20). Out of a gratitude for Christ, living out principles of truth and love, "and with a zeal for the glory of God, and the honor of his Gospel," believers need to emulate each other and strive to serve the Lord with the whole life and with all the ability that is within. (Gill) "Christ purifies His people with this very purpose in mind, namely, that it shall be a people for His own possession 'with a zest for noble deeds,' deeds which proceed from faith, are done according to God's law and unto His glory (cf. I Peter 3:13)." (Hendriksen)

Lenski summarizes the verse when he writes, "that Jesus 'ransomed us from all lawlessness,' i.e., paid the price to buy us free and take us away from all lawless living (ungodliness and worldly lusts, v. 12) 'and cleanse us for Himself as a people select, zealous for all excellent works.'"

2:15 These things speak and exhort and reprove with all authority. Let no one disregard you. *These things* ("*tauta*") refer to all the commands Paul has given in the verses above. He wants to make sure they are repeated over and over, with full reasoning power and conviction. The church is a body of Christians who have different problems and who do not mature at the same pace. As well, all believers do not face the same temptations or issues. Exhortation is a continuing process by the elder leadership.

Speak ("*laleo*," used as a present active imperative) is the most common word for simply *talking* or *telling*. Paul wants this to be an ongoing process that continually reminds the saints of what he has cautioned about. It might be translated, "*keep on telling*" them about what I said.

Exhort is the common word *parakaleo* that should probably be translated *counsel*. It is a favored word used by the apostle, and in its noun and verb forms, it is used nine times in the Pastorals (1 Tim. 1:3; 2:1; 4:13; 5:1; 6:2; 2 Tim. 4:2; Titus 1:9; 2:6, 15), and sixty-four times in his other letters. Here it is a present active imperative and may be translated, "*be continually advising ...*"

Reprove ("*elencho*," used as a present active imperative) is the strongest and most forceful of these three imperatives. It is often translated, "to rebuke, correct, censure, punish, convict." "It designates fatherly or divine correction and [even] punishment for the purpose of improvement." (EDNT) (See 1 Tim. 5:20; 2 Tim. 4:2; Titus 1:13). Many pastor/elders are reticent to correct those in the assembly who are wayward. They are pastors fearful of the sheep. They argue, that if they speak out, the immature sheep will seek other pastures. But the job of the elder is to pastor, and, to oversee what is happening with the flock. The elders must be prepared to stand up and reprove those who need it no matter what the consequences. This does not mean that they should embarrass someone who is morally or spiritually slipping. This can first be done in private. But so often, it must be done!

With all authority. *Authority* ("*epitage*") is a strong word that means "to command, give orders, direction." It is used of the orders given by authority from one in high rank. It is the word used when Christ forcibly and powerfully gave commands to the demons (Mark 1:27). It is used to describe the binding *"concrete instruction"* of Christ the messianic teacher (1 Cor. 7:6, 25). It is used to speak of Paul's apostolic authority (2 Cor. 8:8). That same force is used here for the authority given Titus. "Speak with unhesitating confidence in the truth!" "The minister is an ambassador of the great King he represents. The truth inspires him with power." (PHC) "Do these things 'in the most authoritative manner possible.'" (Nicoll)

Let no one disregard you. *Disregard* is a compound verb from *peri* (*"around, beyond"*) and *phroneo* (*"to think, consider"*). "Let no one *think around* you," or "Let no one *think beyond* you," in the sense of writing off your abilities, thoughts, or authority. In classical Greek the word can mean *"to be contemptuous, to defy, to despise."* (L&S) This verb is also used here as a present active imperative, as the previous three verbs above. "Be continually on guard not to let others write you off." "Let no one think around you (and so despise you). ... [it] implies the possibility of one making mental circles around one and so 'out-thinking' him." (Robertson) Those who have spent any time at all in the ministry know that there are some in the congregation who are always playing games. They plan and plot against the pastor. They are continually being contentious and bringing on strife. "There is jealousy and strife among you, are you not fleshly, and are you not walking like mere men?" (1 Cor. 3:3b). "Speak with decision, and rebuke and punish if need be with vigor, remembering the dark character of the people with whom you have to do." (Ellicott)

Conclusion

Paul ends the chapter with the command to teach in both doctrine and ethics. "These are your themes." "Titus is not to communicate them objectively and diffidently as if they were mere cold facts." (Stott) There must be heart and soul in what he says, and there must be godly and biblical reasons behind the commands he utters. It will be an awesome moment, when at the Bema, ministers will ask the Judge, "Did I lead them correctly?"

Chapter Three

More Practical Teaching Based
On Sound Doctrine

C. Demonstrating Sound Doctrine, 3:1-8

3:1 Remind them to be subject to rulers, and authorities, to be obedient, to be ready for every good deed. Though Christianity was new and radical, in that the converts did not give homage to the Roman gods, Paul still urges the believers not to rebel against the government, but instead be cooperative and obey the authorities. He even urged them to be helpful whenever possible. This would certainly be difficult in a pagan environment that could quite easily become hostile to the followers of Christ. The apostle's argument in these verses forms a link with chapter 2.

With these words "he turns to consider what the behavior and attitude of believers should be towards government and society in general." (Ritchie)

Because the Jewish people often revolted against first the Greeks and then the Romans, the apostle knew of the consequences that could fall upon the new faith. "From many passages it is evident that the Apostles had great difficulty in keeping the common people subject to the authority of magistrates and princes." (Calvin)

Remind them. *Remind* ("*hypomimnesko*," present active imperative) is a compound verb with *hypo* and *mimnesko*. The prefix *hypo* could be used in the sense of "*agency, cause.*" (EDNT) *mimnesko* means "*to remember, remind, recall.*" "To cause one to remember." (Wuest) The word could mean then, "*by way of reminding.*" Paul had written about these issues previously. He had addressed the issue in some detail in Romans 13:1-7. He adds in the 1 Timothy letter that he wants "prayers, petitions and thanksgivings, be made on behalf of all men, for kings and all who are in authority, so that we may lead a tranquil and quiet life in all godliness and dignity" (2:1-2).

It seems as if Paul's ultimate motive is that he wants no problems to surface that would hinder the Gentile population from coming to Christ. He earlier wrote that God "desires all men to be saved and to come to the knowledge of the truth" (v. 4). With the present imperative, he seems to want Titus to continually remind those under his charge of this responsibility to government leaders when possible.

The apostle Peter writes virtually the same thing as Paul. "Submit yourselves for the Lord's sake to every human institution, whether to a king as the one in authority, or to governors as sent by him .... For such is the will of God that by doing right you may silence the ignorance of foolish men.

Act as free men, and do not use your freedom as a covering for evil" (1 Pet. 2:13-16).

To be subject. ("*hypotasso*," present middle infinitive) Again, *hypotasso* is one of Paul's favorite words. (See 2:5, 9.) "Used here in the direct middle voice, 'to put one's self in subjection to or under the authority of' some person." (Wuest) With the present tense, the apostle is stressing the continual nature of this submission. Also, with the middle voice he makes this an issue of personal responsibility. But shortly, another factor will come into play. What if the Romans authorities require the Christians to worship the Emperor? Church history tells us this demand would come to pass soon. Then the issue of conscience and the worship of God alone will be put to the test. Daniel's three friends faced this issue (Dan. 3:1-30) when they refused to bow to Nebuchadnezzar's image, and said to him, "O king, ... we are not going to serve your gods or worship the golden image that you have set up" (v. 18). Following their miraculous deliverance from the furnace, Nebuchadnezzar blessed God, testified of the angelic rescue, testifying how the three had trusted the Lord, even still they had "yielded up their bodies so as not to serve or worship any god except their own God" (v. 28).

Though the Church will be raptured before the tribulation, there will be those who come to Christ in that horrible time. They will have to face the same decision about worshipping the image of the beast (Rev. 13:15-16). Martyrdom will carry many to glory during that period, such as the 144,000 who are "purchased from the earth ... and purchased from among men as first fruits to God and to the Lamb" (14:3-4).

To rulers, to authorities. *Rulers* ("*arch*") and *authorities* ("*exousia*," powerful, having *authority*). Since there is no conjunction *and* ("*kai*") between the words *rulers* and *authorities*, some grammarians believe this reads, "Principalities [rulers] which are authorities." (Vincent) The English word *arch* is related to *ruler*. "To be at the top of the heap!"

Authority refers to the one who wields the control, "the power exercised by rulers or others in high position by virtue of their office." (NIGTC) "Intended doubtless, to include all classes of governing powers, but without meaning, apparently, to denote by the one a lower, and by the other a higher grade." (Fairbairn) The apostle's reminder was very needful because of the seditious character of the Cretans. (Nicoll)

> The island had, when St. Paul wrote to Titus, been some century and a quarter under Roman rule. Their previous government had been democratic; and historians, like Polybius, who have written of Crete, have dwelt particularly on the turbulent and factious spirit which animated their people; added to which, the many Jews who we know formed a very large part

of the Christian Church there, always impatient of a foreign yoke, would in such an atmosphere of excitement be especially eager to assert their right to be free from the hated rule of Rome. (Ellicott)

To be obedient. *Obedient* ("*peitharcho*," present active infinitive) is a compound verb from *peitho* ("*to persuade, convince*") and *archeo* ("*to rule*"). "The idea of *magistrates* is contained in the word itself." (Vincent) Thus, "*to obey magistrates.*" In the New Testament this word is "used absolutely of the obedient behavior of believers ... in personal relationships and before God." (EDNT) "As your Cretan folk are naturally intractable, be careful to insist on obedience to the constituted authorities, and on the maintenance of friendly relations with non-Christians." (Nicoll) But as has been mentioned, this obedience cannot be absolute if it touches on spiritual, moral, or conscience issues. Too, there is the issue of freedom of speech and the witnessing of the objective facts relating to Jesus.

No government has the right to throttle what is true or what is spoken from the heart. This biblical principle was established by Peter and John as they were brought before the religious rulers in Jerusalem. They said to the Jewish Council "Whether it is right in the sight of God to give heed to you rather than to God, you be the judge; for we cannot stop speaking about what we have seen and heard" (Acts 4:19b-20).

To be prepared. Paul uses the simple "*to be*" verb *eimi* as a present infinitive. "To be continually" *able, prepared* ("*hetoimos*"). This word has a rich and wide range of meaning. It can mean "*equip, made available, stand ready.*" It is used of soldiers who are ready and eager to move into combat. It is used like here in 2 Timothy 2:21 with ethical and religious significance, "*ready*" for every good work" for the honor and glory of the Lord. It is used in a Messianic sense in Luke 1:17, "Making ready a "*prepared*" people through the task of bringing about repentance. This is in reference to the work of John the Baptist as predicted in Isaiah 40:3. It is used this way in the other Synoptics, the *preparation* of the way of the Lord. (BAG, EDNT)

For every good work. This phrase is in the singular, "*each good work.*" The context has to do with civil authorities and government, and the demand that may be placed on the citizens. Paul's point is that the Christian may be asked to carry out a specific task or job assigned by the leadership or governors of the town. No matter what the task, except if it is immoral, should be cheerfully executed. "Whenever the need presents itself—think of epidemics, wars, conflagrations, etc.—believers must be ready to show their good spirit, in thorough co-operation with the government which protects them." (Hendriksen)

3:2 To malign no one, to be peaceable, gentle, showing every

consideration for all men. The apostle continues his directives that Titus is to pass on to the churches on Crete. The believer in Christ must watch his attitudes and his words. He must never defame or slander anyone. He is never to utter anything false or color his words in any way that would do harm. He should never injure another or practice injustice. For any human being to do this in a perfect way, is a miracle. Human nature wants to strike out and put others down. Only one who is born again has the inner power to make positive conduct a part of his actions, his soul and spirit. Christians will live imperfectly, to be sure. But as they strive to do what is right, what a change will take place in society!

To malign no one. *Malign* is the Greek word *blasphemo*, "*to slander, wrongly accuse.*" As a present infinitive it could be translated, "Do not be going about *reviling, disparaging* another." "Do not be *denouncing, defaming.*" Paul knew it was so easy to talk about others. The human spirit often wants to put others down in order to lift up self. "We should not make the bad traits of [another's] character prominent, and pass over all that is good." (Barnes) (See also Col. 3:8; 1 Tim. 6:4)

To be peaceable, gentle. *Peaceable* is the Greek word *amachos* which is used only here and in 1 Timothy 3:3. It is a compound from the Greek negative *a* and *machos, to fight.* The verb in classical Greek, *machomai*, is translated *to be warlike, fight.* Originally, the word meant "invincible." (Robertson) The masculine noun *machimos* refers to a *warrior, one fit for battle.* (L&S) "Do not go around as one who is always *fighting.*" Be a nonfighter. (Lenski) Paul is not referring to warfare or defense of family and home. He is speaking about human behavior and personal relationships. The broad context may still touch on how to treat government leaders but it certainly refers also to neighbors and fellow citizens. *Gentle* is *epieikeia* and means *kind, forbearing, benevolent.* "1 Peter 2:18 demands of slaves not only to be submissive to the good and *gentle*, but also to the 'overbearing.'" (EDNT) This kind of person is humble, stands beside the poor, and is called a son of God. He is willing to be mistreated and scorned. Titus is to remind believers "to be conscientious and considerate citizens, because ... *we* were ourselves once anti-social, but *He* (God) saved and changed *Us*." (Stott)

Showing every consideration for all men. Showing ("endeiknymai," present middle participle [deponent]) can be translated "to prove, demonstrate." It is a compound from en ("within, by means of") and deiknymai ("to clarify, explain, unveil, reveal"), thus, "by means of demonstrating" or showing consideration ..." The Greek word prautes means consideration. The Christian cannot simply talk a good line, but has to reveal an attitude of genuine consideration for everyone. Is it possible to fake honest consideration? Certainly. In Greek secular life, consideration was often laughed at and seen as feigned, hypocritical and false concern for someone else, driven by self-interest. In the New Testament it must be genuine. (MacArthur)

When someone has sinned it is easy to judge them and to cast stones. The "religious" can then become judgmental and critical without thinking about their own weaknesses. Paul knew this when he wrote, "If anyone is caught in any trespass, you who are spiritual, restore such a one in a spirit of gentleness; each one looking to yourself, so that you too will not be tempted" (Gal. 6:1).

> The Christian spirit is forbearing and kindly, not urging its rights to the uttermost, lest by doing so it should stir up wrath and bitterness. Instead of indulging a passionate severity, it disarms opposition by meekly enduring wrong. ... If God is so kind and beneficent to all, we ought to be meek and gentile towards each other. (PHC)

3:3 For we also were once foolish ourselves, disobedient, deceived, enslaved to various lusts and pleasures spending our life in malice and envy, hateful, hating one another. Interestingly, the apostle includes himself in this emotional indictment. He too once lived like this, but God rescued him spiritually but also morally. He received inner peace and no longer had to pretend that he was sinless or a faithful law keeper. We often fail to see Paul in this light. It is a reminder of how even the most humanly righteous can be imperfect, but too, it shows the richness of the grace found in the Lord Jesus Christ, that one could be so transformed in the way the apostle Paul was.

Foolish (*anoetos*) is a rare word used only six times (Luke 24:25; Rom. 1:14; Gal. 3:1, 3; 1 Tim. 6:9; Titus 3:3). It means *to lack intelligence, to be foolish*. A related word, *anoia*, means *lacking understanding*, to have *foolishness* "expressed in unreasoning rage," or, to be filled with madness and folly (Luke 6:11; 2 tim. 3:9). Paul may be describing "one who is really out of it morally and spiritually; one who simply cannot get it together." The way he describes this here is how the world actually acts, unless the Holy Spirit takes over and brings conversion. Because of the Fall of Adam, human beings now have a darkened foolish heart (Rom. 1:21), and have become fools (v. 22). Without Christ people have depraved minds (v. 28), are filled with unrighteousness, evil, strife, deceit (v. 29), and are without understanding (v. 31a).

Disobedient (*apeithos*) is a compound word with the negative particle *a* and the word *peithos*, that means *convincing, persuasive*. It has also the idea *to trust, believe*. As a verb *apeitho* could mean *to mislead*, but probably also it may carry the idea *to be unconvinced about, to be unpersuaded*, or *to not* *fully trust, to not depend on. Disobedient* can certainly be the meaning here, and if so, it carries the thought of *rebellion*, or *to balk* at doing what is right. "Unwilling to be persuaded, contemptuous of God's will, spurning belief, hardened heart." (Ritchie) Wuest says they are *"impersuasible, uncompliant."*

Deceived (*"planao,"* *to mislead*). The word is a present passive participle implying that the lost could be continually fooled or seduced by lies and error. It could even be said they were misled by self-deception. "A life in the service of vice, typical of the existence of Gentiles, can be compared to the disoriented lives of those who have gone astray." (EDNT) "All who are estranged from God must therefore wander and go astray during their whole life." (Calvin)

Enslaved The word is *douleuo* meaning *to serve* or *work as a slave*. Here it is used as a present active participle. It is not used as a passive voice as if the slavery was coming upon them. Instead, the word is used in the active voice: "They are slaving away at *various* (*"poikilais"*) sins." They have *various ways* of practicing *lusts* (*"epithumiais"*) and *pleasures* (*"hadontias"*). These last two nouns are in the dative case. The entire participial clause could read: "They are the ones who are slaving away with all kinds of lusts and pleasures," or "They are the ones who are habitually serving in various ways lusts and pleasures." (See 2 Tim. 3:6) "The term here used for pleasures—pleasures, namely, of a groveling or sinful kind ..., the idea of doing service or being in bondage to such things." (Fairbairn) (See also Luke 8:14; James 4:1, 3; 2 Peter 2:13)

As unbelievers, our nature was once set only on sinning. "Although the unsaved, natural man willfully chooses to sin, he does so because his very constitution is sinful, and he has neither the desire nor the ability to be anything but sinful. He is therefore both willingly and inevitably *enslaved* to sin in its many and *various* forms." (MacArthur) Paul spells out this "total depravity" in many of his letters: "God gave them over in the lusts of their hearts" (Rom. 1:24); "God gave them over to degrading passions" (v. 26); "God gave them over to a depraved mind" (v. 28); "There is none who seeks for God; all have turned aside" (3:11b-12a).

Spending our life actually comes from one verb, *diago*, used here as a present active participle. This word can be used to describe drawing a straight line. From this, the word came to mean *to continue to stay in a certain state or path*. (L&S) Or, *to keep going in the same direction.*

The lost make no change of direction toward God. They stay in their sins and continue on in the same course. Lost people remain in the natural state unless touched by God (Eph. 4:31; Col. 3:8).

In malice and envy, hateful. *Malice* is the simple Greek word *kakos* with the basic meaning *evil*. *Envy* (*phthonos*) has the common meaning of *jealousy* (Rom. 1:29; Gal. 5:21, 26; 1 Tim. 6:4; 1 Pet. 2:1). Both words convey how the wicked of the world act. This was once characteristic of all believers before they came to Christ. How terrible for believers to continue practicing their sins along the line of a destructive course! But too often maturity comes slowly with Christians.

This is not what Paul wants to see happen in the lives of those born again. *Stygetos* (*hateful*) is used only here in the New Testament. It is a very emotional word that can be translated *detestable*. In classical Greek the word means *abhor*, with the added idea of expressing oneself with strong feelings of *abomination*. It means to show *hatred* not simply feel it. (L&S) Greek words that are related in form show the effect on the person who is hating. These words are translated "*to be sad, gloomy, sullen.*" One may be hateful just so long. The results will come forth in the personality. The word carries the thoughts of "*odious, fulsome, offensive, disgusting, repulsive. ...* The unconverted sinner by means of his attitude to God and man causes *loathing.*" (Hendriksen) For the unbeliever

> there was no brotherly love; no true affection for others. There was ill-will felt in the heart, and it was evinced in the life. This is an apt description of the state of the heathen world before the gospel shines on it, and it may be regarded as the characteristic of all men before conversion.... When a Christian is tempted to unkind thoughts or words towards others, nothing is more appropriate for him than to reflect on his own past life. (Barnes)

Hating one another. Here the apostle uses one of the most common Greek words for hate (*miseo*). He uses it as a present active participle. "The ones who are continually hating one another." This participial phrase is either used to describe the results of how those who are lost treat each other, or it is used to indicate the cause of all of the sins he has just listed before. A.T. Robertson believes it is in the "active sense and natural result of being 'hateful.'" Others agree. "'Hating one another' marks the climax in the active operation of mutual antagonisms that hasten the dissolution of the bonds of human society." (EBC) "It was our natural hatefulness which begot mutual hatred." (Alford) Whichever, the hate and wrath in the heart is powerful, boiling over "to a desire of revenge" against others. We all once lived with seething tensions between our neighbors.

Since we have been there, there should now be pity and sympathy for those still trapped in such sin. (Poole) The Lord desires to bring peace to the heart and soul of the child of God. He stated emphatically, "Peace I leave with you; My peace I give to you; not as the world gives do I give to you," (John 14:27). Paul added, "Now may the Lord of peace Himself continually grant you peace in every circumstance. The Lord be with you all!" (2 Thess. 3:16).

3:4 But when the kindness of God our Savior and His love for mankind appeared, ... With the *but* ("*hoti*") Paul sets forth a contrast from what the past life was like. God made a change in the believer's Position by "the washing of regeneration and renewing by the Holy Spirit" (v. 5). A new person and a new outlook will be created.

With this transformation, the apostle will urge the believer to "be careful to engage in good deeds" (v. 8) in contrast to what was practiced before. Christianity is both a belief and a walk; it teaches a new Position in Christ *and* a new Experience with Christ! It cannot simply be a dead belief system. All of this begins with the *kindness* ("*chrestotes*") or "essential goodness" of God. In this verse, "The contrast is startling. In verse 3 man is the actor, but in verses 4-7 man is ... the recipient, and God becomes the Actor." (BKC) He is the One who reaches out to His lost subjects. "How unsearchable are His judgments and unfathomable His ways!" (Rom. 11:33).

God our Savior. As already pointed out, this is a common statement by Paul and other apostles (1 Tim. 1:1; 2:3 4:10; Titus 1:3; 2:10, 13; 2 Pet. 1:1; Jude 25). In the New Testament it was first mentioned by Mary in Luke 1:47: "And my spirit has rejoiced in God my Savior." God is first called the Savior in Psalm 17:7, with twelve other references that say the same. On two occasions in the Old Testament, the Lord makes it clear "there is no savior besides Me" (Isa. 43:11; Hosea 13:4).

In 2:11 Paul seems to reach back into the Old Testament to confirm the work of God as Savior. "For the grace of God has appeared, bringing salvation to all men." This of course was the provision of salvation found only in the Lord Jesus. He is also our Savior!

Since God makes it clear that there is no Savior besides Him, to say Jesus was also a Savior would be a mistake, unless He is also God. This truth throws further light on the doctrine of the Trinity. Jesus is very God, and very Man!

And His love for mankind appeared *Love for mankind* is actually a compound Greek noun, *philanthropia*, from *phileo* ("*to love, befriend*") and *anthropos* ("*man, mankind*"). It is used here and in Acts 28:2 as a noun, and as an adverb in 27:3. In both places in Acts the thought is of showing *humankindness*. Because God cares for people, He sent His Son Jesus to die for the sins of humanity.

Calvinists who hold to "limited atonement" or "particular redemption" say that here in Titus 3:4 Paul is simply arguing that God simply sent His Son to die for human beings, but that hidden in the larger context, this means only for the elect who would be drawn from the human race. But many Calvinists realize that limited atonement is not what the Scriptures are teaching. The death of Christ would be sufficient for all, but none would of themselves come to the Lord. The elect would come, however, drawn by the work of the Holy Spirit.

When some scholars argue that the atonement was sufficient for all, many Calvinists think this smacks of universalism or the teaching of Arminianism. But this does not have to be so. The Bible seems clearly to teach that Christ's work at the cross was sufficient for all but applied only to the elect. There appears to be a semantic issue in which two sides are talking past each other.

There are verses, such as the 3:4 that are teaching the sufficiency of salvation for mankind. But there are also verses that are speaking to the issue of unconditional election and predestination. Without contradiction, both emphases are biblical. These passages indicate that Christ died for all: (2 Cor. 5:19; Col. 1:26-29; 1 Tim. 2:4, 6; 4:10; Titus 3:4; Heb. 2:9; 2 Pet. 2:1; 3:9; 1 John 2:2; 4:14)

Appeared. *Appeared* is an aorist passive indicative of *epiphano*. (See 2:11) The *epiphany* is the "*display the revelation, the manifestation*" of the grace of God in Christ. It is the "*shining of the light*" of God's love for His creatures. The word *ephiphano* is singular in number but it refers to both the Lord's *kindness* and His *philanthropia*. Both words are independent and have articles, but together they constitute the whole, the singular "*appeared*" or *epiphany*. The passage might read, "The *kindness* and the *mankindlove*, combined together and thus *appeared*."

The second *appearing* is when Jesus comes as King. Paul urges believers to be careful of how they walk "until the appearing of our Lord Jesus Christ" when He comes down to earth as the "only Sovereign, the King of kings and Lord of lords" (1 Tim. 6:14-15). "Not only has the saving grace of God appeared *unto all* (ch. ii. 11), but it has revealed itself as kindness and love to man as man." (Vincent)

3:5 He saved us, not on the basis of deeds which we have done in righteousness, but according to His mercy, by the washing of regeneration and renewing by the Holy Spirit. This is one of the most important and profound verses on the doctrine of salvation in all of Paul's letters. The verse is packed with important concepts that help us understand the nature of our redemption. In verse 4, the apostle tells us *why* God saved us, here he explains *how* He accomplished our regeneration.

He saved us. *Saved* is an aorist active indicative of *sozo*, meaning God "*rescued, delivered, spared*" us from judgment. The aorist tense makes this completed action. It is an effective aorist. (Robertson) What God set out to do, He effectively accomplished.

The salvation process is finished, completed, though there is the final redemption, either by the rapture or by death, the death of the believer. "The aorist tense of the verb, signify that this salvation has already taken

place and that it has delivered the Christians from what they were."
(NIGTC) "The aorist tense records the past saving act; we now possess his
salvation, although it is still incomplete, awaiting its consummation at
Christ's return." (EBC)

Not on the basis of deeds which we have done in righteousness. *On
the basis* is the preposition *ek*. Actually, "Not from the source (*ek*) of works,
specifically *the* [works] by means of [self] righteousness which we performed." "In His act of saving us God could not take and did not in any
way take into consideration any works that had been done by us." (Lenski)
Here in this passage, Paul is using righteousness ("*dikaiosyne*") in a broad
sense. Our righteousness in no way measures up to please the Lord. How
we evaluate righteousness is not even close to the standard He has. "The
order eliminates any thought of salvation due to personal merit and magni-
fies God's sovereign grace." (EBC) The *we* ("*hameis*") is emphatic, pointing
to the fact that *we* were helpless and totally unable to please God. "The
implication is: there were no such works. Neither Paul nor anyone else had
ever performed such a work, for before God and his holy law *all*—both Jews
and pagans—are by nature 'under sin' (Rom. 3:9)." (Hendriksen)

> No norm exists according to which a righteous judge, in par-
> ticular God, could declare us righteous; if any judge ever did
> such a thing he would thereby condemn himself as being
> unrighteous; his verdict would be false. In other words Paul
> says more than that we did not meet the righteous require-
> ments of any code of true moral law. We deserved utter con-
> demnation as being unrighteous in all our works. ... His act of
> saving us was *in toto* an act of mercy. (Lenski)

"The basis for our salvation is stated both negatively and positively.
Negatively, He saved us 'not by works (*ergon*) of righteousness (*dikaiosune*)
which we have done'. God could never deal with us on this principle since
all our works, apart from conversion, are unrighteous." (Ritchie) As Isaiah
writes, "all our righteous deeds are like a filthy garment; and all of us with-
er like a leaf, and our iniquities, like the wind, take us away" (Isa. 64:6).

But according to His mercy. In the Greek text, the passage reads: "*but
according to His mercy, He saved us.*" The *but* (*alla*) is contrastive. "Our
works could not save us *but* by His mercy ..." *his* is in the emphatic position. *Mercy* (*eleos*) is the pity of the Lord for His helpless and sinful creatures. There is nothing in us that can generate or cause the Lord to be *merciful*. Showing *mercy* is something He does because of who He is. He is all
merciful. This *mercy* is the basis of our salvation. "God has mercy and pities
our miserable condition and delivers us from it." (NIGTC) Which comes

first from the Lord, His love or His mercy? Ephesians 2:4 seems to indicate that His mercy, or pity, comes forth from His love. "God being rich in mercy, because of His great love with which He loved us." In this Ephesians passage the apostle goes on and writes that we are saved by grace through faith (v. 8), not as a result of works" (v. 9). He adds that this salvation is a gift of God (v. 8b).

By the washing of regeneration by the renewing of the Holy Spirit.
Washing (*loutron*). Both "Greek and Jewish usage also resonates with the sense of purificatory washings." (EDNT) One might expect *baptism* (*baptizo*), but *loutron* carries the stronger meaning of ritual or religious cleansing. Besides here in Titus, the word is used three other times in the New Testament (2 Cor. 11:2; Eph. 5:26, 27). The verb *louo* occurs five times in the New Testament in a purely nonreligious meaning. In classical Greek the word *louter* simply means a "place of bathing," and *loutron* can also mean the same but also the "water for bathing."

> In Titus 3:5 baptism is defined as the "washing (*loutron*) for the regeneration and renewal that the Spirit effects." Observe that it is not the washing that effects renewal. The washing is the occasion when the Spirit creatively works in the individual, just as he made the community of disciples the Body of Christ at Pentecost (Acts 2:33) and at the end will produce a new creation (Matt. 19:28).[24]

A better view is that this "ritual" *washing* does indeed bring about the renewal. This *washing* by the Holy Spirit accomplishes two things, both *regeneration* and *renewing*. "*By the Holy Spirit*" is actually a subjective genitive. (Robertson) Both words are governed by the one preposition *of* ("*dia*"). Notice that the washing is performed by the Holy Spirit and would then be a metaphor for spiritual cleansing not the actual application of physical water. Water in itself cannot create a new person as the words *regeneration* and *renewing* imply.

Regeneration (*palingennesia*) is a compound noun from *palin* (*again*) and *gennesia* (*generation, origins, birth*). *Renewing* is also a compound noun from *ana* (*up, again*) and *kainoseos* (*new*). Thus, making new again, a renewing, renovation. (Barnes)

Paul is saying that the Holy Spirit spiritually cleanses in the salvation process by "*again birthing* and *again newing* the child of God. Wuest argues that the first has to do with the cleansing of the sinner by the blood of Christ and the second has to do with the cleansing for the daily walk. Or, the first effects justification and the second sanctification. However, it is not impossible that the grammar allows for the two words to be synonymous,

"The washing of regeneration *that is* the renewing by the Holy Spirit." "Both 'rebirth' and 'renewal' may be regarded as dependent on 'washing' to form one concept. Then the washing of rebirth is further described as a renewal wrought by the Spirit." (EBC)

"The washing referred to is wholly spiritual. It is that of *regeneration and renewing*, regarded as one concept." (Hendriksen) But not all commentators agree. Ellicott translates it "the laver of regeneration but also of renovation by the Holy Spirit." In some ways, it may not matter. The picture seems to be clear that the Holy Spirit is doing a new inner work to bring about salvation. "Here 'washing' means 'laver' ..., but a closer consideration of the word confirms that it refers to the act of washing rather than to the water in which the bath is taken." (Ritchie)

Jesus refers to this when He told Nicodemus "unless one is born again he cannot see the kingdom of God" (John 3:3). Further in the conversation with this man, the Lord made it clear that the washing of water was the work of the Spirit (v. 5). This verse should read, "unless one is born of water, EVEN the Spirit, he cannot enter into the kingdom of God." Later in the book of John, Christ emphasized the washing of the Spirit again. The one who believes in Him, "'From his innermost being will flow rivers of living water.' But this He spoke of the Spirit, whom those who believed in Him were to receive; for the Spirit was not yet given, because Jesus was not yet glorified" (7:38-39a).

This laver washing by the Holy Spirit was promised in the New Covenant. The New Covenant was first prophesied for Israel in Jeremiah 31:31 and would be a covenant that would replace the Mosaic Law Covenant (vv. 32-37). It would provide a washing (Ezek. 36:25) and a new heart and a new spirit within (v. 26), which would probably be the Holy Spirit of God (v. 27). Like a new birth, God's Spirit placed within would bring the Jewish people alive spiritually (37:14).

The sacrifice of Christ would ratify this New Covenant. At the last supper with His disciples, the Lord said "This cup which is poured out for you is the new covenant in My blood" (Luke 22:20). Though this New Covenant was predicted first for Israel, the church now benefits from it. Now believers in Christ have been "made ... adequate as servants of a new covenant, not of the letter but of the Spirit; for the letter kills, but the Spirit gives life" (2 Cor. 3:6). And, all believers have been placed into the spiritual body of Christ, by which we are washed and through which we are given spiritual gifts (1 Cor. 12:12-13).

3:6 Whom He poured out upon us richly through Jesus Christ our Savior. *Whom* (*ou*) is the relative pronoun that is both masculine and neuter (genitive case, singular), and can be translated masculine (*whom*) or neuter (*which*). The pronoun references back to the Spirit that just happens to be a neuter word in Greek. But the deity and personality of the Holy Spirit is so well established in the Bible that *ou* is correctly translated here as a masculine *whom*.

He poured out is from *ekcheo* (aorist active indicative) and means to "pour out like water, to stream forth." (L&S) Paul is describing the giving forth of the Holy Spirit who is the agent of the new birth, regeneration and renewal. It is possible that the apostle has in mind the launching of the New Covenant and the coming of the Spirit at Pentecost (Acts 2). The use of the aorist tense shows that Paul is thinking about that event. (Nicoll) In Acts Luke says the believing disciples were "all filled with the Holy Spirit" at that time (v. 4), but also, he writes that Peter quoted Joel 2:28-30 where the Lord said "I will pour forth of My Spirit upon all mankind" (Acts 2:17). *Pour forth* here is also *ekcheo*. The disciples were filled (or controlled) by the Holy Spirit, but later Peter adds they were also baptized by the same Spirit (11:15-17).

The filling and baptizing work of the Spirit are not the same functions. The baptismal work of the Spirit places the believer into the spiritual body of Christ. Though the disciples were "saved" in Old Testament terminology, they had not been placed into the union with the risen Christ, which would be a particular work in the dispensation of the Church. For the disciples of Jesus, and other disciples (19:1-6), this work of Spirit baptism came long after they had given their lives to God. Acts is recording the time of the transition in which the Lord was establishing the new personal relationship.

Now believers in Christ are placed into the spiritual body of Christ at the point of belief (1 Cor. 12:12-18), and there is no delay in this work nor in the receiving of the Holy Spirit. "The language intentionally conjures up images of the day of Pentecost (cf. Acts 2:17). God's purpose in pouring out the Holy Spirit was *so that, having been justified by His grace*, believers *might become heirs having the hope of eternal life*." (BKC)

Richly is the Greek word *plousios* and means *abundantly, fully, without restriction, without reservation*. There is no holding back the work of the Holy Spirit with the believer. The child of God receives the *immeasurable* and *unlimited* involvement of the grace of the Spirit. Spiritually speaking, the Spirit makes believers *wealthy* by His activities in their lives. "'Richly' means in abundant measure so as to effect the results that God, our Savior, desires." (Lenski) The Spirit "is represented, not simply as given, but as poured out,—nay, poured out richly, in order to convey some idea of the plenteous beneficence of the gift. This rich bestowal is peculiar to New Testament times; and here, as elsewhere, it is expressly connected with the mediation of Christ, who as Savior has opened the way for it, and Himself sends forth the Spirit as the fruit of His work on earth." (Fairbairn)

By adding the fact that the Spirit was poured out *upon us* (*"epi hamas"*), indicates that the "immediate reference is to the experience of St. Paul and other Christians" then and even now. (Nicoll) There was an outpouring at Pentecost but there is a continual giving of the Spirit to our own present generation of Christians, at the immediate moment of accepting Jesus as Savior.

> The sense is, that the Holy Spirit had been imparted richly to ALL who were converted, at any time or place, from the error of their ways. What the apostle says here is true of all who become Christians, and can be applied to all who become believers in any age or land. (Barnes)

Through Jesus Christ our Lord. *Through* (*"dia"*) implies *by means of*, or *through the agency of*. The apostle has written "with reference to the kindness of God in saving us and imparting to us his *enabling* Spirit: *which* (or *whom*, namely, this Spirit) *He* (namely, God the Father) *poured out upon us richly through Jesus Christ our Savior*. Note how in this passage God the Father, God the Spirit, and God the Son are beautifully combined." (Hendriksen)

3:7 So that being justified by His grace we would be made heirs according to the hope of eternal life. This verse seems to tie back to the "kindness of God" (v. 4) who "saved us" (v. 5). "His mercy" tells us on what basis He saved us, and the work of the Holy Spirit tells us what means He employed. Now here in verse 7 Paul puts it all together.

Being justified (*dikaio*) is used here as an aorist passive participle. This is the only place in the Pastoral epistles that Paul writes of justification of the believer. He uses the word in 1 Timothy 3:16 to describe how the Spirit *justified* the life of Christ. But the NASB rightly translates the word as *vindication* in that context. In His witness, the Lord Jesus "was *vindicated* in the Spirit." *Being justified* means that we were "declared righteous" or "legally acquitted" before the bar of justice of the all holy God. What an awesome sight! The aorist tense indicates that this is a completed transaction. The passive voice shows that the Lord imputed this justification to us. The participle points out the fact that we are seen now in this justified state.

In a sense, we were declared by Him as sinful, unrighteous, and enemies. But now, because of the work of Christ on the cross, we are set free and given the righteousness of Jesus applied to our account. We were given "even the righteousness of God through faith in Jesus Christ for all those who believe; ... being justified as a gift by His grace through the redemption which is in Christ Jesus" (Rom. 3:22, 24). And, Paul adds, "But to the one who does not work, but believes in Him who justifies the ungodly, his faith is reckoned as righteousness" (4:5).

By His grace. The word *grace* ("*charis*") was used as a common greeting, such as in 1:4: "Grace and peace from God the Father and Christ Jesus our Savior." But there is also the doctrine of *grace* by which we are saved and even blessed on a continuing basis. The Lord saved us according "to His own purpose and grace which was granted us in Christ Jesus from all eternity" (2 Tim. 1:9). In the Pastorals Paul writes of that saving *grace* that originates from God the Father (1 Tim. 1:14; Titus 2:11; 3:7).

Though it is true that "The grace by which man is justified is usually spoken of as that of God the Father" (Nicoll), this is not always the case. Saving *grace* as well comes from the Lord Jesus (Gal. 1:6): God "who called you by the grace of Christ." He also refers to the *grace* for living that comes from Christ (2 Tim. 2:1). "God in grace and at infinite cost procured our justification and by the same grace bestowed it upon us. We as believers are not only God's *chosen one's*, 'God's elect' (1:1) and God's *clean one's*, 'the pure' (1:15), but also God's *cleared one's*, 'being justified'." (Ritchie)

We would be made heirs. After being saved we are not left to our own devices. *We would be made* is the aorist active (deponent) subjunctive of *ginomai*, that means "to become" in the sense of receiving a new status. *Ginomai* is related to the verb *gennao* that means "*To beget, give birth, bring forth.*" (EDNT) "We have been birthed as the children of God and as such we are now His heirs." However, the way the subjunctive is translated, it sounds as if we had not attained yet to our new position. It sounds as if "we might become heirs," as if reaching this new level was only a potentiality or possibility. But this is not so. "We regard the aorist as ingressive: 'we got to be.' Once getting to be such heirs means that we remain what we got to be." (Lenski)

Heirs comes from the compound noun *kleronomos*, from *kler* ("lot, share, portion") and *nomos* ("law") used as "to declared legally." An *heir* is one who is rightfully and legally declared to receive an inheritance. Being made an heir is one of Paul's favorite ideas. (Vincent) Elsewhere Paul writes of the guarantee or "earnest of our inheritance" (Eph. 1:14) and of "the riches of the glory of His inheritance in the saints" (v. 18). This inheritance is an eternal promise (Heb. 9:15), it is incorruptible (1 Pet. 1:4), it is not the results of law keeping (Gal. 3:18), but it is described as a reward, not yet earned, but given as a gift from the Lord (Col. 3:24).

According to the hope of eternal life. The apostle has shown how by the new birth and regeneration we become the children and sons of God. Thus we are made *heirs* even by spiritual birth (John 3:8). Yet *heirs* have not enjoyed their inheritance. It is not yet paid out to them. "Paul therefore says: 'We got to be heirs in accord with eternal life's hope.'" (Lenski) The preposition *kata* (*according*) "says that what we got to be is 'in accord' with this hope. The genitive is objective: hope 'for life eternal.'" (Lenski) *Hope* (*elpis*) better carries the thought of *anticipation*. We know these things are true and we are not simply speculating or wishing that eternal life were real. We are absolutely certain and yet we must wait until God opens the door of eternity to us.

> Our salvation is as yet hidden; and therefore he now says that we are heirs of life, not because we have arrived at the present possession of it, but because hope brings to us full and complete certainty of it. (Calvin)

3:8 This is a trustworthy statement; and concerning these things I want you to speak confidently, so that those who are believing God will be careful to engage in good deeds. These things are good and profitable for men. Titus is here urged to speak out boldly in order to fortify the believers in Christ so that they would produce fruit that would result in blessing to others. Paul's expression *this is a trustworthy statement* simply reads in Greek *faithful the word* ("*pistos ho logos*"), or, "what I am saying is dependable, reliable."

Concerning these things. All the apostle has said ("*concerning these things*"), he desires Titus to repeat and continue in regard to the Cretans. He wishes *those who have believed* what God has said, would then live a spiritually productive life. *Good works* ("*kalon ergon*") must follow the proclamation and declaration that the Christians say they hold to. They cannot live as hypocrites. In God's mysterious providence, He has ordained *good works*. We are "created in Christ Jesus *for* good works, which God prepared beforehand so that we would walk in them" (Eph. 2:10). (Italics mine)

I want you to speak confidently. *Speak confidently* is the compound verb *diabebaioomai* from *dia* ("through, thoroughly") and the present active (deponent) infinitive of *bebaioomai*. The compound verb means "to assert strongly, establish, strengthen, confirm." By the present tense Paul wants them "to be constantly and strongly asserting" these principles to the Cretan churches. "*constantly*, not *continually*, but *uniformly* and *consistently*." (Vincent)

Those who have believed. *Believed* ("*pistuo*") is a perfect active participle. Paul is saying, "I want you to strongly confirm those who believed in the past and are now existing in that belief." They have a problem, however. They need to:

Engage in good deeds. *Engage* ("*phrontizo*") is only used here in the New Testament and it means to "*be concerned, be worried, take care*" to apply themselves to good deeds. (EDNT) With the present active subjunctive the apostle is saying that they should now begin that process, with no delay.

Phrontizo is a strong word that says they are to throw themselves into this activity. The lost on Crete has heard their proclamation of Christ, but they have also observed their hypocrisy and inconsistency in their living.

> *Phrontizo* denotes the application of earnest and continued thought, a careful striving of soul in this direction, that the belief in the doctrines of the gospel should be substantiated by a steady performance of its commanded duties. (Fairbairn)

The issue of *good deeds* requires some thought. While Paul focuses on justification by faith (Rom. 3:28), the apostle James was concerned about the practical Christian walk and the evidence of faith by good works (James 2). Paul points out that, positionally and in regard to salvation, we are not saved by good works. Being justified by faith, he writes, human boasting is excluded and believers are delivered by the "law" of faith (Rom. 3:27). The apostle then adds, "We maintain that a man is justified by faith apart from works of the Law" (v. 28).

Reading James carefully we see that there is no conflict with Paul. James is discussing in chapter 2 "justification by works" as it benefits others. He describes a hypothetical case, "if a man comes into your assembly with a gold ring ..." (James 2:2). He points out the prejudice one might show to the poor man in dirty clothes in contrast to the rich man. He argues against showing partiality (v. 9) and of breaking even one law that would destroy the whole law (v. 10). James then asks, "What use is it" if one says he has faith but no works? (v. 14). *What use is it* (*ti to ophelos*) is used in verses 14 and 16. *Ophelos* should be translated *profit* meaning "what *furtherance, help, advantage*" (L&S) if one makes claims of salvation but shows no sign of it in helping others. In verse 14 the apostle James writes "Can faith save him?" It may be that James is referring to the one in trouble or in need. Can our faith by itself warm that one without clothes (v. 15) or feed the hungry person (v. 16)? Not unless something comes forth from the one declaring his faith. James seems to tie up his argument with, "You have faith and I have works; show me your faith without the works, and I will show you my faith *by my works*" (v. 18). (Italics mine)

These things are good and profitable for men. The reference is to the *good deeds*. They substantiate the care the Lord has for others, but they also show that the love of Christ is being expressed through the giving and charity of the believers. One can imagine that the Cretans had some time to make up.

After the evangelism on the island, the small assemblies seemed to have floundered in carnality and lack of leadership. This is why Titus is returning and commissioned by Paul with a very difficult task, that is, to mature the churches so that they may become beacons of Christ and so that they may be a blessing to the lost. Without being profound, he says in a very simple way that these *works* are just *good* ("*kala*"). He could not get anymore basic than that! But he also adds *profitable*!

Profitable (*ophelimos*) is only used by Paul in the Pastoral letters. It is used twice in 1 Timothy 4:8: "Bodily training is *useful* only for some things, while godliness is *of value* in every way." (EDNT) And in 2 Timothy 3:16 the apostle says the Scriptures are "*useful/ profitable* for teaching." (EDNT) By simply saying *for men* he must not only have in mind the members in the churches but also the lost.

> These good works are for the believers themselves and, even more significantly as far as the emphasis of this passage is concerned, for the unsaved sinners around them who are drawn to Christ by the exemplary lives of those He has graciously transformed. (MacArthur)

D. Avoiding Those Who Oppose Sound Doctrine, 3:9-11

In this paragraph Paul does not want Titus to become embroiled in wrangling and arguing about Judaistic beliefs and issues over the Law. He warns Titus that he will have to face factious and perverted men who have evil intentions. He could be snared in verbal debates with some of the Jews who despise the simple gospel that in their minds subverts the requirements of Moses. There always seems to be around those who wish to destroy and who cannot stand deep but plain truth. These are the false teachers he had written about earlier (1:10-16).

3:9 But avoid foolish controversies and genealogies and strife and disputes about the law, for they are unprofitable and worthless. With the particle *de* (*but*) Paul "contrast this statement and its contents with what immediately precedes." (NIGTC) The word *avoid* is the present middle imperative of the compound verb *peritstemi*, with the preposition *peri* (*around*) *and histemi* (*to stand,* place) With the middle voice it means "*to turn around, to turn away from,* or *to avoid.*" (EDNT) This "verb that has within its basic meaning the concept of 'around' and which in the middle means 'go around so as to avoid,' and more succinctly 'avoid, shun.'" (NIGTC) "Do not get yourself trapped in their arguments but turn away from them." (See 2 Tim. 2:16, 2:23)

Foolish controversies (*moras zetesis*) may also here be translated as *foolish investigations*, but possibly the thought is *stupid discussions*. Paul deals with the same problem in 1 Timothy 6:4 and 2 Timothy 2:3. In 2 Timothy 6:4, Timothy is encouraged by the apostle to not get trapped in senseless and "unnecessary investigations." Here in Titus the thought probably means *dumb* and *senseless debates*.

Genealogies and strife and disputes. Paul adds *genealogies* and *strife* and *disputes* concerning the Law. All three words may refer to the heated discussions over the Law, the Pentateuch of Moses. *Strife* (*eris*) and *disputes* (*mache*) are both intense and strong words. *Eris* means "*quarrel*," and *mache* is *battle* and comes from the word *machaira* which means a sword. The apostle is describing an all out assault and war that is instigated by the Jewish extremists on Crete. They will do and say anything to destroy the message of the gospel. The apostle wrote more in detail about this problem when he told Timothy not "to pay attention to myths and endless genealogies, which give rise to mere speculation rather than furthering the administration of God which is by faith" (1 Tim. 1:4).

Here in his letter to Titus, Paul adds that such arguments "*are unprofitable and worthless*". Unprofitable (*anopheles*) is used only here and in Hebrews 7:18 and means "*useless, unsuitable.*" Worthless (*mataois*) can be translated "*vain, futile.*" The apostle is not mincing words. He is using emotional descriptives to paint a picture of the subversion attempted by some in the Jewish community. Those bringing on such opposition were probably highly intelligent and learned scholars who hoped to destroy the message of Christ.

These men "disturb and embitter the feelings; they lead to the indulgence of a bad spirit; they are often difficult to be settled, and are of no practical importance if they could be determined." (Barnes) What kind of arguments were being set forth in their defense of Judaism over Christianity? No one can say for certain but H. D. M. Spence writing in Ellicott's Commentary (8:178-79) seems to have the most plausible and possible answers:

While Timothy remained at Ephesus, Paul urged him while away in Macedonia, to stop certain men "not to teach 'strange doctrines' or 'heretical beliefs'" (1 Tim. 1:3-11). These were probably mythical legends added to Old Testament history, Judaistic false ideas that were leading to Gnosticism. In the Jewish schools some were teaching that an oral Law had been given at Sinai from the time of Moses and handed down. This "Law was upon the lip" and was a supplement to the written Word. Supposedly, this code was preserved by memory or on a secret roll and taught orally. These works were committed to writing by rabbi Jehuda in the second century under the name of the Mishna, or repetition of the Law. The Mishna and the Gemara, with a second Gemara was finished in Babylon around the fifth century A.D. Altogether, these works were known as the Talmud.

The reference to genealogies is probably a reference to the recorded names in Numbers, and to which wild allegorical interpretations had been assigned. Such fanciful meanings had already been assigned by Philo, whose religious writings were becoming at this time known and popular in many Jewish schools. Paul wished to put a stop to this influence. He saw it as separating the Jewish and Gentile converts in the churches. A life and death struggle seems to have developed between the apostle, the other apostles, and the Rabbinical schools. Paul felt if these heresies entered the teaching going on in the churches, the truth would be diminished and the congregations would shrink to narrow Jewish sects promoting unbiblical and incomplete Judaism. This is why he wrote that such teachings were *worthless*.

Gill adds that the doctrinal struggle within Judaism raged between the schools of Hillell and Shammai

> which occasioned great contentions and quarrels between the followers of the one, and of the other, as both the Misnah and Talmud show: ... the Syriac version renders it, *the contentions and strife's of the scribes*; the Jewish doctors, who were some on the side of Hillell, and others on the side of Shammai.

3:10 Reject a factious man after first and second warning. *Reject* is a present active (deponent) imperative from *paraiteomai* that means "*to reject, avoid, refuse.*" The prefix *para* "gives a nuance of aversion or repudiation." (EDNT) *Factious* is the Greek word *hairetikos* from which we get *heretic*. The word comes from *haireo*, meaning "to take, to take for one's self, to choose, prefer." "The noun means, 'fitted or able to take or choose, schismatic, factious.' A heretic is one therefore who refuses to accept true doctrine as it is revealed in the Bible, and prefers to choose for himself what he is to believe." (Wuest)

The warning (*nouthesia*) is actually an *admonition*, an *exhortation*. *Nouthesia* is related to the Greek word *mind*, thus, "strongly place in their minds that what they are saying is wrong and rejected."

> A heretic is a man ... self-willed, and contending for his own theories, though they are opposed and contradictory to the universally received doctrines. ... if he refuses to be advised and continues recalcitrant, leave him to himself— have nothing more to do with him, either in admonition or intercourse. (PHC)

By **first and second** warning, Paul is urging that the man be given a chance to change his mind and to think over his false teachings. But then if he continues, he must be rejected. Paul is placing before young pastors, such as Titus, the directive that they should act with firmness and authority. Some pastors cower down when being challenged doctrinally. They are afraid of the sheep. Possibly they are trying to avoid being a bully to the congregation, but there is a time when those who are wrong must be silenced.

3:11 Knowing that such a man is perverted and is sinning, being self-condemned.. By writing *knowing (oida,* perfect active participle) Paul is indicating that he, and maybe even Titus, have come to an understanding about such men. The perfect participle would point to the fact that they progressively came to a point of realizing what these men were really like. The language throughout this verse is extremely strong. (Fairbairn)

Perverted (*ekstrepho,* perfect passive indicative) is a graphic word from *ek* meaning *out* and *strepho* meaning "to turn, turn around." It can mean "to turn outward, to turn inside out." The word is used only here in the New Testament and has the force of "to twist, to pervert." (Robertson) With the perfect tense, the apostle may also be indicating the fact that these men progressively learned to act this way. The word "signifies to turn out of, ... the proper way or course; and when used, as here, in the passive of one who, notwithstanding even a second admonition, persists in following his self-willed line of action." (Fairbairn) The thought is more than simply to turn away from the right path, it means to be turned inside out. (Vincent) The word "denotes a complete inward corruption and perverseness of character." (Ellicott) "Argument with a man whose basal mental convictions differ from your own, or whose mind has had a twist, is mere waste of breath." (Nicoll)

Is sinning (*hamartano,* present active indicative) is the simple word for such an activity. Being in the present tense, Paul pictures such a person as presently so altered spiritually, that he is now simply going about continually practicing his evil.

Being self-condemned ("*autokatakritos*") is actually three Greek words put together from *auto* ("self"), *kata* ("against"), and *kritos* ("judged"). The meaning is to bring judgment against yourself. Your actions are then self-condemning. "The factious person, who is twisted by his constant sinning, will manifest his wicked condition by his own words and actions, therefore by becoming self-condemned." (MacArthur)

> His own course, in attempting a division or schisms in the church, shows him that it is right that he should be separated from the communion of Christians. He that attempts to rend the church, without a good reason, should himself be separated from it. (Barnes)

V. Paul's Salutation, 3:12-15

Paul's final words are to the point and without much elaboration. He reveals very little of his final plans, though he mentions four fellow disciples who are part of his support in the service of Christ. As he closes this letter, he is more than likely somewhere in Macedonia. Whether this is Philippi or not is uncertain. It is fairly certain he is not in Nicopolis since he writes in verse 12 that he plans to winter *there.* However, it is clear that he wishes to spend the colder months with Titus. Nicopolis was probably chosen because it was the most famous of what is called the "Victory Cities." The metropolis was so named because of the victory of Augustus over Antony in the fall of 31 BC. Augustus was encamped on the northern promontory and Antony on the southern. The decisive battle was actually fought at sea.

Verse 12 is the only New Testament reference to Nicopolis, though from this one mention, many scholars believe that the apostle planned to use it as a center for further evangelism. The city was actually a center for the west coast of Acarnania and Epirus. Though there were two other cities named Nicopolis, one in the region of Cilicia and one in the area of Thrace, this one near the area of Epirus is the one most likely in view. This key center would have been perfect for reaching the entire western region of this part of larger territory know as Achaea. The circumstances by which Paul resolved to go to Nicopolis, and his reason for communicating this to Titus, is unknown. It is even more unclear whether he actually made it to the city.

From Rome, sometime later, Paul wrote to Timothy that he had recently gone through Miletus and Corinth (2 Tim. 4:20). It is possible that he would have passed through Corinth to Nicopolis. Some conjecture that he actually reached that city, and that he was arrested there while carrying out his witness. From there, some argue, he was arrested and sent to Rome.

3:12 When I send Artemas or Tychicus to you, make every effort to come to me at Nicopolis, for I have decided to spend the winter there. Little is known about *Artemas,* who is mentioned in Church history and tradition as the bishop of the city of Lystra. The name seems to be a shortened form of Artemidoros, meaning "a gift of Artemis." It is possible, because of this designation, his parents worshipped the Greek goddess Artemis who was the protector of both humans and animals. Here in this verse, it appears as if Paul is planning on both Artemas and Tychicus to take the place of Titus on the island of Crete.

Tychicus is well known as a companion and helper to the apostle Paul, and is mentioned in Acts 20:4; Ephesians 6:21-on; Colossians 4:7; and 2 Timothy 4:2. Tychicus, whose name means *fortunate,* originally resided in Asia Minor (Acts 20:4). As a loyal worker, he traveled with the apostle on his third missionary journey. Along with Onesimus, he carried the apostle's letter to the church at Colosse (Col. 4:7-9) and related to the believers there the personal condition of this great servant of the Lord. Paul also sent Tychicus to Ephesus on at least one occasion and possibly to Crete on another. Church tradition says that he died a martyr's death.

Make every effort to come to me. *Make effort* is the verb *spoudazo* (aorist, active, imperative) means *"to make haste, make every effort."* With the aorist tense, Paul would seem to be giving this some sense of urgency. The apostle probably understood that his world was closing in on him. He knew his time was short and he wanted to see Titus one more time. Both men coming to Nicopolis would have to travel about the same distance. This city was an ideal location and suitable meeting-place.

I have decided to spend the winter there. Because the winters could be harsh, Nicopolis provided a little warmer weather from the cold blowing down from the north. Since Paul did not know how much longer he could minister, he may have planned for Titus to launch from here further west, say to Spain, with the gospel. "It seems probable that Titus actually reached Nicopolis, and performed some evangelistic work in Dalmatia, to which he returned at a later time." (Hendriksen)

3:13 Diligently help Zenas the lawyer and Apollos on their way so that nothing is lacking for them. *Diligently* is the adverb *spoudaios* that is related to the verb *spoudazo* used in verse 12. *Spoudaios* is translated *hurriedly, eagerly, earnestly.* (EDNT) Though not brought out in this verse, it is as if Paul senses the storm clouds on the horizon. He seems concerned about his fellow workers as if the task before him must be finished quickly.

Help is from the verb *propempo* (aorist active imperative), a compound of *pro* (*before*) and *pempo* (*to send, equip*). The word is translated *"to send forth, out* as one equipped for a journey." (EDNT) Paul wishes that these two men be thoroughly supplied with all they need for the task before them. The aorist tense and the imperative mood of command may well indicate the sense of urgency the apostle has in mind. The first of this verse may carry the thought, "quickly and hurriedly equip these men and send them on their way."

Zenas the lawyer is only mentioned here in the New Testament. His name seems to be a contraction of Zenodorus. Some feel the term *lawyer* ("*nomikos*") indicates he was a Jew who was learned in the Old Testament law. But more than likely his Greek name indicates he was a jurist in the Roman courts. The Latin terms would be *juris consultus* or *jurisperitus.* Hyppolytus cites a tradition that he was a member of the Lord's seventy disciples, and later became the bishop of the city of Diospolis.

Apollos is better known in the New Testament. His name means *destroyer.* Apollos was an Alexandrian Jew who came to Ephesus after Paul's first visit. He was taught by Priscilla and Aquila. Well educated in the Old Testament Scriptures, he was a forceful speaker, though he needed to better understand the new revelation of Christian doctrine. He is mentioned in Acts 18-19; 1 Corinthians 1:12; 3:4-6, 22; 4:6; and 16:12. He greatly strengthened the believing brothers by using the Word of God to demonstrate that Jesus was the Messiah (Acts 18:28). Though no one can say for certain, he may have been the author of the book of Hebrews. A disciple of John the Baptist, he later became the close friend of the apostle Paul. Had he chosen, he might

> have rivaled or even superseded St. Paul in his supreme authority over the churches planted along the Mediterranean sea-board. But Apollos seems resolutely to have declined any such rivalry, and to have lived ever as the loyal and devoted friend of the great Apostle; who, however, always seems to have treated the learned and eloquent Alexandrian as an equal power in the Church of Christ. (Ellicott)

So that nothing is lacking. These men were to be expedited and outfitted for a journey. This implies that they were to be supplied clothing, money, and baggage. We cannot assume these men were with Titus now, for Paul would then have sent them salutations and would have stated whither they were to travel. "They were with Paul, had received their directions from him, and carried this letter to Titus who was to help in sending them on. We have no means of knowing their ultimate destination, not even whether both were bound for the same place." (Lenski)

3:14 Our people must also learn to engage in good deeds to meet pressing needs, so that they will not be unfruitful. At first glance one may think that Paul has begun a new subject and simply pulled these thoughts out of thin air. But the fact that his companions in the ministry were to be helped along and be lacking in nothing, must have triggered his thinking in regard to the activities of all the believers in Christ, as to their service of good deeds in supporting the gospel ministry and those who were traveling about doing missionary work. In no way is Christianity to be a passive faith. It would change the world by the passion for helping others. The support and care among believers, though never lived out in perfect form, would mark in a distinctive way those who love Jesus.

Our people ("*hemeteros,*" plural, masculine) is an unusual and rare possessive pronoun that simply means *ours* but with the expanded though, "*those who belong to us.*" It is adequately translated *our people* but the thought really conveys closeness, relationship, and intimacy. The apostle adds *also (kai)* or *ours also.* Though he has the Cretans in mind, by the "also" the command is applicable for believers everywhere. "If Titus was not to forget fellow-laborers, how incumbent it was upon the saints generally. The whole weight was not to fall alone upon the shoulders of Titus; others were to share the responsibility. Too often the practical side of the work of the assembly is left to a minority." (Ritchie)

Must learn is the very unusual Greek verb *manthano* (present active imperative) that means *"to learn by doing, by practice."* The apostle is saying, "Our own must learn how to perform good deeds by continually doing them." "The thought is that of learning by use and practice, to acquire the habit of ... This injunction needs to be heeded in a day when believers give so much of their time and energies to their own things and seem indifferent not only to lost sinners, but also to needy saints." (Ritchie)

To engage *("proistemi,"* present middle infinitive) is a compound verb from *pro (before)* and *histemi (to stand, to place, to set)*. With the middle voice Paul is saying they are to *be themselves setting forth* good deeds. The thought can also mean *"To devote themselves"* to this task, the same as in verse 8. The word can also be translated *to maintain, to practice*. Or, "to take the lead" and "to stand forward, in the front line." (Lenski) Believers are to so carry out good works in order

> to glorify God, testify their subjection to him and gratitude
> for mercies received; to show forth their faith to men; to adorn
> the doctrine of Christ, and a profession of it; to recommend
> religion to others: to stop the mouths of gainsayers, and put
> to silence the ignorance of foolish men. (Gill)

In good works *("kalos ergon,"* as a plural*)* is described here as something that believers must learn to do. We forget that Christians must be trained in righteousness and in righteous acts. Surprisingly, it is the apostle of justification by faith who stresses the showing forth of good works. He writes about practicing good works twenty times in his epistles. James, the apostle who stresses caring out Christian works, does not use the adjective *good* in the fourteen times he writes about living forth charitable *works*. It is as if James believes the reader knows what he means. "Throughout the Pastorals *kala erga* consistently means 'good works' in the widest sense of fine actions or righteous deeds, so that it probably means the same here as well. ' Our people' must demonstrate that they are such, that they truly belong to Paul's following by giving themselves to good works." (Stott)

To meet pressing needs. The word *pressing (anankaios)* is related to the verb *anakazo* that is often translated with the sense of *compelling*. Another form of the word becomes the equivalent of *thlipis* that carries the thought of troubles and tribulations. The apostle's point is that people are suffering under duress and need relief. In this "distressful" and pressured environment, in which believers were being persecuted, the church could not stand by in idleness.

So that they will not be unfruitful. Paul uses the *hina* clause, the negative *me,* and the present subjunctive of the *to be* verb *eimi.* "They should not be going about in their spiritual lives living as unfruitful Christians." *Unfruitful ("akarpoi,"* or *"without fruit")* explains itself. There is nothing being produced in the life. Though the Lord Jesus says we should expect spiritual fruit (Jo. 15:1-4), it is certainly possible for Christians to be fruitless and impotent in practicing righteous acts. Though Paul does not go into details in this passage, Jesus made it clear that the believer must be in spiritual union and fellowship with Him in order to produce fruit. He said "The branch cannot bear fruit of itself unless it abides in the vine, so neither *can* you unless you abide in Me" (v. 4). He made it clear that He was the vine and without Him we could do nothing (v. 5).

3:15 All who are with me greet you. Greet those who love us in *the* **faith. Grace be with you all.**

Greet is the deponent verb *aspazomai.* Though the etymology of the word is uncertain, a connection seems to exist with *spao* that means *to attract.* "In the widest sense, the greeting is the opening of communication between individuals." (EDNT) Since that open door of communication has already been opened in their common faith centered around the Lord Jesus, the apostle is urging that it remain open and that their love will continue to be shared.

Love here is *phileo (present active participle)* and not *agapao.* Paul is stressing their comradeship and companionship. With the present participle, he is emphasizing the fact that such care and concern for Paul and his companions is continual. It also characterizes their feelings. He could count on these believers to show an ongoing concern that does not cease. Wuest capitalizes *Faith* (*pistos*) as in "The Faith."

Paul is placing the truth of Christianity into one description. "The belief that Christ is the Son of God and that He died for His own." Of course that Faith has so many other facets to it! In its widest sense, it encompasses the entire body of truth, from the Old into the New Testament.

Grace be with you all. Paul uses the article *he* in front of *grace* ("*charis*"). Grace is *giving, giving forth favor.* This grace is really to come upon them from God. Human grace or giving is so limited and temporal. But the apostle certainly has more in mind with this word then simply physical favor and kindness. "Titus is asked to convey the greetings of Paul and of his companions to those who are filled with affection for them in the sphere of the Christian faith." For those who read this letter, "God's favor in Christ for those who have not deserved it" is certainly strong. (Hendriksen)

With you all carries a more pronounced thought with the preposition *meta* that has the force of "in the midst of." This grace is to permeate the group, operate both within the individuals and without in their collective activities for the Lord. They are to experience His presence and His continual favor.

Paul usually closes his epistles with the names of those who sent words of affection, or, to whom he is addressing. But it would seem here that Titus knew those with Paul, and also that he himself had been traveling with him. "He evidently refers not to those who were residing in the place where he was, but to those who had one with him from Crete as his companions." (Barnes)

In the Greek text a subscription has been added that reads, "It was written to Titus, ordained the first bishop of the church of the Cretians, from Nicopolis of Macedonia." No one knows the age or source of this addition. It has been generally judged as having been added by writers who knew nothing of the background of the letter. Titus was not placed on Crete to be a bishop.

To write of "the church of the Cretians" is certainly inaccurate because doubtless there were many churches there and Titus was to build up all the congregations. Paul was actually with him earlier and left him there to complete the work he originally started. "There is no evidence that Titus was 'bishop' there at all in the prelatical sense of the term, or even that he was a settled pastor." (Barnes)

Bishop in a hierarchical meaning did not come along in church government until a later time. This subscription, in the nature of notes and comments, is certainly not a part of inspired Scripture. But it has consistently done damage in perpetuating error and misunderstanding about the nature of the early church.

Paul's concluding benediction about grace ties in with how he began the letter, with God's grace (1:4). The apostle continually teaches that grace alone brings salvation (2:11) and brings out godly living (v. 12). Grace begins the first and last chapter of each of the apostle's letters, "as also in 1 and 2 Peter and Revelation and at the beginning of 2 John and the end of Hebrews. The word expresses God's unmerited favor in Christ in its soteriological significance for the believer, saving, sanctifying, and empowering." (NIGTC)

Endnotes

1 Donald Guthrie, *New Testament Introduction,* 607.

2 The reader is urged to examine 13-68 of Homer Kent's *The Pastoral Epistles* (Chicago: Moody Press, 1986) and 253-260 in Henry Thiessen's *Introduction to the New Testament* (Grand Rapids: Eerdmans, 1943) from which most of this material is taken.

3 *Epistle to the Philippians,* section iv.

4 *Stromata,* II. xi.

5 *On Prescription Against Heretics,* chap. Xxv.

6 The specifics may be found on 53, 54 in Knight's *Commentary on the Pastoral Epistles,* and on 1001 – 1010 in Guthrie's *NT Intro.*

7 *Ecclesiastical History* 2.25.5, quoted by Knight, 54.

8 In fact, some commentaries on the PE address them in that order.

9 Kent, 14.

10 D. Edmond Hiebert, *An Introduction to the New Testament, Vol. Two,* 329.

11 Ibid, 328.

12 Ibid, 355,356.

13 George W. Knight, *The Pastoral Epistles,* 6.

14 The information in this paragraph is taken from Ibid, 7.

15 Knight, 9.

16 Colin Brown, ed., *Dictionary of New Testament Theology,* 3 Volumes. Grand Rapids: Zondervan Publishing House, 1975, 1:127.

17 Mal Couch, gen. ed., *A Biblical Theology of the Church.* Grand Rapids: Kregel Publications, 1999, 175.

18 Ed Glassock, *The Husband of One Wife: Requirements In 1 Timothy 3:2,* Bibliotheca Sacra, 145, no. 540 (July-September 1983): 247.

19 Ibid, 253.

20 Ibid, 256.

21 Mal Couch, *A Biblical Theology of the Church,* 286.

22 Ibid, 182.

23 Ibid, 182.

24 Colin Brown, ed., The *New International Dictionary of New Testament Theology,* 3 Volumes. Grand Rapids: Zondervan Publishing House, 1975, 1:153.

Abbreviations

Most Used Commentaries and Other References

(Alford)   Henry Alford, *The Greek Testament,* 2 Vols. (Chicago: Moody, 1958), Vol. 2.

(BAG)   William Arndt, Wilbur Gingrich, *A Greek-*
English   *Lexicon of the New Testament* (Chicago: University of Chicago Press, 1959).

(Barnes)   Albert Barnes, *Notes on the New Testament,* 14 Vols. (Grand Rapids: Baker, 1885), Vol. 12.

(BKC)   John F. Walvoord, Roy Zuck, *Bible Knowledge Commentary, New Testament* (Wheaton: Victor Books, 1983).

(Calvin)   John Calvin, *Calvin's Commentaries,* 22 Vols. (Grand Rapids: Baker, 1989), Vol. 21.

(Couch)   Mal Couch, *A Biblical Theology of the Church* (Grand Rapids: Kregel, 1999).

(EBC)   Frank E. Gaebelein, ed., *The Expositor's Bible Commentary,* 12 Vols. (Grand Rapids: Zondervan, 1978), Vol. 11.

(EDNT)   Horst Balz, Gerhard Schneider, *Exegetical Dictionary of the New Testament,* 3 Vols. (Grand Rapids: Eerdmans, 1994).

(Ellicott)   Charles John Ellicott, *Commentary on the Whole Bible,* 4 Vols. (Grand Rapids: Zondervan, 1959), Vol. 4.

(Fairbairn)   Patrick Fairbairn, *Commentary on the Pastoral Epistles* (Grand Rapids: Zondervan, 1956).

(Gill)   John Gill, *Gill's Commentary,* 6 Vols. (Grand Rapids: Baker, 1980), Vol. 6.

(Hendriksen)   William Hendriksen, *Thessalonians, Timothy and Titus* (Grand Rapids: Baker, 1983).

(Lenski)   R. C. H. Lenski, *St. Paul's Epistles, Titus* (Minneapolis: Augsburg, 1961).

(L&S)   Henry George Liddell, Robert Scott, *A Greek English Lexicon* (Oxford: Clarendon Press, 1996).

(MacArthur)   John MacArthur, *Titus* (Chicago: Moody, 1996).

(Nicoll)   W. Robertson Nicoll, *The Expositor's Greek Testament* (Grand Rapids: Eerdmans, 1988), Vol. 4.

(NIGTC)   George W. Knight III, The New International Greek Testament Commentary, The Pastoral Epistles (Grand Rapids: Eerdmans, 1992).

(PHC)   *The Preacher's Complete Homiletic Commentary,* 31 Vols. (Grand Rapids: Baker, n.d.), Vol. 29.

(Poole)   Matthew Poole, *Commentary on the Holy Bible,* 3 Vols. (Peabody, MS: Hendrickson, n.d.), Vol. 3.

(Ritchie)   T. Wilson, K. Stapley, *What the Bible Teaches, Titus* (Kilmarnock, Scotland: John Ritchie, 1983).

(Robertson)   A. T. Robertson, *Word Pictures in the New Testament,* 6 Vols. (Nashville: Broadman, 1931), Vol. 4.

(Stott)   John Stott, *Guard the Truth* (Downers Grove, IL: IVP, 1996).

(Thayer)   Joseph H. Thayer, *Greek-English Lexicon of the New Testament* (Grand Rapids: Baker, 1992).

(Vincent)   Marvin R. Vincent, *Word Studies in the New Testament,* 4 Vols. (Peabody, MS: Hendrickson, n.d.), Vol. 4.

(Wuest)   Kenneth S. Wuest, *Wuest's Word Studies,* 4 Vols. (Grand Rapids: Eerdmans, 1998), Vol. 2.

Part III

Suggested Doctrinal Statement for Churches

It is important that a church has a complete statement of faith, or doctrinal position. It is our belief that this statement must be complete in regard to the major truths of Scripture. It must also address cultural philosophies that can hinder the work of the church. The following doctrinal statement is from *Tyndale Theological Seminary and Biblical Institute*, and is provided as a framework.

Doctrinal Statement

The Scriptures

We believe all Scripture, Old and New Testament, is inspired by God. This refers to the original autographs as written by the prophets and apostles. Thus, the Bible is inerrant and without mistakes in the original words. We believe all Scripture points to the Lord Jesus Christ and reveals the mind of God to man, and the only way of Salvation through Christ. The Scriptures also are the only guide for our practical moral and spiritual instruction.

Mark 12:26, 36; 13:11; Luke 24:27, 44; John 5:39; Acts 1:16; 17:2-3; 18:28; 26:22-23; 28:23; Rom. 15:4; 1 Cor. 2:13; 10:11; 2 Tim. 3:16; 2 Pet. 1:21

The Interpretation of Scripture

Though in some ways, interpretation of Scripture would not be considered "doctrine," yet it is extremely important as to the method that one approaches in the study of the Bible. In this sense, interpretation becomes an essential doctrinal issue.

"Hermeneutics" is the science of interpretation. There are evidences in both the Old and New Testaments as to the method that Biblical truth is to be interpreted. Conservative, normal, and literal hermeneutics takes a very tried and true approach to understanding the Bible that should include observation, interpretation, and application. It would argue for but one sense or meaning for each passage of Scripture. As well, normative hermeneutics leaves no room for a new "complementary hermeneutics" approach in the popularly labeled system of Progressive Dispensationalism.

Though taking the Word of God literally, and at face value, in classical hermeneutics there is room for poetry, figures of speech, illustrations, types, and symbols. But these literary devices do not take away from the foundational or normal interpretative understanding of Biblical truth. Normal interpretation also argues for progressive revelation, i.e., that the Holy Spirit over a period of time revealed certain truths in a progressive fashion. For example, the revelation of Jesus Christ starts in Genesis but is not fully complete until the book of Revelation. Literal interpretation is in opposition to allegorical interpretation. Though the Apostle Paul in Galatians "creates" an allegory in order to make an isolated point or illustration (4:21-26), allegory as a system

246

is but an unacceptable philosophical approach to understanding the Word of God. It is clearly contrary to proper Biblical interpretation.

Luke 1:1-4; 24:35; 44-46, 48; Acts 10:8; 17:11-12; 26:6-7; 26-27

The Godhead

We believe that the Godhead eternally exists in three persons - the Father, the Son, and the Holy Spirit - and that these three are one God, having the precise same nature, attributes, and perfections and worthy of precisely the same honor, confidence, and obedience.

Mt. 28:18-19; Mark 12:29; John 1:14; Acts 5:3-4; 2 Cor. 13:14; Heb. 1:1-3; Rev. 1:4-6

God's Eternal Purpose

We believe that according to the "eternal purpose" of God (Eph. 3:11) salvation in the divine reckoning is always "by grace through faith," and rests upon the basis of the shed blood of Christ. We believe that God has always been gracious, regardless of the dispensation, but that man has not at all times been under an administration or stewardship of grace as is true in the present dispensation of the Church.

Cor. 9:17; Eph. 3:2; 3:9; Col. 1:25; 1 Tim. 1:4

The Sovereignty of God

Though God is Absolute Sovereign over all creation and history, He is not the author of sin. Yet in some mysterious way, His decrees include all that takes place in the universe. God has a "determined plan for the whole world" and no one can alter His purposes. What He has planned that He will do. And, He "works out everything in conformity with the purpose of His will"; "Surely as I have planned, so it will be, and as I have purposed, so it will stand."

Sovereignty also extends to the providence of God whereby He sustains all creatures, giving them life and removing life as He pleases. In sovereignty, all things were created for the glory of God and all things exist for Him. The sovereignty of God also extends to the doctrine of divine election whereby those chosen by the council of the Lord's own will, shall come to Him in faith. And yet, even though difficult to reconcile in human understanding, the sovereignty of God does not remove the responsibility of man.

Isa. 14:26-27; Isa. 46:11; Eph. 1:11; Isa. 14:24; Deut. 32:39; Rev. 4:11;

Jn. 6:37, 39, 44; Eph. 1:3-18; II Thess. 2:13; Habakkuk 1:6, 11; Acts 2:22-23, 36

Angels, Fallen and Unfallen

We believe that God created an innumerable company of sinless, spiritual beings, known as angels; that one, "Lucifer, son of the morning" - the highest in rank - sinned through pride, thereby becoming Satan; that a great company of the angels followed him in his moral fall, some of whom became demons and are active as his agents and associates in the prosecution of his unholy purposes, while others who fell are "reserved in everlasting chains under darkness until the judgment of the great day."

Isa. 14:12-17; Ezek. 28:11-19; 1 Tim. 3:6; 2 Pet. 2:4; Jude 6

Man, Created and Fallen

We believe that man was originally created in the image and after the likeness of God, and that he fell through sin and as a consequence of his sin, lost his spiritual life, becoming dead in trespasses and sins, and that he became subject to the power of the devil. Paul adds that the lost are mentally blinded by Satan, the god of this world, and that the truth of the gospel is veiled from those who are destroying themselves. The Word of God makes it clear, there is no one who seeks after God. So God has given mankind over to the lusts of the heart and to a depraved mind. The Apostle further argues that men who live to indulge the flesh and the mind with lusts, are by nature the children of wrath, and in life, walk after the course designed by Satan, the "spirit" presently working in the sons of disbelief. Theologically, this "deadness" and darkness of mind and heart along with all the sins that come forth, has been rightly called Total Depravity. Following the sin of Adam, man could only produce descendants who would be sinners. Therefore all mankind is under the death sentence and penalty of sin and thus are all condemned. This doctrine is important because it stands in opposition to the philosophy of humanism that is the moral and spiritual scourge of modern man. Only through the reconciliation of Christ, by His death, are human beings who are enemies of God being saved. The result is that sinners are justified by Christ's blood, and are rescued from the wrath of God.

II Cor. 4:3-4; Rom. 3:11; Rom. 1:24, 28; Eph. 2:2-3; Rom 1:28; Rom. 5:12-18; Rom. 5:10; Gen. 1:26; 2:17; 6:5; Ps. 14:1-3; 51:5; Jer. 17:9; Eph. 2:1-6

The First Advent of Christ

We believe that, as provided and purposed by God and as pre-announced in the prophecies of the Scriptures, the eternal Son of God came into this world that He might manifest God to men, fulfill prophecy and become the Redeemer of a lost world. To this end He was born of the virgin, and received a human body and a sinless human nature.

We believe that in fulfillment of prophecy He came first to Israel as her Messiah-King, and, being rejected of that nation, He gave His life as a ransom for all according to the eternal counsels of God.

We believe that, according to the Scriptures, He arose from the dead in the same body, though glorified, in which He had lived and died, and that His resurrection body is the pattern of that body which ultimately will be given to all believers.

Luke 1:30-35; John 1:18; 3:16; Heb. 4:15; John 1:11; Acts 2:22-24; 1 Tim. 2:6; John 20:20; Phil. 3:20-21

Salvation Only Through Christ

We believe that, owing to universal death through sin, no one can enter the kingdom of God unless born again; and that no degree of reformation however great, no attainment in morality however high, no culture however attractive, no baptism or other ordinance however administered, can help the sinner to take even one step toward heaven; but a new nature imparted from above, a new life implanted by the Holy Spirit through the Word, is absolutely essential to salvation, and only those thus saved are sons of God.

John 1:12; 3:16; Rom. 1:16-17; 3:22; Gal. 3:22

The Extent of Salvation

Though the saved one may have occasion to grow in the realization of his blessings and to know a fuller measure of divine power through the yielding of his life more fully to God, he is, as soon as he is saved, in possession of every spiritual blessing and absolutely complete in Christ, and is therefore, in no way required by God to seek a so-called "second blessing," "second work of grace," or a "second baptism."

1 Cor. 3:21-23; Eph. 1:3; Col. 2:10; 1 John 4:17; 5:11-12

Eternal Security

We believe God keeps eternally all those He has elected and called to salvation and that none are lost. God will, however, chasten and correct His own in infinite love; but having undertaken to save them and keep them forever, apart from all human merit, He, who cannot fail, will in the end present every one faultless in Christ, and on His merits, before the presence of His glory and conformed to the image of His Son.

We believe that believers can have eternal assurance that they are the children of God and thus, are eternally kept. This assurance gives confidence and helps the believer grow in inner peace and maturity.

John 5:24; 10:28; 13:1; Eph. 1:3-17; 1 John 5:13; Rom. 8:29; Eph. 1:3-17

The Holy Spirit

We believe that the Holy Spirit, the Third Person of the Trinity, though omnipresent from all eternity, took up His abode in the world in a special sense on the day of Pentecost according to the divine promise, dwells in every believer, and by His baptism unites all to Christ in one body, and that He, as the indwelling One, is the source of all power and all acceptable worship and service.

We believe that speaking in tongues was never the common or necessary sign of the baptism nor of the filling of the Spirit.

John 14:16-17; 16:7-15; 1 Cor. 6:19; Eph. 2:22; 2. Thess. 2:7; Acts 4:8, 31; Rom. 8:23; 1 Cor. 13:8

The Great Commission

We believe that it is the explicit message of our Lord Jesus Christ to those whom He has saved that they are sent forth by Him into the world to make known Christ to the whole world.

Mt. 28:18-19; John 17:18; Acts 1:8; 1 Pet 1:17; 2:11

The Blessed Hope

We believe that the next great event in the fulfillment of prophecy will be the coming of the Lord in the air to receive to Himself into heaven both His own who are alive and remain unto His coming, and also all who have fallen asleep in Jesus, and that this event is the blessed hope set before us in the Scripture, and for this we should be constantly looking.

John 14:1-3; 1 Cor. 15:51-52; 1 Thess. 4:13-18; Titus 2:11-14

The Apostasy of the Church

Without designating a specific time table, the Apostle Paul warns of a "falling away" from the faith that will lead to a heeding of deceitful spirits and the teachings of demons Paul simply says it will occur in the "later times" and produce hypocrisy and a searing of the conscience. This apostasy will be religious and moral in nature and will happen prior to the rapture of the Church and before the revelation of the son of destruction, the Antichrist. Paul further teaches that the seeds of apostasy are present in the Church but they will also completely mature in the last days, which he describes as "difficult times."

The Apostle Peter continues the theme of the apostasy that will come upon the Church in the future, that is, during the "last days" when men will be mockers asking "Where is the promise of His coming?"

Some argue, as is true, that the apostasy is ever-present and not simply a future departure from the Word of God. Yet, the Bible still predicts a future religious phenomenon whereby the truth is maligned and the righteous will be exploited by greed and false words.

II Tim 4:1; I Tim 4:2; II Tim 3:1-7; II Thess. 2:1-5; II Tim. 3:1; II Pet. 2:1-2; II Pet. 3:3; II Pet. 3:4; II Pet 2:2-3

The Tribulation

We believe that the rapture of the church will be followed by the fulfillment of Israel's seventieth week during which the church, the body of Christ, will be in heaven. The whole period of Israel's seventieth week will be a time of judgment on the whole earth, at the end of which the times of the Gentiles will be brought to a close. The latter half of this period will be the time of Jacob's trouble, which our Lord called the great tribulation. We believe that universal righteousness will not be realized previous to the second coming of Christ, but that the world is day by day ripening for judgment and that the age will end with a fearful apostasy.

Dan. 9:27; Rev. 6:1 - 19:21; Jer. 30:7; Mt. 24:15-21

The Second Coming of Christ

We believe that the period of great tribulation in the earth will be climaxed by the return of the Lord Jesus Christ to the earth as He went. The millennial age will follow, with Satan bound. Israel will be restored to her own land and the Abrahamic Covenant will be fulfilled by the consummation of its three divisions - Land (Palestinian Covenant), Seed (Davidic Covenant), and Blessing (New Covenant finally brought to complete fruition). The whole world that survives will be brought to a complete knowledge of the Messiah.

Deut. 30:1-10; Isa. 11:9; Ezek. 37:21; Jer. 31:31- on; Mt. 24:15 - 25:46; Acts 15:16-17; Rom 8:19-23; 11:25-27; Rev. 20:1-3

The Eternal State

We believe that at death the spirits and souls of those who have trusted in the Lord Jesus Christ for salvation pass immediately into His presence and there remain in conscious bliss until the resurrection of the glorified body when Christ comes for His own, whereupon soul and body reunited shall be associated with Him forever in glory; but the spirits and souls of the unbelieving remain after death conscious of condemnation and in misery until the final judgment of the great white throne at the close of the millennium, when soul and body reunited shall be cast into the lake of fire, not to be annihilated, but to be punished with everlasting destruction from the presence of the Lord, and from the glory of His power.

Luke 16:19-26; 23:42; 2 Cor. 5:8; Phil. 1:23; 2 Thess. 1:7-9; Judge 6 - 7; Rev. 20:11-15

Dispensationalism

We believe that the Bible presents the fact that God has not always dealt with mankind the same way in every age. According to Biblical terminology these distinct periods are called "administrations" in regard to the purpose of God or "stewardships" concerning the responsibility of man as originated from the New Testament usage of the Greek word, *oikonomia*. We believe that classical or traditional dispensationalism is the system that best represents the Biblical teaching on this matter. Classical or traditional dispensationalism is distinguished by:

- A consistent literal interpretation

- A clear distinction between Israel and the Church

- Taking into account progressive revelation

- Recognizing the glory of God as the ultimate purpose of God in the world.

Eph.1:10 3:2, 9

On Current Issues

We believe that corruptive influences have always been working against the Church, the body of Christ. Along with anti-moral forces, Tyndale repudiates the man created philosophies of secular humanism, materialism, evolution, and feminism. This includes the influences of secular psychology. While some truths may be imprinted into what man can observe, basically, they are counter to the revealed truths of Scripture.

Tyndale believes that much of what is commonly identified with the "Church Growth" movement encourages, perhaps unintentionally, dependence upon the flesh and worldly methods, rather than means ordained by God. Tyndale acknowledges that, in this age of grace, the Head of the Church has given His servants great freedom to trust Him for creative strategies and methods as they pursue by the Spirit the fulfillment of our Lord's mandate, the Great Commission. However, Tyndale repudiates dependence on the flesh and upon worldly strategies in all aspects of the Lord's work.

More than a detestable lifestyle, homosexuality is hedonism which claims its own rights no matter what the consequences. Some churches are confused and say, "we don't have to accept the practice but we must love the person." When men and women blatantly jeopardize the lives of others and defiantly shake their fists at God and human authority, tolerance reaches a limit. Though God detests every sin, those sins that destroy human life, He moves against, giving them "over to a depraved mind, to do those things which are not right." If homosexuals repent before God and ask for forgiveness, as found only in Christ, they should be accepted and supported. Christians must continue to fight against the socialization of homosexuality in government and education. Believers must also continue to witness about God's gracious ability through Christ to rescue even from the most detestable of sins.

Lev. 18:22; 20:13; Rom. 1:28, 1:18-32; 1 Cor. 6:9; 1 Tim 1:8-11

Women and Ministry

We believe that in the body of Christ men and women stand spiritually equal and constitute the Church universal. We believe women have had and always will have their God-given gifts and roles within this body. Accordingly, as the primary role of believing men is to be husbands and fathers, so the primary role of women is to be wives and mothers. But modern secular feminism has destroyed the importance of these positions and blurred the differences between men and women. Tyndale encourages women to have personal ministries. But the Scriptures are clear that male leadership is called to the local church positions of deacon, elder, and pastor-teacher. No amount of debate can water down what the Bible says about the individual and distinct callings of both sexes, in regard to gifts and positions. Tyndale equally encourages women to pursue diplomas but the role of pastor-teacher is Biblically reserved for men.

1 Tim. 2:9-15; 3:1-13; Titus 1:5-9; 2:1-8; I I Cor. 14:34-35

Openness of God

Tyndale repudiates the theories known as the "Openness of God". This theory proposes that God does not exhaustively know the future, that He learns as He observes the unfolding of history, and that He is "open" to the free actions of His creatures, altering His plans in response to the exercise of their free agency and previously unknowable acts. This theory violates both the omniscience of God and the fact that in sovereignty, He has ordained all things. In fact, this theory may be classified as heretical.

Progressive Dispensationalism, Preterism

Tyndale repudiates the theories of Progressive Dispensationalism. The central disturbing tenet in this view is that the Lord Jesus Christ is now spiritually reigning on the throne of David in heaven. The Scriptures do not teach this view. The Lord is seated at the right hand of the Father presently in glory, but this is not the prophesied Davidic rule that will take place in time and history. Progressive Dispensationalism arises from a faulty, inconsistent and complementary hermeneutic, and a misplaced desire for rapprochement between Dispensational and Covenant Theologies.

Tyndale repudiates the theories of Preterism. Preterism is an eschatological viewpoint that places many or all Eschatological events in the past, especially during the destruction of Jerusalem in A.D. 70. Preterism, in it's full or "consistent" form asserts that Christ's second coming has already occurred, that the Scriptures do not speak of any future eschatological events, and that we are now living in the New Heavens and the New Earth. Tyndale believes that the Preterist view is exegetically unsupportable and represents a compromise with Liberal Theology by downgrading the veracity of prophetic scriptures.

Other books by Mal Couch

Classical Evangelical Hermeneutics
ISBN Prefix #0-8254-2367-8
Pages: 372
Edition: paperback

> Words...grammar...syntax...context — all of these elements form the basis for hermeneutics, the principles and practice of interpreting works of literature. Here is a set of written tools and guidelines for an accurate interpretation and understanding of Scripture. Topics covered include: A history of interpretation and the various hermeneutical traditions in Christian history; An examination of dispensational hermeneutics in the early church; The importance of the doctrine of inerrancy in Bible interpretation; and Understanding symbols and types in biblical prophecy.

Biblical Theology Of The Church
ISBN Prefix #0-8254-2361-9
Pages: 336
Edition: hardcover

> One of the most popular topics among Christians is how to "do Church." Should it be traditional of contemporary? What should the music be like? Should it target a specific group? Often lost in this discussion are far more crucial and basic questions such as, "What does God intend for the church to be? What does the Bible say about the function and organization of the local church?" A Biblical Theology of the Church takes up the task of defining the mission and function of the local church from a biblical perspective. As noted in the Introduction, "This should be the finest hour for the gospel and for the church of Jesus Christ. At every turn there are urgent opportunities to share the truth in both word and deed. The gospel should be going forth as never before, and believers in Christ should be growing in spiritual maturity. The church should be foundationally solid and a strong bastion proclaiming God's sovereignty and will. Local congregations should be centers of light and places of refuge where comfort and hope is dispensed and renewed."

The Fundamentals For The Twenty-First Century
ISBN Prefix #0-8254-2368-6
Pages: 656
Edition: hardcover

In the early decades of the twentieth century, a prophetic series of books took a bold stand in the debate over the essential meaning of Christianity. With the publication of The Fundamentals: A Testimony to the Truth, a new term entered religious language, fundamentalism, which then meant an adherence to the fundamental doctrines of biblical Christianity. Nearly a century later, biblical Christianity faces similar challenges, both from within and without its ranks. The term fundamentalism and the faith it represents have been debased by cultural change, entrenched secularism, and theological confusion. This new landmark work, with contributions from thirty-four notable Bible scholars, pastors, and teachers, sets forth a distinctively biblical agenda for the Christian faith in the twenty-first century.

Issues 2000
ISBN Prefix #0-8254-2363-5
Pages: 160
Edition: paperback

The evangelical faith that produced the historic work, The Fundamentals, in the early 20th century finds itself, once again, challenged by cultural change and theological confusion.

A Bible Handbook To The Acts Of The Apostles
ISBN Prefix #0-8254-2360-0
Pages: 464
Edition: hardcover

Numerous evangelical scholars combine their insights to present an in-depth look at the major doctrinal themes of Acts from a dispensational perspective. It also provides definitions and identifications of the people, places, and terms used in the Acts of the Apostles. Includes numerous charts and maps. This book combines the best of a Bible handbook and a biblical theology.

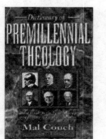

Dictionary Of Premillennial Theology
ISBN Prefix #0-8254-2351-1
Pages: 448
Edition: hardcover

More than fifty scholars combine their expertise to present a historical and topical dictionary of premillennial theology.